Spanish Sausages
Authentic Recipes
And Instructions

Stanley Marianski, Adam Marianski

Bookmagic LLC
Seminole, Florida

Spanish Sausages, Authentic Recipes And Instructions
Stanley Marianski, Adam Marianski

ISBN: 978-0-9904586-6-1

Library of Congress Control Number: 2018914174

Bookmagic, LLC.
http://www.bookmagic.com

Printed in the United States of America.

Contents

Introduction

Why write a book on making Spanish sausages? For a very good reason - there are none. For exactly the same reason in 2008 I have written *The Art of Making Fermented Sausages* which has since introduced thousands of newcomers to making salami type products at home. At first glance it may be assumed that there is not much to write about, after all everybody knows that chorizo is a Spanish sausage and this is where their knowledge of Spanish sausages ends.

There is a negligible amount of information on Spanish sausages in English, but when one visits Spanish sites and forums he discovers the whole world of products that are waiting to be explored. No country in the world has a larger assortment of blood sausages than Spain, there are wonderful sausages such as longaniza, fuet, salchichón, sobrasada, androlla, botillo, morcón, cooked butifarra, and a wide selection of common sausages known as *salchichas* which are the Spanish equivalent of widely known products such as mortadella, frankfurter, hot dog, bratwurst or liver sausage.

There has never been any information about Spanish sausages in English and surprisingly nothing of much significance in Spanish, at least not after 1983. Even the Spanish books written in the past offered only few recipes with general information, very limited instructions and hardly any explanations.

To be fair there are a few small Spanish books describing Spanish sausages, but they provide very general information. Saying that a sausage contains pork meat and spices, is stuffed in natural casings and is subsequently dried is hardly a detailed recipe. Such general information abounds left and right on the internet and is offered by meat stores, meat plants, supermarkets and blogs, however, they do not offer instructions on making those sausages. Meat plants and butchers do not want to divulge the information for fear of competition, and supermarkets and bloggers offer a pretty photo, but still do not know how the product is made.

My hope is that the reader will be pleasantly surprised seeing 200 detailed recipes in this book. All materials, ingredients and detailed processing instructions are included as well as their general descriptions and where they originated.

Making dry sausages requires more knowledge so topics of crucial importance were reprinted from our *The Art of Making Fermented Sausages* where deemed to be necessary.

By reading this material one can get a full understanding of the manufacturing process, however, it is assumed that the reader already has some basic sausage making skills.

The book was started in the USA and finished in Madrid. Plenty of research was perrformed: the National Library of Spain was frequently visited, as well as many local meat trade shows. Being fluent in Spanish I have selected information from the most reliable sources.

When traditional sausages were made in the past starter cultures did not exist, however, they offer a benefit of more reliable and safer production. It is explained in the book how a starter culture can be added to a recipe without changing ingredients or processing procedure. Items like thermometers, humidity, acidity and moisture testers are easily available online and make home processing easier and more enjoyable. The purpose of this book is to explain to the reader how he can make Spanish sausages at home, regardless of the climate and the outside conditions.

Stanley Marianski
November 2018.

Chapter 1

Spanish Sausages

History of Spanish Sausages

In prehistoric times, about 3000 B.C., meat was already preserved in Egypt with salt. The procedure was simple: meat was sliced thin, salted and dried in air. With time we learned the benefit of smoking, thinking it preserved the meat, although it was the drying that accomplished the task. The smoke played an important part in the process by inhibiting growth of bacteria, keeping insects at bay and providing a well liked flavor.

The oldest ever reference to a sausage mentioned in written literature comes from Homer's Odyssey written in the ninth century B.C., book XX, verse 25:

"And as a man with a paunch pudding, that has been filled with blood and fat, tosses it back and forth over a blazing fire, and the pudding itself strains hard to be cooked quickly; so he was twisting and turning back and forth, meditating how, though he was alone against many, he could lay hands on the shameless suitors."

The above is the first written record of the grilled sausage. In the first century A.C., Italian author Marcus Gavius Apicius mentions "botellus" (*small sausage*) in his famous work "De re coquinaria" (*On the Subject of Cooking*) which many sources link to Spanish *botelo* or *botillo del Bierzo*. Other sources give credit to Spanish monks from Monasterio de Carracedo as they mention "botellus" in their writings in the Middle Ages.

Of most significance was an anonymous cookbook written in XIII century Andalusia just before the king Don Fernando III liberated Spain from Morrocan Arabs who dominated the Iberian Peninsula from 1147 to 1269. The book was called Spanish-Arabic Cuisine (*La cocina hispano-magrebí*) and included an entire part dedicated to meat recipes: sausages, meat balls, liver spreads, ground meats and usage of spices. In 1324 appeared The Book of Sent Sovi (*Libro de Sent Sovi*); the oldest surviving culinary text in Catalan. This very practical book contained sections about seafood, poultry and wild game among other topics. XV century is the point when home sausage making takes off on a grand scale. Cows are grown for milk and meat, but they feed on pasture out of sight. They are slaughtered in slaughter houses and commercially distributed.

Pigs, however, feel comfortable and safe with humans so they are close by. Even during wars when inhabitants of villages ran away to hide in a forest, the pigs did the same where they were able to feed themselves without any help. When the situation normalized, the pigs would return to the village.

In the winter time, usually around Christmas a pig would be slaughtered *which was a kind of local celebration known as "la matanza" (the slaughter)*. It was a social event where families and neighbors participated together sharing duties, tasks and knowledge. This fiesta would go for a few days where a whole pig was transformed into a variety of products following simple sanitary rules.

Parts that spoil first like blood and offal meat (liver, heart, kidney, spleen, lungs, cleaned entrails) would be processed on the first day into blood and liver sausages. Other meat trimmings and fat would be made into sausages and noble parts such as hams, loins and pork belly would be salted and preserved for later.

Christopher Columbus' discovery of America in 1492 opened the door to a myriad of foods previously unknown in Spain: peppers, potatoes and new spices like allspice from Jamaica. The most important for sausage production was pepper which grew quite well on Spanish soil and in time became the "pimentón" which is an absolute must have ingredient for chorizos, sobrasadas and other Spanish sausages giving them characteristic color and flavor. Sausages became popular not only with villagers but with royalty as well:

King Carlos IV, nicknamed "the hunter" due to his love for the sport displayed great affinity for sausages which has been immortalized in the following story. On one of his hunting trips in the mountains of Salamanca province, the king became hungry and discovered that his bag did not contain any provisions. Then by a stroke of luck in the village of Candelario, he encountered a peasant named Uncle Rico (*Tio Rico*) who was carrying a variety of sausages to deliver them to town. The king found them delicious and started to devour them one by one. With his hunger gone and being in a good mood the king granted the peasant permission to be the official supplier of sausages to the palace. The story is depicted in a famous painting by Ramón Bayeu "Choricero de Candelario" (sausage maker from Candelario) which is displayed in Prado Museum in Madrid.

Spanish King Alfonso XII (1874-1885) was so fond of salchichón de Vic that he always had this sausage in his kitchen.

Iberian Pig

Best Spanish hams, loins and sausages are made from iberian pork that comes from black Iberian pigs (*cerdo ibérico*) which roam free in Spanish oak forests (*dehesa)*. For most of the year they feed on grass, but from October to February when the oak trees drop mature acorns, the pigs feed exclusively on oak acorns (*belotas*) and occasionally on chestnuts. This fattening period is known as *la montanera*. During this time a pig gains well over a pound (0.67 kg) of weight each day by consuming about 8-10 kg (20-25 lbs) acorns daily.

Photo 1.1 Ibérico pigs.   *Photo courtesy www.dehesa-extremadura.com*

Photo 1.2 Early morning in dehesa forest.
Photo courtesy www.dehesa-extremadura.com

Photo 1.3 There are four types of
oak trees growing in Spain: *encina,
alcornoque, roble* and *quejigo*. The
most popular are *encina* and *alcornoque*
each producing differently tasting
acorns. Photo courtesy
www.dehesa-extremadura.com

Oak acorns have been the perfect food for Iberian pigs. Smaller *encina* acorns are much sweeter than larger *alcornoque*s. Oak acorns are very hard but edible and were commonly milled to an oak powder and then used as flour to bake oak bread. Or they were made into a liqueur called "beso de bellota" (Oak Acorn Kiss) which is still sold today.

The texture and flavor of pork fat is easily influenced by the pig's diet. As a result its meat is interlaced with thin fat-like veins similar to a high quality marbled steak. As fat is the carrier of flavor, the final result is the development of a wonderful meat.

Photo 1.4 Ibérico loin.   **Photo 1.5** Ibérico ham.

In March, soon after the fattening period the pigs are processed. To preserve the forest and to provide enough acorns to meet each pig's voracious appetite, the number of oak trees and the number of pigs are carefully controlled. There are 1 million hectares (2,470,000 acres) of oak forests just in the region of Extremadura and 1 hectare (2.4 acres) of forest is dedicated to two pigs. There are wide open spaces between the trees that gives pigs plenty of exercise. For comparison purposes, a typical commercially raised american pig is given about 2 m (10 square feet) of space, sometimes cannot even turn around and its diet is enriched with antibiotics and growth hormones.

Certain recipes require iberian pork which is available only in Spain, however, in 2014 a plane loaded with 149 Spanish iberian pigs arrived at the USDA Quarantine Station in Rock Tavern, NY. More transports followed and there are farms in Texas and Georgia where iberian pigs are being raised. There are plenty of oak trees in the American southern states and the climate is very suitable. It is a question of time when Spanish hams and sausages will be produced on a larger scale in the USA.

Geographical Location and Climate Conditions

The traditional sausage making process was greatly influenced by the location of the manufacturing facility. Latitude and elevation control temperature. Proximity to sea, rivers and lakes affect humidity. Mountains have influence on temperature and wind, the time of the year affects conservation of the product. All those factors played a crucial part in home production. Today we can control parameters such as temperature, humidity, air speed or smoke temperature in computer controlled chambers, but in the past we had to work with mother nature together. Even so, the above mentioned equipment due to its cost, is used by commercial producers and not by a typical hobbyist.

Spain is not a huge country, about 500 km in length and 1000 km at its widest point. With Portugal on the left, most of Spain is also about 500 km wide. Eastern Spain faces the Mediterranean Sea, north-western Atlantic Bay of Biscay and northern Spain shares Pyrenees Mountains with France. There are not many lakes or rivers. Overall the country is blessed with proper conditions for drying due to mild temperatures and constant prevailing winds. In northern parts temperatures can drop very low, but that is corrected by warming the drying chambers with slow-burning wood. Another solution was hanging sausages above a wood-fired kitchen stove or moving them to a different area. Taking under consideration a physical location where sausages are made, we can generalize sausages into two groups:

1. Sausages made in the eastern region of Iberian peninsula, basically the Spanish Mediterranean coast. Starting from top: the northern Catalonia (Barcelona, Girona), Valencia (Alicante, Castellon, Valencia), southern Aragon (Teruel), Murcia (Cartagena, Murcia), the eastern part of Castile-La Mancha (Albacete and Cuenca), eastern Andalusia (Almería, Granada and Jaén), and Balearic Islands (Majorca, Minorca, Ibiza).

A little use of pimentón and preference for cooked sausages are the factors that distinguish this area, also known as "Levante," from other regions in Spain. In this area pimentón is seldom added, except for the Balearic Islands whose famous "sobrasada" always includes a hefty dose of it.

There are not known chorizos that originate from the Levante area of Spain. Catalonia is known not only for its cooked *butifarras,* but for some of the greatest dry sausages as well: *Salchichón de Vic, fuet, and secallona.*

2. Sausages made in other regions: Extremadura, Castilla La Mancha, Castile-León, Community of Madrid, Galicia, Asturias, Cantabria, País Vasco, La Rioja, Navarra, and Arragón are made with or *without pimentón* and are usually uncooked.

Morcillas (blood sausages) are cooked and made everywhere. There is a small number of dry morcillas: Asturiana, Serrana, de Badajoz, de Calabaza, de Despojos. This breaks the cooking rule and makes them quite unique.

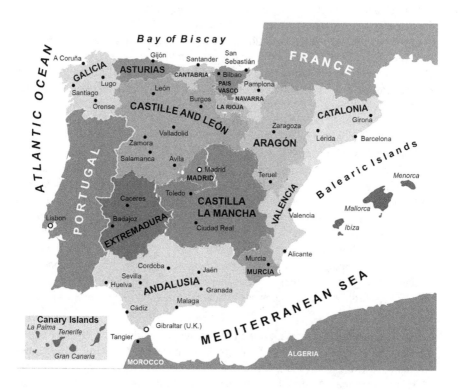

Fig. 1.1 Regions of Spain.

Naming Spanish Sausages

Anybody hearing the name salami can visualize this type of sausage and most people hearing the word chorizo know it is a Spanish sausage. However, the world of sausages becomes confusing when we see descriptions such as embutido, salchichón, salchicha, longaniza, longanissa, morcilla, morcilla negra, morcilla blanca, botelo, butelo, butifarra, botifarra, botagueña, morcón, chorizo blanco, sobrasada, lomo embuchado and others. All those sausages are demystified in the pages that follow.

There are 17 autonomous regions in Spain and each one produces meats and sausages. The sausage name usually starts with the sausage type and is followed with the name of the region where the product was made. Examples of morcilla:

Morcilla Asturiana – denotes a blood sausage from Asturias.

Morcilla Extremeña – blood sausage from Extremadura.

Morcilla Toledana – blood sausage from Toledo (Toledo is the city in the province of Toledo, Castile - La Mancha region.

Morcilla Gallega – blood sausage from Galicia.

Morcilla Riojana – blood sausage from La Rioja.

Morcilla Riojana de Arroz - blood sausage with rice from La Rioja.

Morcilla Dulce Riojana - sweet blood sausage from La Rioja.

Morcilla Dulce Canaria - sweet blood sausage from Canary Islands.

Morcilla de Cebolla de León - blood sausage with onions from León.

Morcilla de Cebolla Valenciana - blood sausage with onions from Valencia.

The Spanish regions are: Andalusia, Aragon, Asturias, Balearic Islands, Basque Country, Canary Islands, Cantabria, Castile-La Mancha, Castile-Leon, Catalonia, Extremadura, Galicia, La Rioja, Madrid, Region de Murcia, Navarre and Region de Valencia.

Spanish sausage names have been left in original, but the English equivalent follows in parenthesis or in text. This way it will be easy to get more information about particular sausage on the Internet, if one so desires. Most known sausages are not translated into English: Bratwurst, Bockwurst, Liverwurst, Salami, Salami Milano, Pepperoni, Mortadella, those sausages are completely different from each other, yet the consumer understands what product he is getting. It is best to leave Spanish names alone, all that is needed is to get familiar with 6-8 major groups (morcilla, chorizo, longaniza, salchichón, butifarra etc), after all they are already known in Spanish speaking countries. Renaming them will only create confusion.

Definition of Embutido

To have a better understanding of Spanish sausages, it is necessary to master the confusing definition of the *embutido*. Spanish verb "embutir" translates into "to stuff" or to fit. As all sausages are stuffed into a suitable casing they are rightly called embutidos. Whole pork loins that are stuffed in casings are also known as *embutido* although loins are usually called l*omo embuchado* as "embuchar" is another name for stuffing minced meat. Fresh sausage, dry sausage, hot dog, mortadella, frankfurter, bratwurst, blood sausage, liver sausage, grilled sausage, smoked sausage – they all are e*mbutidos*. In short, if we see the word *embutido*, we can safely assume it is a some kind of a sausage.

South American-Latin American-Caribbean and Filipino Sausages

All these countries owe much of their culture to mother Spain and culinary arts are not an exception. Not surprising, all Spanish sausages are popular there although different climatic conditions have a profound influence on the methods of their manufacture. Most sausages made in Spain were air dried as the country was blessed with dry prevailing winds for most of the year but in other Spanish speaking countries the climate is hot and humid so choosing air drying as the main processing method would be severely limited. An exception would be Argentina and Chile which are large countries with many climatic zones. Making dry sausages in Latin American countries or hot and humid tropical islands of the Caribbean Basin offers many challenges, unless drying takes place in controlled chambers.

All those countries add vinegar (sometimes wine) as these acidic fluids help to preserve food at least to a certain degree. Mexican sausages are much hotter than those made in other countries and recipes call for a hefty dose of hot peppers. Adding vinegar is quite common too. Many countries (Cuba, Dominican Republic, Philippines) always faced energy problems and a large percentage of the population did not own refrigerators. A very common method was to keep sausages in barrels filled with lard. Dominican longanizas included orange juice and were usually dried in the sun. Locals often come up with ingenious solutions, for example Nham, uncooked, fermented semi-dry Thai sausage very popular in Asia. It is made from fresh lean pork, pork skins, cooked rice, fresh garlic, eye bird chillies and is wrapped in banana leaves. Garlic is added at 5% (50 g/1 kg material) and this large amount inhibits the growth of undesired bacteria. Nevertheless any kind of sausage can be successfully produced if we can apply and maintain right temperatures and humidity.

Application of Smoke in Spanish Sausages

Let's quote 1967 edition of The Spanish Meat Encyclopedia:

"Neither our industry nor our market prepares or accepts smoked products, however, in some areas there are available small quantities of smoked herrings packed in drums."

"Our butchers (la chacineria) quite often smoke meats: however, in no case the application of smoke is considered to be a unique and characteristic technique of meat preservation, for our butchers, the smoke is just a factor, not particularly important one, that is incorporated in process of curing sausages. Smoked meats, smoked fish, totally smoked, are not prepared in Spanish food industry, smoked delicacies are products of northern countries."

The application of smoke was reserved for heating the drying chamber in winter months when temperatures were dropping low. The chambers were heated by slow burning wood and that produced cold smoke during part of the process.

Official Classification of Spanish Meat Products - Boletín Oficial del Estado, Real Decreto 474/2014, June 13.

The official list of Spanish meat products is presented in Boletín Oficial del Estado, Real Decreto 474/2014, 13th June. All popular meat products and sausages are briefly described as well as basic information about manufacturing processes such as salting, curing, fermenting, cooking, drying, canning and others. The Spanish word "cured" covers individual steps like fermenting, drying, and maturing (ageing), however, "drying" takes place during fermentation, drying, aging/maturing and even changes in a product during storage.

Detailed instructions about making sausages which are on this list are provided in Chapter 4 - Spanish Sausage Recipes.

Androlla - *sausage*. Spare ribs cut to smaller pieces (bones included), spices, marinated, stuffed in casings, dried in the presence of smoke.

Androlla Maragata - *sausage*. Lean pork, pork skins, no bones, ground, marinated, stuffed in casings, smoked and dried.

Bacon - pork belly, smoked.

Baiona curada - *sausage*. Pork cuts cured with salt and nitrite, mixed with spices, stuffed in natural casings and dried.

Bisbe, Bull - *sausage*. Cooked meat, fat, tongue, occasionally offal meat, salt, pepper, stuffed in large diameter casings and cooked. Sometimes, pork blood is added.

Bispo - *sausage*. A typical product from Pyrenean valleys made with pork masks and head meat, tongues, lean pork which are cooked in water, then the meat is separated from bones, cut or ground, mixed with spices, stuffed in pork caecum (blind cap) and cooked.

Blanquet - *sausage*. Lean pork, pork head meat, eggs. Stuffed in casings and dried.

Bolas - blood, pork fat, bread, spices, pine nuts. All mixed and shaped into round balls, then cooked in water.

Borono - cooked meat product made from pork fat, suet, blood, onions, corn or wheat flour, parsley.

Botelo or **Botillo** - *sausage*. Spare rib meat (bones included), pork tails, bone meat, stuffed into pork blind caps or stomachs.

Budin de **Cerdo** - lean pork, fat, offal meat, fried, cooled and canned.

Butifarra - *sausage*. Pork meat, back fat, offal meat including lungs, heart, and kidneys. Meats are cooked, ground, mixed with spices, stuffed in pork casings and cooked.

Cabeza de jabalí - *sausage*. Head cheese made from *pork* head meat.

Cachuelas - pork liver fried in pork fat with garlic, onions, pimentón, spices. Liver is chopped, all is mixed and cooked.

Callos - cooked beef, veal or sheep stomachs. Also cooked pig stomachs and casings.

Camalot - *sausage*. Lean pork, dewlap, back fat, pork liver, pork blood, pepper pimentón, and spices. Meats ground and mixed with all ingredients. Pork skin is wrapped around the meat mixture and cooked. This irregularly shaped grey colored sausage weighs between 0.5-4.0 kg (1-9 lb).

Chicharrones, Budin - Fried or baked pork fat, occasionally sheep fat. Offal meat sometimes included.

Chireta - *sausage*. Sheep heart, pork lungs, pork lean meat and fat, all cooked and ground. Then, the meats are mixed with rice, parsley, garlic, pepper, cinnamon and sweet pimentón. Stuffed in sheep casings and cooked.

Chistorra - *sausage*. A combination of cut/ground pork, or pork and beef, pork fat, containing pimentón, stuffed into small diameter natural or artificial casings and subsequently dried/natured. The diameter of the finished sausage should not exceed 25 mm, the texture should display an intense red color and the flavor be typical of the product.

Chóped - a fine paste of meat, mainly pork, with visible larger pieces of show-meat.

Chorizo criollo - *sausage*. White chorizo (*no pimentón*) made with ground pork and fat, spices, stuffed into natural or artificial casings, may be submitted to a short drying/maturing process or not, which will contribute to desired color and flavor. The sausage may be be submitted to heat treatment (*optional*).

Chorizo cular - *sausage*. Lean pork, fat, spices, may include garlic, white wine and olive oil. The sausage mass is stuffed into large diameter (40-60 mm) pork casings, usually pork bungs. When cut its texture should display intense red color of lean meat with specks of fat resulting in a marbled appearance.

Chorizo de cebolla - *sausage*. Meat, fat, diced onion, spices.

Chorizo de entraña - *sausage*. Pork jowls (cheeks), spices, stuffed into casings.

Chorizo de Pamplona - *sausage*. Pork meat and fat, occasionally pork and beef even other permitted meats, all ground very finely. May exhibit mold on outside, lean meat and fat particles should be easily visible, the orange tinted fat resembling grains of rice. Lean meat displaying vivid red color.

Chorizo de Teror, Chorizo Palmero and **Chorizo de Perro** - *sausage*. Made of pork, not submitted to drying nor maturing, characterized by a soft spreadable texture.

Chorizo rondeño - *sausage*. Pork meat and fat, stuffed into a natural casing in the form of a ring and submitted to a short drying process of 5-7 days.

Chosco - *sausage*. Pork tongue, loin and lean pork, stuffed into casing.

Chuleta de Sajonia - pork chops, marinated with spices, cooked and usually smoked.

Emberzao - pork fat, blood, chopped onions, pimentón, all mixed with corn flour, formed into balls and wrapped with cabbage leaves. The leaves are tied with twine and cooked.

Embuchado - lamb casing wrapped around in the form of a firm ball and cooked or grilled. Then sliced and served.

Fardeles - cooked pork liver, lean pork, kidneys, pepper, parsley, cinnamon, pimentón, all is mixed and made into portions that are wrapped with pork caul membrane (epiplon).

Farinato - *sausage*. Pork fat, bread, flour, pimentón, stuffed into casings.

Fariñón - *sausage*. Pork fat, blood, onions, pimentón, beaten egg, corn flour, oregano. Stuffed into a large pork casing and cooked.

Flamenquín cordobés - pork roulade filled with pork loin, sliced ham and sheets of back fat. Usually breaded and fried.

Figatells - *sausage*. Lean pork, liver, kidneys, spices. Stuffed into casings.

Fuet - *sausage*. A type of salchichón, stuffed in small diameter casing, usually covered with white mold.

Galantina - fine meat paste, usually from poultry.

Girella or Chireta - *sausage*. Sheep offal meat, lungs, heart, occasionally liver, casings, pork belly. Meats are ground, combined with rice, sometimes egg, and mixed with garlic, parsley, pepper, other spices, stuffed into sheep stomach and cooked.

Gordilla or Madeja - a small diameter lamb casing rolled around a ball of sheep fat.

Güeña - *sausage*. Pork by-products, pork belly, offal meat, ground and mixed with spices (pepper, pimentón, cinnamon, cloves, garlic). Stuffed into 20-24 mm sheep casings, linked every 10-15 cm (4-6").

Hamburguesa - ground meat mixed with spices (hamburger).

Imperial de Lorca - *sausage*. A type of longaniza made with pork meat and fat. Meats are ground, mixed with spices, stuffed in natural casings and dried.

Jamón de pato - duck ham. Duck breast, marinated with salt, seasoned with pepper and dried.

Lacón - pork front leg, dried and matured.

Lomito - head of loin, dried and matured. Smaller and fatter than loin.

Lomo adobado de cerdo - whole loin, well trimmed of tendons and skin, marinated with salt, (spices included or not), marinade may be injected, and then the loin is baked.

Lomo embuchado - *sausage*. Salted loin, marinated with salt and spices, stuffed into natural or artificial casings and dried/matured. The product is made from a whole piece of loin or from its individual muscles firmly stuffed together.

Lomo de Sajonia - pork loin marinated with salt and spices. Cooked and usually smoked.

Longaniza - *sausage*. Ground meat mixed with spices and stuffed into small diameter casings.

Longaniza de Aragón - *sausage*. Pork meat mixed with spices, stuffed into 25-40 mm casings, 20-70 cm (8-26") long, forming "U" shaped loop. Dried and matured.

Longaniza imperial - *sausage*. A type of longaniza, 30-40 mm diameter, shaped in a loop form, covered with white mold.

Longaniza de Pascua - *sausage*. A type of salchichón made from lean pork, back fat, lean pork with attached fat (*lardeo*), beef, mixed with spices and stuffed into small (less than 25 mm) natural or artificial casings. Submitted to drying/maturing process of no less than 5 days.

Longaniza de Payés - *sausage*. Lean pork, pepper, sugars. Dry sausage covered with mold.

Lunch - fine meat paste with pieces of lean pork and back fat.

Magreta - fatty product made with skinless fatty meat trimmings and fat cuts. Marinated and cooked or baked.

Mondejo - *sausage*. Green vegetables, eggs, sheep casings or stomach and sheep fat. Stuffed into sheep casings.

Morcilla - *sausage*. Blood is the main component of blood sausage.

Morcilla blanca - *sausage*. Lean meat, pork belly, tongue, eggs, diced bread, spices, no blood added, all are stuffed into natural or artificial casings and cooked.

Morcilla de calabaza - *sausage*. Blood, back fat, cooked pumpkin and onions, spices. All stuffed into natural or artificial casings and cooked.

Morcilla de cebolla - *sausage*. Onions, fat, pork blood, occasionally rice, spices. All stuffed into natural or artificial casings and cooked.

Morcilla lustre - *sausage*. Blood, often cooked lungs, chopped heart, pork belly, cumin, parsley, mint. All stuffed into natural or artificial casings and cooked.

Morcilla rondeña - *sausage*. Cumin and cloves give this sausage a characteristic sweet flavor. Stuffed into natural or artificial casings forming a loop, and cooked.

Morcilla serrana - *sausage*. Blood, pork belly, pepper, garlic, and pimentón. All stuffed into natural or artificial casings and cooked.

Morcón - *sausage*. Pork shoulder, lean pork, coarse ground, mixed with pepper, pimentón and garlic and stuff into a large pork casing (blind cap or stomach).

Mortadela - *sausage*. A fine paste of pork meat occasionally other animals, usually with diced fat, spices, and often with show-material such as pistachios, olives or peppers.

Mortadela bolonia - *sausage*. A fine pink color paste of pork meat with visible and well defined cubes of fat.

Mortadela cordobesa - *sausage*. A fine paste of pork meat with visible grain-of-rice size cubes of fat and pitted olives.

Mortadela siciliana - *sausage*. A fine pink color paste of pork meat with visible grain-of-rice size cubes of fat.

Morteruelo - meat paste made with pork liver, small wild game, poultry, diced bread and spices.

Moscancia - sausage. Blood, beef suet, onions, pimentón. All mixed, stuffed into beef casing and cooked. Garlic can also be added and optionally beef suet may be replaced with sheep fat.

Panceta or tocineta - pork belly (interlaced layers of fat and meat) which can be prepared and cooked in different ways.

Pantruco - back fat, chopped onions, beaten eggs, corn flour, pimentón, ajo, parsley. Formed into meat balls and cooked.

Patatera - *sausage*. Pork fat, potatoes, pimentón, garlic. All mixed and stuffed into casings.

Perro - *sausage*. Pork head meat, back fat, skins, blood, pepper, cinnamon, cloves. The meats are ground, mixed with all ingredients, stuffed into pork or beef casing and using twine tying sections 25-35 cm (10-14") long.

Relleno de Huéscar - *sausage*. Pork, chicken, dry ham, eggs, bread, parsley. garlic. Meats ground, mixed with all ingredients, stuffed into pork casings and cooked in water.

Roulada - a fine paste of pork or other meats, with cubes of fat.

Sabadeña - *sausage*. Cooked casings, spices are stuffed into casings and submitted to a short drying process.

Sabadiego or **chorizo sabadiego** - *sausage*. Pork meat, beef meat or both, blood, onions, spices. Stuffed into casings, smoked and dried.

Salami - *sausage*. Pork meat or combination of meats, hard fat, spices, ground finely and stuffed into casings forming straight sections. Sausages usually covered with mold.

Salchicha - *sausage*. A typical common and small sausage made from ground meat, spices, and stuffed into casings.

Salchichón de Málaga - *sausage*. Pork meat, beef or both, pork fat, spices. Meats are ground and stuffed into 30 mm or bigger natural casings, and submitted to drying/maturing process.

Salchichón de ajo/al ajillo - *sausage*. Cooked sausage made from meat and back fat, mixed with spices and garlic.

Secallonas, **somalles**, **petadors** - sausage. Small diameter dried and matured sausages, usually less than 30 days.

Sevillana - meats, olives, pepper, spices. Ground, mixed, canned and heat treated.

Torteta - blood, flour, lard, bread, almonds, hazel nuts, pine nuts and others. All mixed, packed into mold and heat treated.

Zarajos - casings from a young or baby lamb, marinated, then spun around a grape vine stick or similar axis.

The meat products listed above are only general descriptions of a particular product, so the word "chorizo", "longaniza" or "morcilla" does not identify a particular sausage. As there are 17 regions in Spain, each one with many municipalities, there are dozens of longanizas chorizos or morcillas, each with its own name and combination of ingredients, for example *Longaniza de Aragón, Longaniza Murciana, Longaniza Navarra* or *Morcilla Andaluz, Morcilla Asturiana, Morcilla de Cebolla Valenciana, Morcilla Dulce Canaria.* This naming convention applies to all products, be it morcilla, chorizo, longaniza or other sausages.

European Certificates of Origin

Throughout Europe there is a huge assortment of great foods. When a product acquires a reputation extending beyond national borders it can face competition from other products which may pass themselves off as the genuine article and take the same name. Our hats go off to the French who invented the idea in the 1930's to protect their regional wines. The system used in France from the early part of the twentieth century is known as the appellation d'origine contrôlée (AOC). Items that meet geographical origin and quality standards may be endorsed with a government-issued stamp which acts as an official certification of the origins and standards of the product to the consumer. In 1992, the European Union created the following systems to promote and protect food products:

Photo 1.6 Protected Designation of Origin (PDO) - covers the term used to describe foodstuffs which are produced, processed and prepared in a given geographical area using recognized know-how.

Example: Jamón de Huelva (ham) - Spain.

Photo 1.7 Protected Geographical Indication (PGI) - the geographical link must occur in at least one of the stages of production, processing or preparation.

Example: Salchichón de Vic (dry sausage) - Spain

Photo 1.8 Traditional Speciality Guaranteed (TSG) - does not refer to the origin but highlights traditional character, either in the composition or means of production.

Example: Jamon Serrano (ham) - Spain

This system is similar to the French Appellation d'Origine Contrôlée (AOC) system, the Denominazione di Origine Controllata (DOC) used in Italy, and the Denominación de Origen system used in Spain. The purpose of the law is to protect the reputation of the regional foods and eliminate the unfair competition and misleading of consumers by non-genuine products, which may be of inferior quality or of different flavor. These laws protect the names of wines, cheeses, hams, sausages, olives, beers, and even regional breads, fruits, and vegetables.

As such, foods such as Gorgonzola, Parmigiano Reggiano, Asiago cheese, Camembert de Normandie and Champagne can only be labelled as such if they come from the designated region. To qualify as Roquefort, for example, cheese must be made from the milk of a certain breed of sheep, and matured in the natural caves near the town of Roquefort in the Aveyron region of France where it is infected with the spores of a fungus (*Penicillium roqueforti*) that grows in those caves. Italy has a long history in the production of traditional fermented sausages, and almost every part of the country offers many great products, some of which have been awarded Protected Designation of Origin and Protected Geographical Indication certificates. In order to preserve the original taste and flavor, these products are made without starter cultures and sold on local markets. European Certificates of Origin don't come easy and only a few countries were able to obtain them for meat products.

Indication of Quality

Traditionally made sausages were made from leaner meats than commercially produced products of today. In addition, mass produced sausages contain ingredients such as starches, antioxidants, nitrates, curing accelerators, colorants, protein concentrates, color stabilizers, sugars, hydrocolloids (gums), powdered milk, phosphates and more. All those ingredients decrease production time, lower costs and extend the shelf life of the products to give supermarkets sufficient time for selling them. To buy the best quality sausage read the label. A good indication of quality is the casing - is it natural or synthetic. All sausages carrying European Certificates of Origin are stuffed in natural casings and do not contain chemicals.

Photo 1.9 Sobrasada de Mallorca. Label attached to protective wrapping. Each sausage has its own serial number. The list of ingredients is also included.

Photo 1.10 Chorizo de Cantipalos. Label attached directly to twine. Sausage has its own serial number. The list of ingredients is also included.

Spanish Sausages Carrying European Certificates of Origin

There are hundreds of manufacturers making thousands of different quality sausages, and as long as they are safe to the consumer they can be sold. However, a sausage carrying the Protected Geographical Indication (PGI) mark must conform to a set of stringent regulations so there is no doubt to its quality no matter where it is sold.

Photo 1.11 Sobrasada de Mallorca, PGI 1996.

Photo 1.12 Sobrasada de Mallorca de cerdo negro (from black pig) PGI 1996.

Photo 1.13 Salchichón de Vic; Longanissa de Vic, PGI 2001.

Photo 1.14 Botillo del Bierzo, PGI 2001.

Photo 1.15 Chorizo Riojano, PGI 2010.

Photo 1.16 Chorizo de Cantipalos, PGI 2011.

Photo 1.17 Chosco de Tineo, PGI 2011.

Photo 1.18 Morcilla de Burgos, PGI 2018.

Each of these sausages is described in detail in Chapter 4 - Recipes.

Spanish Sausages Today

Unfortunately, artisan sausage making in Spain follows the same trend as in other countries; young people move to large cities and are less inclined to maintain family traditions which includes general cooking skills and making sausages. However, people living in rural areas still gather together to celebrate the "la matanza" ritual the same way it has always been done. In addition in areas recognized for the superb sausages there are numerous shows and festivities, for example "*chireta* festival" in Aragon or "*la festa de androlla*" in Galicia. Spain is famous for a number of original sausages: *chorizo, longaniza, sobrasada, lomo embuchado, salchichón, fuet, morcilla, androlla, botelo* or *buche de costillas* and others.

Cooked sausages like *salchichas* or liver sausages are made in other European countries and although they carry different names, they differ little from Spanish ones as they are made with the same technology, from similar meats and spice combinations. It is only fair to give special recognition to *morcilla* as there is no other country with such a variety of blood sausages as Spain.

Dry fermented sausages account for about 15% of all meat products produced in Spain. Pork is the most common meat, although beef and lamb are also occasionally used. A wide variety of raw-fermented and dried sausages are produced and the methods of production, choice of materials and spices have been strongly influenced by geographical location and climate conditions. Today, with the advance of technology, the importance of climate and location plays a lesser role, at least for commercial producers as parameters such as temperature, humidity and air flow are computer controlled in drying chambers.

Home production still relies on traditional methods, however, even hobbyists today use nitrite curing salts and starter cultures. What separates Spanish sausages from others is: meat selection, heavy usage of locally grown paprika (*pimentón*) and marinating meats with spices (*adobo*).

Following the same trend that is happening in other countries little butcher shops are pushed out of existence, at least in large metropolitan areas, by huge supermarkets that carry a variety of foods on one floor. They do not manufacture their own cheeses, hams or sausages, but buy them at wholesale prices from the manufacturers. It is impossible for a small store to compete with giants like *El Corte Inglés* or *Museo de Jamón*, the last one not being a museum but a combination of a huge meat store and a restaurant. A customer can buy a sample of ham, loin or one of many sausages and enjoy it with wine or beer. Once teaming with life markets like *Mercado de la Cebada,* established in 1875, are having only a few remaining butcher and fish stores which carry a wide assortment of quality products, but a few customers are walking around.

Out in the country small butchers face less competition from large industry giants for whom starting a big supermarket may not be the best investment. Butchers in large cities who have a chance of continuing business are those who own their stores and have a local trusted clientele.

Photo 1.19 Jamonería Lopez Pascual in Madrid was established in 1919. Alberto Lopez is the third generation family member that runs the store.

Chapter 2

Types of Spanish Sausages

The official list of Spanish meat products and sausages known as Boletín Oficial del Estado, Real Decreto 474/2014 was presented in the previous chapter. It lists 29 meat products and 58 sausages which are popular in Spain. Out of this list there is a certain number of products which are favored by a consumer and those will be described in a more detail.

Spanish sausages can be divided as:

Hard sausages - not cooked just dried, characterized by firm texture, can be sliced paper thin, majority of products exhibiting vivid red color, can be stored at room temperature for a long time.

Soft cooked sausages - these are Spanish versions of sausages which can be found in other European countries: blood and liver sausages, mortadella, frankfurter. They all have similar composition and follow similar processing technology. They have longer shelf life than fresh sausages, but still need to be refrigerated.

Soft fresh sausages - processing of these sausages ends with the stuffing step. They have a short life and must be refrigerated. They must be fully cooked before serving. These are very simple to make products and are not even listed in the official list of Spanish sausages.

The consumer does not think about how sausages are grouped, he simply likes some more than the others. Sausages which have gained the biggest acceptance by the consumer are described in this chapter. Many of these sausages are known not only in Spain, but in other countries of the world. A large percentage of Spanish products are dried what results in a long shelf life. This makes them attractive to supermarkets as they have plenty of time for selling them without worrying about spoilage.

The official classification of Spanish sausages as presented in Spanish Food Code *(Código Alimentario Español), Decreto 2484/1967.*

Secion 3 - Meat Products *(Derivados carnicos)*

3.10.23 Sausages *(Embutidos).*

The definition of the sausage *(embutido)* applies to prepared meat products, comminuted or not, subsequently cured or not, containing edible meat parts and fat, products of vegetable nature, flavorings and spices, and stuffed into natural or artificial casings.

The classification of sausages:

3.10.24. Sausages made with meat *(Embutidos de carne).*
3.10.25. Sausages made with offal meat *(Embutidos de visceras).*
3.10.26. Sausages made with blood *(Embutidos de sangre).*
3.10.27. Sausages formed into blocks *(Fiambres).*

Raw sausages *(Embutidos crudos).* Sausages which are only marinated, mixed and stuffed into casings, matured or not, dried and smoked or not. Free of connective tissues, cartilage or suet.

Cooked in water sausages. *(Embutidos escaldados).* Sausages prepared from finely comminuted meat, cooked for different times in water at 70-80° C (158-176° F) and then smoked or not.

3.10.24 Sausages made with Meat *(Embutidos de carne).*

Sausages made with meat as specified in paragraph 3.10.1. They can be "pure" *(puros)* or "mixed" *(mezcla)* depending whether they are made from one type of meat (for example pork only) or with meats from different animals (for example pork and beef). Their texture can be be hard, soft or pasty. Their color can be red or white, depending on whether they contain pimentón.

Traditional products:

Chorizo-Embuchado-Salchichón-Salchichas-Salchicha type Frankfort (Frankfurter)-Salchicha type Viena (Wiener)-Butifarra-Butifarrón-Sobrasada

Boletín Oficial del Estado is the set of all regulations that regulate industry, food, cosmetics and all aspects of life in Spain. In United States it is called Code of Federal Regulations (CFR).

The latest Spanish regulations **for dry (cured) sausages** were established in **BOE-A-1980-6080**, on February 7, 1980 and are quoted in our book where applicable.

Chorizo

From Spanish Government Official Regulations *(Boletín Oficial del Estado), BOE-A-1980-6080m, February 7, 1980, Section 2:*

Chorizo is a mixture of comminuted pork, or pork and beef, pork fat, salt, pimentón, other spices, authorized flavorings and additives, stuffed into natural or artificial casings, submitted to sufficient drying and maturing, smoked or not, to obtain the characteristic red color (with the exception of white chorizos) and characteristic taste and flavor.

Chorizo must include **pimentón**. When chorizo is made *without* pimentón but conforms to all requirements for making chorizo it is called *chorizo blanco* (white chorizo).

General Characteristics

Chorizos exhibit a firm texture, cylindrical shape, more or less round, presented in different methods depending how they are linked (straight, tied in series with twine, U-shaped), generally looking rough on outside, the casing well adhered to the meat. When cut, the slices are clean with uniform texture holding its shape well, fat particles can be easily distinguished from lean. Chorizos exhibit characteristic color and flavor due to spices, flavorings and processing steps.

When chorizo sausage is stuffed into 40 mm or larger casings it can be called *chorizo* only; if it is stuffed into casings smaller than 40 mm but bigger than 22 mm it can be called *chorizo* or *longaniza*, and if it stuffed into casing smaller than 22 mm it must be called *longaniza*.

Photo 2.1 Chorizo.

Ingredients

Ingredients commonly used are salt, pimentón, garlic, black or white pepper, nutmeg, oregano, powdered milk, sugar, curing salts.

Chorizo is the most popular Spanish fermented dry sausage. Chorizo is a small, intensely orange-red sausage which is cured (dried, but not cooked), and often cold smoked. Smoke is applied not for the flavor, but as a part of the drying process, usually to warm up the chamber when the temperature drops low.

Pimentón was brought to Spain by Christopher Columbus so chorizos made before 1493 did not include it and were light colored. In time pimentón has become the most important ingredient for making quality chorizos. Certain chorizo recipes require that only the best quality Pimentón de La Vera be used, for instance Chorizo de Cantipalos - *"If it does not contain pimentón de La Vera it is not Chorizo de Cantipalos."* Hot and sweet pimentón are often mixed together.

Originally, chorizo was made with lean pork, usually loin, however, today it is a coarsely ground sausage with a generous proportion of fat. There are exceptions, for instance in Chorizo de Pamplona the meat is finely ground. Chorizo de Pamplona and Chorizo de Soria in addition to pork also include beef.

Chorizo de Cantipalos

This classic, dry chorizo originates in the municipality of Cantipalos in the province of Segovia in Castilla and León, Spain.

From 2011 Chorizo de Cantipalos carries protective geographical indication certificate (PGI).

Chorizo Riojano (*Chorizo de la Rioja*) is made in the autonomous community of La Rioja in Spain. The sausage carries Protective Geographical Indication (PGI 2010) award.

Photo 2.2 Chorizo riojano.

Chorizo de Pamplona

From Spanish Government Official Regulations *(Boletín Oficial del Estado)*, *BOE-A-1980-6080m, February 7, 1980, Section 3:*

Chorizo de Pamplona is a mixture of comminuted pork, or pork and beef, and pork fat ground through 3 mm plate, salt, pimentón, other spices, authorized flavorings and additives, stuffed into natural or artificial casings forming straight sections, submitted to sufficient drying and maturing with smoke; the fully cured sausage must have a diameter of 40 mm or more, the surface slightly grainy and the slices should display easily visible grain-of-rice sizes of pink fat, the sausage having characteristic taste and flavor.

Photo 2.3 Chorizo de Pamplona is easy to recognize due to its finely comminuted meat. It looks almost like salami, however, it is made with pimentón so its color and taste are different.

Chorizo de Cerdo Ibérico *(Chorizo made with Iberian pig meat)*

From Spanish Government Official Regulations *(Boletín Oficial del Estado)*, *BOE-A-1980-6080m, February 7, 1980, Section 5:*

Chorizo de Cerdo Ibérico is a mixture of comminuted meat and fat that must come from Iberian pig only, salt, pimentón, other spices, authorized flavorings and additives, stuffed into natural or artificial casings, submitted to sufficient drying and maturing, with or without smoke, to obtain the characteristic red color and characteristic taste and flavor.

Iberian meat is what separates this chorizo from others and to enforce conformity to official regulations meat inspectors have the right to inspect production facilities of any factory that produces this sausage.

Traditional method of making chorizo

There are many regions, provinces and municipalities in Spain and each has its own chorizo. This results in dozens of names, different spice combinations, thicknesses and lengths of the sausages, however, the processing technology remains basically the same for all of them. Best meat for chorizo comes from heavy pigs weighing about 150 kg (330 lb). Lean pork (70-80%), back fat (20-30%). Salt, sweet and hot pimentón, garlic and oregano. No addition of sodium nitrite, sodium nitrate or sugars was allowed, however, adding those ingredients is practiced today. Traditional production took place in winter months when low temperatures allowed the slaughter of the pig and processing of its meat in the streets at a comfortable and unhurried pace. Then the stuffed sausages were transferred to a drying chamber which was often heated by burning oak wood.

Meat selection - lean pork (70-80%), back fat (20-30%). Meat must be well trimmed and all tendons, sinews and gristle removed.

Cutting/grinding (*Picado*) - meat is ground through 8-10 mm (3/8") plate. Fat can be ground through the same plate or manually diced into cubes which will result in a better visual distribution when the sausage is sliced. To avoid smearing, fat should be partially frozen.

Mixing with salt and spices - ground meat is mixed with all ingredients: salt, pimentón, and garlic are required, oregano is also usually included, pimentón is applied in large amounts, 20-30 g/1 kg of meat. Sweet and hot pimentón are added together depending on desired hotness of the sausage. This sausage paste known as *adobo* is then marinated in a refrigerator what is known as *reposo*.

Marinating and **Conditioning** (*Reposo y maceración*) - application of a marinade (*adobo*) - usually for 24 hours at 2-6° C (36-42° F) or in refrigerator.
Stuffing - Chorizo is stuffed in natural casings larger than 22 mm, 40-50 mm being normal. Casings formed into rings with both ends connected with twine to facilitate hanging.

Fermenting/drying (*Estufaje*) - at 22-24° C (72-75° F), 85-90% humidity, with or without smoke, for 48 hours.

Drying (*Secado*) - at 12-15° C (53-59° F), 75-85% humidity, for 7-30 days, depending on diameter.

Commercial processors add nitrite and/or nitrate, sugars, reducing agents and occasionally colorants. The fermenting and drying processes take place in computerized chambers where temperature, humidity and air flow are computer controlled.

What has changed today is that due to refrigerators becoming a common appliance, chorizo and other formerly dry only sausages are made as fresh ones that end up fried, grilled or in stews.

Longaniza

Longaniza is a long pork sausage which can also be found in Puerto Rico, Dominican Republic, El Salvador, Mexico, Chile, Argentina, and Uruguay. In Philippines the sausage is known as *longanisa*. Longaniza is one of the oldest sausages already described in 1529 by Ruperto de Nola in his "Libro de Cocina" (Cookbook), and in 1882 by by Angel Muro in his "Diccionario General de Cocina" (Cooking Dictionary).

Processing steps for making longaniza are the same as for chorizo so both sausages are closely related. The sausage is occasionally smoked, too. Both sausages contain pimentón, however, in some longanizas pimentón is either not included or added in smaller amounts. Longaniza differs from chorizo in that it is longer and stuffed into smaller than 40 mm casings. There is no lower limit, longaniza can be stuffed in 22 mm and even smaller casings, which are not permitted for chorizo.

Photo 2.4 Longaniza, dry cured.

Llonganissa de Vic also known as **Salchichón de Vic** is the best known Spanish longaniza. It is made in the province of Barcelona. Llonganissa de Vic carries PGI, 2001 classification. The first references written about sausage from Vic date back to 1456. In the past, this product was produced in the farms located in the Plana de Vic as a method of preserving meats, taking advantage of the suitable climate conditions of the area.

LLONGANISSA•DE
VIC
INDICACIÓ GEOGRÀFICA
PROTEGIDA

Chorizo and longaniza can be distinguished by shape and size:

- chorizo - 30-45 mm, 8-10 cm long, curved links or horseshoe loops (*sarta or herradura*)
- longaniza - less than 40 mm, 30-70 cm long, straight (*cular or vela*)

Fresh longaniza is available in Spanish supermarkets. It is usually stuffed into 22 mm sheep casings and must be cooked before serving. When salchichón is stuffed into casing smaller than than 40 mm, it may be called *longaniza imperial*.

Manufacturing

Meat selection - depending on region longaniza can be made from lean pork, semi-fat pork, including some offal meat (lungs, heart), beef. The choice of spices is also more diverse and longanizas include pepper, garlic, pimentón, nutmeg, aniseed and vinegar. In Catalonia, dry longaniza goes by the name *llonganissa*.

Cutting/grinding - meat is ground through 6 mm (1/4") plate which is smaller than for chorizo due to the smaller diameter of longaniza.

Mixing with salt and spices - salt, pepper, cure #1, sugar, nutmeg, garlic, pimentón or not, anise, white wine. The sausage paste (*adobo*) is then submitted to marinating.

Marinating and **Conditioning** - application of a marinade (*adobado*) - usually for 24 hours at 2-6° C (36-42° F) or in refrigerator.

Stuffing - longaniza is stuffed in long natural casings not larger than 40 millimeters. Sausages tied into 15 cm (6") into forming 100 cm (3') sections or made into rings with both ends tied with twine to facilitate hanging.

Fermenting/drying - at 18-20° C (64-70° F), with smoke or not, for 24 hours.

Drying - at 12-15° C (53-59° F), 75-85% humidity, for 8-10 days.

Photo 2.5 Longaniza de Payés.

Chistorra

From Spanish Government Official Regulations *(Boletín Oficial del Estado)*, *BOE-A-1980-6080m, February 7, 1980, Section 4:*

Chistorra is a mixture of comminuted pork, or pork and beef, and pork fat, salt, pimentón, garlic, and authorized additives, stuffed into natural or artificial casings, submitted to sufficient drying and maturing with or without smoke; the fully cured sausage must have a diameter of no more than 25 mm, and exhibit the characteristic red color, taste and flavor.

As far as materials, ingredients and processing steps are concerned, there is not much difference between Chistorra, Chorizo and Chorizo de Pamplona. Chistorra has the smallest diameter, Chorizo de Pamplona is very finely ground, and most chorizos are coarsely ground. Fresh chistorra is also available. Chistorra is a delicious sausage that can be found in most supermarkets. Both sausages, Chistorra and Chorizo de Pamplona contain more fat than a typical chorizo, in chistorra the fat can reach up to 50%.

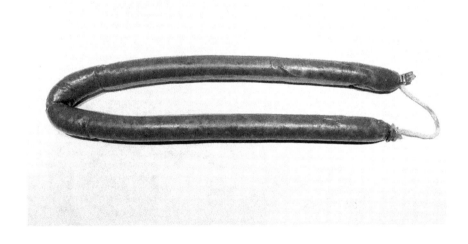

Photo 2.6 Chistorra.

Lomo Embuchado (*Stuffed Pork Loin*)

From Spanish Government Official Regulations *(Boletín Oficial del Estado), BOE-A-1980-6080m, February 7, 1980, Section 8:*

Lomo embuchado *(Stuffed loin) is made from the ileoespinal muscle of the pig (practically free of external fat, silver screen membrane and tendons), salted and marinated (adobado), stuffed into natural or artificial permeable casings, and subjected to the drying and maturing process.*

Processing steps: trimming loin from the outside fat, tendons and membrane commonly known as "silver screen", dry salting or curing in brine, stuffing into natural or artificial permeable casings, tying or clipping both ends, and drying and maturing.

General characteristics: stuffed loin is made from one whole loin muscle. the texture of the loin is firm and resistant to pressing against it, the shape cylindrical, the diameter of the casing 40 mm or more and variable length. The casing adheres well throughout the entire length and may be covered with mold. The slices clean and holding shape, the color red or rosy and the texture uniform and solid without having separate muscles. The taste and flavor characteristic for this product.

Ingredients: salt, pimentón, garlic, black or white pepper, nutmeg and other spices, Stuffed loins have no quality classification, however, the notice is made on the label when the loin is made from iberian pork. They always carry a red label that implies the Extra product (the highest quality). The embuchado loin should be cut into thin slices and eaten raw, sometimes in a sandwich.

Photo 2.7 Ibérico pork loin (*lomo embuchdo ibérico*).

When loin consists of individual muscle cuts and is processed in the same way as a one piece loin, it is called *morcón* and is stuffed into pork blind cap (caecum, "ciego" in Spanish), for example Morcón Extremeño. Morcón de Lorca, however, is an exception as it is made with lean head meat and dewlap.

Many countries produce loins, but they are smoked and cooked, for example Canadian Bacon made in the USA. Why it is called "bacon" remains a mystery, Canadians call it "back bacon" which is also incorrect as it is a pork loin, or "peameal bacon" which is a pork loin rolled in cornmeal. In most countries it is simply a "smoked loin."All those loins are cured, usually with a wet method, then smoked/cooked or just cooked. Lomo is different in that that it is not cooked at all what gives the sausage its characteristic texture allowing it to be sliced paper thin. Its deep vivid red color, induced by large amount of pimentón is unmistakably Spanish and completely different from loins cured with nitrite only.

All Spanish dry products such as chorizo, longaniza, salchichón or fuet are submitted to 24-48 hours of marinating (*reposo y maceración*) which is not a real curing but rather a short conditioning step. Lomo, however, is properly cured with salt using a dry or wet method of curing. After salting the loin is marinated and after that it is stuffed into a casing.

Wet curing - immersing loin in brine made of salt and water. A strong brine of Baume 20° (80° Salometer) is made by dissolving 264 g of salt in 1 liter of water or 2.22 lb of salt in 1 US gallon (3.8 liters) of water. The more salt added to water the stronger the brine. Allocate about 40% (400 ml) of brine per 1 kg of meat. Loin weighing 1 kg (2.2 lb) needs 400 ml (0.42 qt) of brine.

If cure #1, which contains 93.75% salt, is added to brine, this salt should be subtracted from the total salt added for making brine. About 120 g of cure #1 can be added to 1 gallon of water so for making Baume 20° (80° Salometer) we need 2220 g - (0.9375 x 120 g)=2200-112=2088 g of salt.

If the container is much bigger than the loin you may need more brine. Brine is usually made with salt and water only, but often marinade making ingredients are included. Loin is submerged in brine for 3-4 days depending on diameter. Then it is removed and placed in cold water for 24 hours, a few water changes are needed. The loin is drained and hung to dry. Marinade paste is applied when the loin is sufficiently dry or at least tacky to touch.

There is not one standard marinade nor the same production regimen that may be applied to every loin. It is obvious that a larger diameter loin needs more brining, marinating and drying time. The drying will be faster at higher temperatures, lower humidity or stronger air flow. Climate conditions differ from region to region as well as the choice of spices. If oregano grows well in a particular area, the locals will add it to products they make. Spices that are added to marinade are the ones used for making chorizo: salt, pimentón, garlic and oregano. This is the basic combination, however, additional spices like pepper, bay leaf and cumin are often included. To obtain marinating paste they are usually dissolved in liquids such as olive oil, white wine, vinegar or just water.

Marinade (*adobo*) *per 1 kg of meat*: olive oil 60 ml (4 Tbsp), sweet pimentón 30 g (4.5 Tbsp), hot pimentón 6.0 g (3 tsp), vinegar 30 ml (2 Tbsp), garlic 3.5 g (1 clove) cumin 1.0 g (1/2 tsp), bay leaf (1) and oregano 2.0 g (1 tsp). Taste your marinade, there is still time to change its composition, for example adding some lime juice. Salt is not mentioned because it was applied as brine. If for any reasons the brining process is omitted, you must rub in 35 g (6 Tbsp) of salt into the loin before applying marinade paste.

Crush bay leaf and mix with wine adding smashed garlic.

Mix all ingredients until a marinade paste is obtained.

Apply marinade all over the loin until it is covered in thick paste.

Hold loin for 48 hours in refrigerator.

Stuff into pork bungs.

Dry for about 3 months.

Dry curing - common salt is manually rubbed in all around the loin. Simple sprinkling from the shaker will not suffice, the salt must be forcefully rubbed in into all parts of the loin.

Hold the loin at low temperature or in refrigerator for 3 days.

Wash and soak in water for 24 hours.

Drain and dry sufficiently so it can accept marinade paste.

Apply marinade paste and hold in refrigerator for 48 hours.

Stuff into pork bungs.

Dry for about 3 months depending on diameter.

Loins are dried at 12-15° C (53-59° F), usually at room temperature that could oscillate between 15-18° C (59-64° F). Occasionally, they are submitted to the fermenting step at 18-20° C (64-68° F) for 24-48 hours.

The size of the casing is chosen to fit the loin snugly. A little oil is occasionally applied to the surface of the loin to make the operation easier. One end of the loin is tied with butcher twine and the loin is pulled through the casing. Then both ends are tied and a hanging loop is created. Pork bung is a traditionally used casing and its texture (surface holes) is perfect for extended drying. Artificial casings can also be used as long as they are permeable (allow moisture and smoke to go through). Their drying cycle is much shorter, so weigh the loin to verify that it has lost 35% of its original weight.

There are different temperatures for fermenting or drying. They may be at 25° C (75° F), 15° C (59° F) or at 12 °C (53° F), and the drying will continue in each case, however, the flavor of the product will vary. The flavor is the result of many reactions, some due to bacteria work such as fermentation or development of color, some due to breakdown of proteins and fats. At 12° C (53° F) fermentation will be negligible due to the fact that bacteria are less active at low temperature, but at 25° C (75° F) they will metabolize sugar just fine.

When Loin is Done?

In computer controlled chambers loins can be produced in 2-3 months, in home production it will take longer, 3-4 months. Once it loses about 35% of its original weight it may be considered done.

Photo 2.8 Stuffed pork loin (*lomo embuchado*).

Salchichón

From Spanish Government Official Regulations *(Boletín Oficial del Estado), BOE-A-1980-6080m, February 7, 1980:*

Salchichón *is a mixture of comminuted pork, beef, or pork and beef, pork fat, salt, spices, additives, stuffed into natural or artificial casings, submitted to sufficient drying and maturing to obtain stability, and characteristic taste and flavor.*

General characteristics: salchichón has a firm texture which is resistant to pressing against it, the cylindrical shape, the casing adheres well throughout the entire length and may be of variable length depending on whether the links are straight or U-shaped. The slices are clean and holding shape, the color red and the texture uniform and solid with visible fragments of fat and lean. The characteristic taste and flavor of this product depends on meat, spices and processing steps.

Ingredients: salt, spices, garlic, black or white pepper, oregano, nutmeg, non-animal proteins, dry milk, sugars, sodium nitrite.

Salchichón comes in all quality grades: Extra, 1st Grade, 2nd and 3rd Grade.

Photo 2.9 Salchichón is a large diameter and quite long dry sausage, usually stuffed into pork bung or suitable artificial casings.

Photo 2.10 In most cases salchichón is stuffed into straight pork bungs, however, in this photo it is formed into U-loop (*herradura* style).

The smallest diameter of casing allowed for salchichón is 20 mm. If stuffed into a diameter smaller than 40 mm then it may be called *fuet, longaniza imperial, salchichón, salchichonada* or *longaniza de Aragón*. Salchichón is usually stuffed into 40-60 mm pork bungs or artificial casings, 30-50 cm (12-20") long.

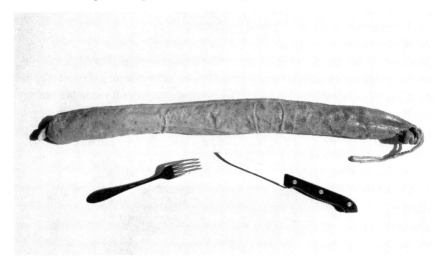

Photo 2.11 Salchichón is a large sausage, this one is 55 cm (22") long.

Salchichón is the Spanish equivalent of Italian salami. Salami probably has a stronger name recognition at least in the USA, however, salchichón is a superb sausage made from first grade meat. After chorizo, salchichón is the second most popular sausage in Spain. Due to its popularity salchichón is produced locally in many areas so different varieties can be expected. The typical ingredients are lean pork, lean beef, pork hard fat, salt, sugar, ground and whole black pepper, nutmeg, cilantro, sherry wine and additives such as nitrite, nitrate, phosphates, which are used by commercial producers. Classical, traditional salchichón is made with black pepper only, no other spices are included. *Pimentón is not added to salchichón*, and this differs the sausage from chorizo. The deep orange-red color of chorizo, cannot be mistaken with the red color of salchichón.

Processing steps: meat is ground, mixed with spices and marinated for 24 hours. The mixture is stuffed into 40-60 mm natural casings. Then the sausages are fermented for 3 days. After that they are dried for 3-5 weeks. Cold smoke may be applied during the drying stage. Typical meat is pork, but recipes with other meats such as ox, veal, or even horse meat can be found in Spanish books. A typical traditional way of making these sausages at home was to mix salt, nitrate and spices with meat and then hang the sausage for 4-5 days in the kitchen or in open air outside. Then the sausage was transferred to a dry and drafty area where it remained for 2-3 months. After that time it was ready for consumption. Salchichón is served as a snack on its own, on sandwiches or in side dishes.

Fuet

Fuet is a smaller version of salchichón so it is a kind of salami stuffed into a smaller, usually less than 40 mm, irregular natural casing, about 30 cm (1') long. Fuet in Spanish means "lash", the word *fuete* means "whip" and the sausage resembles the whip. The sausage is called *fuet* in Spanish Catalan language and *fouet* in French. In pure Spanish Catalan it is often addressed as *longaniza imperial*. This is why fuet is sometimes referred as a smaller version of longaniza which is not correct as longaniza is actually close to chorizo and they both include pimentón. The sausage originates in Catalonia in northern regions of Spain. It is a small diameter sausage, very popular in all areas of Spain and in many European countries. Fuet is sliced diagonally, a little thicker than salchichón. Its main characteristic is that it is covered with white mold. Due to its popularity it is manufactured in many areas so it can be expected that there will be small differences in its composition, especially in commercially manufactured products where fuet includes nuts or figs.

Photo 2.12 Fuet.

General recipe: lean pork (65-75%), back fat (25-35%), salt, sugar, white pepper, black pepper. Sausage is stuffed into 34-48 mm casings and held for 24 hours at 28° C (82° F), 90% humidity. It is dried for 30 days at 12-14° C (53-56° F), 75-85% humidity. Commercial producers will add sodium glutamate, sodium ascorbate, phosphates, sodium nitrite, sodium nitrate, coloring. Fuet is covered in white mold and the casing is tender and easy to peel off, however, many people don't bother with removing the skin as the mold is pleasantly smelling, almost aromatic. The saying that follows says it all:

> "The fungus is always good, it is the perfume of the fuet"
> *(Siempre que el hongo sea bueno, es el perfume del fuet)*

Salami

From Spanish Government Official Regulations *(Boletín Oficial del Estado), BOE-A-1980-6080m, February 7, 1980, Section 7:*

Salami *is a mixture of comminuted pork, beef, pork and beef, pork fat, ground into particles smaller than 3 mm (1/8"). stuffed into straight sections, dried, smoked and matured to acquire characteristic taste and flavor.*

When cut, the slices should display easily noticeable particles of fat and lean.

Spanish salami comes in two grades: Extra and the 1st grade.

Technology of making traditional salami is very similar to that of producing dry sausages such as salchichón or chorizo. Pimentón is not added at all to Spanish salami. Technically speaking, salchichón may be considered to be the Spanish equivalent of Italian salami. High quality *traditionally produced* Italian salami is made *with very little added sugar or none at all.* There is no sugar allowed in traditionally made Hungarian salami, so there is little natural fermentation. Those sausages are called salami in their countries, but if the meat was ground with a larger plate they might be as well called salchichones.

Salami, although of Italian origin, is the sausage which an be found in each corner of the world, including Latin and South America. It is especially popular in Argentina where it is produced on a large scale.

Photo 2.13 Spanish salami.

Secallona-Somalla-Petador-Espetec

Secallona, Somalla, Petador, Espetec - although those names sound mysterious and exotic, the truth is that they all are dry sausages and they all can be called small diameter fuets or longanizas. The manufacturing process is basically the same, what separates them is the size. Longaniza is packed into a large diameter, fuet into medium and secallona into a small diameter casing. Secallona is very dry and wrinkled, somalla is moister. Secallona or somalla are U-shaped, about 50 cm (20") long and usually without mold, unlike fuet which always carries white mold. Petador is the name that is common for those sausages in Catalonian city of Sabadell, 20 km north from Barcelona. Espetec or fuet is basically the same Catalonian sausage.

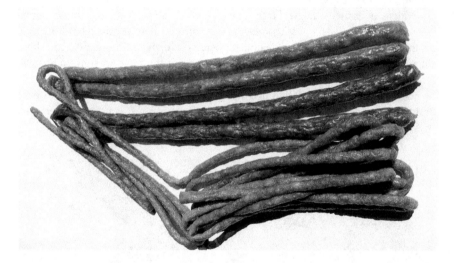

Photo 2.14 Secallona.

Didalets. Didalets, for example *didalets de secallona,* are very short small diameter sausages, about 10 cm (4") long, weighing 10 g (1/3 oz) each what makes them a convenient snack. They can be cooked or fresh sausages, but they are very short.

Photo 2.15 Didalets.

Salchichas

From Spanish Food Code *(Código Alimentario Español-Decreto 2484/1967):*

Salchichas are soft sausages, raw, of red or white color, made from finely comminuted pork or pork and beef (occasionally from sheep, chicken or game), mixed with pork fat and stuffed into 18-28 mm natural or synthetic casings, 28 mm being the maximum diameter."

This definition pertains to a fresh salchicha which be stored for up to 7 days in refrigerator or be frozen, however, they must be fully cooked before serving by frying, grilling or boiling.

Pimentón can be added or not and that influences the color of the sausage which can be red or yellowish. Due to its small size salchichas are often tied off into small units about 50 grams (1.76 oz) each.

Salchichas Frankfurter Type (tipo Francfort) are sausages cooked in water, made from very finely comminuted (emulsified) pork or pork and beef, mixed with pork fat and stuffed into 18-28 mm natural or synthetic casings, 28 mm being the maximum diameter, smoked and cooked in water.

Salchichas which are cooked first and then smoked are called Wieners (tipo Viena).

Only the manufacturer knows what goes into mass produced salchichas; pork, beef, sheep, poultry, de-boned meat plus flours, starches, dry milk, sugar, soy proteins, gums, colorings, antioxidants, sodium nitrite, flavorings, water and anything that is not prohibited by the government as dangerous to our health.

Some well known salchichas: Salchicha Madrileña, Salchicha de Trufas, Salchicha de Ternera, Hot Dog, Frankfurter, Wiener plus hundreds of German sausages such as Bratwurst, Bockwurst, Bierwurst, Weisswurst. The majority of salchichas are cooked in water during processing, however, some like Bratwurst, Salchicha de Trufas, Salchicha de Ternera are fresh type and are usually fried or grilled before serving.

The names of Spanish liver sausages do not start with the word "liver" (*higado* in Spanish), but have salchicha prefix ie. Salchicha de higado (Liver Sausage), Salchicha de higado con trufas (Liver Sausage with Truffles).

Photo 2.16 Salchichas. Salchicha is a term that covers almost any fresh or cooked small sausage.

Butifarra

From Spanish Food Code *(Código Alimentario Español-Decreto 2484/1967):*

Butifarra *is generally a white sausage, made from pork or pork and beef, stuffed into a natural pork or beef small diameter casing and cooked or not, in water.*

Butifarras are popular in Spain regions facing the Mediterranean sea: Catalonia, Balearic Islands, Murcia, Valencia and Andalusia. As the Catalan language differs somewhat from standard Spanish, butifarra produced in Catalonia is spelled *"botifarra."* Butifarras can be found in Colombia, El Salvador, Mexico, Argentina, Uruguway, Chile, Peru, Bolivia and Paraguay. Butifarras are cooked so they are ready to eat sausages, however, they are occasionally added to other dishes or grilled and served with beans. Butifarras are stuffed into small diameter casings, linked every 15 cm (6") or left in a continuous coil. There are two types of butifarra:

- Butifarra Negra - made with blood (*negro* means black), so they are related to morcillas (blood sausages).
- Butifarra Blanca - made without blood. It can be classified as salchicha.

Then there are varieties of butifarras made with: liver (*Botifarra Traidora*), truffles and mushrooms, tongue, onions and pine nuts, rice, bread, parsley and garlic (*La Girella*), butifarra de perol, sweet butiffaras made with honey (*Butiffara Dulce de Gerona*) and very pretty Colombian *Butifarra Soledeña.*

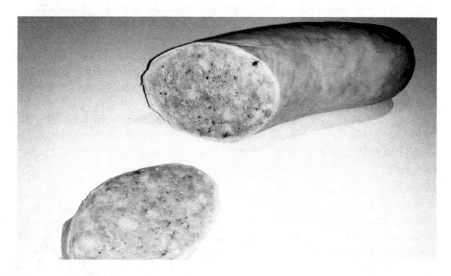

Photo 2.17 Butifarra.

Butifarras are usually made from lean pork, but occasionally other meats are included, even lungs, ears, or tongues, for example Butifarra Traidora. They contain less fat than chorizos or other sausages. Common ingredients are salt, pepper, nutmeg, cloves, garlic, and eggs, however, they may be enriched with mushrooms, truffles, foie gras, and herbs. Pimentón, if used at all, is applied in a small amount.

Butifarrón

From Spanish Food Code *(Código Alimentario Español-Decreto 2484/1967)*:

Butifarrón is a white sausage made from pork or pork and beef, comminuted into small and large pieces, stuffed into pork or beef bungs or middles, or artificial casings, baked (conditioned) in oven at no more than 20° C (68° F), cooked in water below boiling point, and submitted to drying.

Butifarrón is popular in Catalonia, where it is often served in stews and white beans, according to food code it is a white sausage, basically related to butifarra.

There is also Butifarrón Negro (black butifarrón) which is popular in Balearic Islands (Mallorca, Menorca, Ibiza, Formentera). Balearic butifarrón is made with offal meat and a little blood so it is called Butifarrón Negro. It contains salt, pepper, aromatic spices such as cinnamon, cloves, anise, nutmeg, fennel and is cooked in water like any blood sausage. Butifarra and Butifarrón are quite similar, the first sausage much easier to find, at least outside Catalonia.

Photo 2.18 Butifarrón.

Sobrasada de Mallorca

Sobrasada de Mallorca was the first Spanish sausage to receive European protective geographical indication certificate (PGI 21/06/1996). Majorca is the largest of the Balearic Islands and a popular tourist spot due to its warm temperature and pretty beaches with clean water. Majorca has a very rich history that can be compared to a roller coaster ride: Phoentians, then Carthaginians, Romans, Vandals, Christians, Muslims, until finally in 1229 - Catalan King Jaume I of Aragon occupied and conquered Majorca (*Mallorca*) on December 31, after three months of fighting. Wars continued between Catalans, Castillians and Majorcans until in 1479 - Kingdom of Espana was formed by uniting the Kingdom of Castilla and the Kingdom of Aragon, including Majorca (*Mallorca*).

Romans probably brought the first pigs to the island which somehow managed to survive Muslim occupation. It is very likely that later Spanish troops brought some celta and iberian pigs. As a result today we have black majorcan pigs and white pigs that is reflected in two protective geographical indication certificates: one for *Sobrasada de Mallorca* and another for *Sobrasada de Mallorca de Cerdo Negro* (black majorcan pig).

Majorcan Sobrasadas are made from pork, salt, spices and pimentón which can be made from locally grown peppers or with pimentón produced in the mainland, for example from Murcia. Paprika *Tap de Cortí* is the result of grinding the *Tap de Cortí variety of red pepper (Capsicum annuum)*, which is cultivated and processed only in Majorca and is responsible for giving color, aroma and taste to the typical dishes and cold meats of Majorca. It is known in Majorca as *pebre bord* or *pimentón mallorquino,* however, only a small amount of pimentón can be produced in the island. The original sobrasadas did not have the vivid red color as the ones of today as pimentón was not known yet. The first chili peppers came to Spain with Columbus on his return trip in 1493 and were planted in Extremadura. It took a while for pimentón to become a part of Spanish cuisine, but at the end of XVIII century sobrasada and many other Spanish sausages always included this spice.

What probably comes as a surprise to many is that sobrasada is a spreadable sausage which makes it completely different from hard textured sausages like salchichón or chorizo. Due to its soft texture the sausage can be scooped up and spread with a spoon. It is somewhat similar to German Mettwurst or Polish Metka as both sausages are fermented and spreadable, however, they are not dried and must be consumed relatively fast. The differences end there because Majorcan sobrasada has a much deeper red color and different flavor, both being the result of using pimentón.

Note: in order to not introduce smoky flavor Sobrasada de Mallorca should not contain Pimentón de La Vera.
Garlic must not be added to Sobrasada de Mallorca.

There are also sobrasadas made on Spanish mainland, but they cannot carry (PGI) certificate. There is a noticeable difference in quality and they are much fatter.

From Spanish Food Code *(Código Alimentario Español-Decreto 2484/1967):*

Sobrasada *is a raw, soft and red sausage made from pork or pork and beef, pork fat and spices, marinated, stuffed and dried.*

The sausage originates in Spanish Balearic Islands (Majorca, Menorca, Ibiza and Formentera), but is also popular in Murcia, Extremadura and nowadays it can be found everywhere in Spain. Sobrasada is produced from finely chopped lean pork and pork belly, mixed with salt, pimentón and spices. The recipes vary depending on who makes the sausage, but the manufacturing process for PGI protected Sobrasada de Mallorca must confirm to the rules enforced by Majorcan Regulatory Council (*Consejo Regulador*). The sausage is stuffed into large diameter pig casings and the sausages are dried for 4-8 weeks, depending on the diameter of the casing and the texture, color and flavor that is expected. Sobrasada exhibits a vivid red color and its texture is soft enough to be spread on bread. There are two varieties of Majorcan sobrasada:

Sobrasada de Mallorca carries protective geographical indication certificate (PGI 21/06/1996). The sausage must meet the following requirements: lean pork (30-60%), back fat (40-70%), pimentón (4-7%), salt (1.8-2.8%) and a touch of pepper. The following spices are often added: rosemary, thyme, oregano.

Sobrasada de Mallorca de Cerdo Negro carries protective geographical indication certificate (PGI 21/06/1996). All meat must come exclusively from black pig (*cerdo negro*) that grows locally on the island of Mallorca, and only natural casings are allowed.

Photo 2.19 Sobrasada mallorquina. Photo taken at Sobrassada de Mallorca *www.sobrasadademallorca.com* booth at the Meat Attraction Show in Madrid, September 18, 2018.

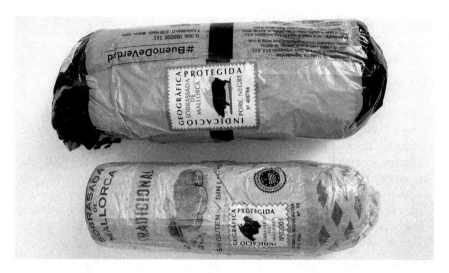

Photo 2.20 Majorcan sobrasada can be found all over Spain.

Sobrasada is packed into different casings such as pork middles, pork bungs, pork caps or even pork stomachs.

Photo 2.21 Packed into blind cap.

Photo 2.22 Sobrasada is a soft spreadable sausage which is served on a roll, very often with honey or apricot marmalade.

3.10.25. Sausages Made with Offal Meat (*Embutidos de visceras*).

Sausages made with offal meat (embutidos de visceras) are sausages that besides the meat, contain pieces of cooked entrails and offal meat which are then stuffed.

Sabadeñas, longanizas gallegas, and *salchichas de higado* also belong to this group. Liver sausages are most prominent example of this group.

Why Use Offal Meat

The question may arise as to why there are so many different, almost unappetizing meat cuts in certain sausages. They are generally termed "offal" meat: liver, heart, pancreas, tongue, pork head, snouts, dewlap, spleen, kidneys, lungs, stomach and tripe. Slaughtering and processing the pig takes longer than a day. When the animal's arteries are cut, blood starts gushing out and is immediately collected. Blood and liver spoil fastest so in the past, without access to refrigerators, the most practical way to save those cuts was to process them as soon as possible and that is the reason why some sausages are made with offal meat.

Photo 2.23 Once the noble cuts of meat like ham, loin, pork belly are removed, there is a large amount of back fat, internal fat as well as skins remaining. All those meats are cooked, separated from bones and used for making head cheeses, blood and liver sausages.

Photo 2.24 Cooked offal meat would be separated from bones, mixed with fillers (rice, bread, grouts, onions), spices, blood, stuffed into casings and cooked again.

Salchicha de Higado *(Liver Sausage)*

Spanish liver sausages borrow the prefix of *salchicha* and combine it with the word liver (*higado* means liver in Spanish), for example: Salchicha de Higado (liver sausage), Salchicha de Higado de Cerdo (pork liver sausage), Salchicha de Higado de Oca (goose liver sausage). You will find dozens of liver sausages in Germany or Poland, even in the US, but they are hard to find in Spanish stores. The production of liver sausages has not taken off in countries with hot climates, as it was difficult to preserve those sausages, at least in the past when there was no refrigeration. Surprisingly, liver patés are popular and can be purchased in fancy delicatessens. They are made with pork, poultry or rabbit liver, pork fat and spices. Then they are placed in molds and slow cooked in water or baked in oven, usually in a double pot filled with water (*al baño maría*).

    Liver purchased in a supermarket is quite clean, but make sure that there are not any glands, tendons, membranes or connective tissue left remaining. Soak the liver in water to remove any traces of blood. For the same reason liver is scalded briefly or immersed in hot water, however, do not cook liver as it will lose its emulsifying properties. The liver must be processed raw.

Photo 2.25 (above) Liver sausage.   **Photo 2.26** and **2.27** Liver paté.

3.10.26. Sausages Made with Blood (*Embutidos de Sangre*).

From Spanish Food Code *(Código Alimentario Español-Decreto 2484/1967):*

***Blood Sausages** (Embutidos de sangre) are semi-soft or soft sausages, raw or cooked, with blood as the main component to which are added meat, entrails, fat, lard and different products of vegetable nature, and stuffed into large diameter casings.*

To this group belong different types of *botagueñas* and *morcillas*. No other country has a richer and more diversified selection of blood sausages than Spain. Blood sausages are popular in most countries of the world except the USA. They carry their own descriptive name: Germany-Blutwurst, Poland - Kiszka Krwista or Kaszanka, England - Black Pudding, France - Boudin Noir, nevertheless, Spanish morcillas are in a class by themselves.

Morcilla (*Blood Sausage*)

Blood sausage is a sausage that contains blood. The name morcilla comes from the adjective *morcillo* which denotes something *black with reddish hairs* like a breed of a horse. The majority of morcillas are processed in hot water, however, there are some which are only dried. A classic Spanish morcilla is made with blood, fat and onions. Additionally they often include a filler material: rice, potatoes, pumpkin, bread, bread crumbs and flour. Buckwheat or barley groats so popular in Polish, German or Russian blood sausages are not popular in Spanish morcillas. Filler material such as potatoes, pumpkin or rice is introduced at about 30%. To get 3-4 kg of cooked pumpkin about 15-16 kg of raw pumpkin is needed.

IGP MORCILLA
DE BURGOS

Photo 2.28 Morcilla de Burgos is the best know blood sausage in Spain. It was awarded European Protected Geographical Indication (PGI) certificate in 2018.

Onions can be added raw or cooked. A rule of thumb says that onions are introduced at:

  1 part raw onions and 2 part filler material, for example cooked rice
  1 part *cooked* onions and 1 part filler material

Rice, pumpkin, potatoes and vegetables can be prepared and cooked a day earlier, garlic and spices during production. Popular ingredients are salt, pepper, sweet and hot pimentón, oregano, garlic, parsley, cumin, hot pepper, sugar and aromatic spices such as cinnamon, nutmeg, cloves, anise and quite often pine nuts. All materials and ingredients are mixed and the resulting paste is known as *bodrio*.

Morcillas on average contain about 30% of ground fat or lard. This creates difficulty in obtaining uniform paste during mixing. In traditional home production this problem was solved by melting the fat on a very small fire and then mixing it with other ingredients before it solidified again. Then the sausages were stuffed into 36-40 mm natural casings, usually pork, but beef or even sheep casings were used. After stuffing the sausage is fully cooked in water so it is ready to eat. Prick morcilla with a needle and if there is no blood visible the sausage is cooked. Morcillas are often eaten raw and cold the next day but tastes better fried or baked. Morcilla is served with potatoes and fried onions, with bread, pickles and mustard and often becomes an ingredient in Spanish pork and bean stews, the best known is Fabada Asturiana. Blood sausages go well with apples, often the apples are cored, filled with blood sausage mix and baked in an oven resulting in a very attractive presentation.

Sweet Blood Sausage (*Morcilla dulce*)

A popular variety of blood sausage is Sweet Blood Sausage (*Morcilla Dulce*) which is made with blood, sugar, flour, dry wheat bread, wheat flour, nuts, raisins, figs and aromatic spices, cinnamon being a must. Sweet blood sausage is produced in many Spanish regions for example in La Rioja and in Canary Islands. In Argentina it is known as Morcilla Vasca.

A general recipe: pork blood, cream or full milk, dry wheat bread or rolls, wheat flour, dry figs, raisins, pine nuts. Sugar, pepper, cinnamon, cumin, ground star anise, and ground cloves. Mix blood with sugar and milk, add crushed rolls and let them soak. Add remaining ingredients and spices, mix. Lastly add enough flour so the mix is soft, but not running. Stuff into 36-40 mm casings, make loops and tie the ends together. Cook in water at 80° C (176° F) for 45 minutes. Cool and refrigerate.

Dry Blood Sausage (*Morcilla curada*)

There are some original morcillas which are not cooked, but cured like dry sausages. After the paste (*bodrio*) was obtained it was processed like regular dry sausages ie., submitted to marinating (*reposo*) for 12-24 hours. Then the sausages were dried.

Morcilla Blanca (*White Blood Sausage*)

There is a variety of morcilla known as Morcilla Blanca which is usually made without blood so technically speaking it is not a blood sausage. The processing steps remain the same as the ones for black morcilla, however, without blood the sausage develops a lighter color (*blanco* means white in Spanish). Although calling the sausage White Blood Sausage (Morcilla blanca) if there is no blood inside makes little sense, nevertheless this nomenclature is not limited to Spanish sausages, but it is also used in other countries.

England – White Pudding (English call blood sausage a "pudding", i.e. Black Pudding or White Pudding).
France – Boudin Blanc (blanc means white in French).
Poland – Biała Kaszanka (biały means white in Polish, blood sausage is usually called Kaszanka or Kiszka Krwista).

Occasionally the white blood sausage may include a little blood like in German *Weiße Blutwurst (white blood sausage)* which is made with white colored materials and ingredients (fat, poultry meat, eggs, cream). The color of the sausage will be lighter though not pure white, a kind of pink, but it is called a white blood sausage.

Other Blood Sausages

Not all blood sausages have "morcilla" in the name. Catalonian butifarras which for the most part are cooked sausages often made with blood, for example *Butifarra Negra, Butifarra de Baleares* or *Butifarra Lorquina* from Murcia. *Botagueña* from Navarra is also a blood sausage.

When blood sausage is stuffed into *sheep casing* it is known as ***delgadilla*** (*delgado* means "thin" in Spanish) due to the fact that the diameter of sheep casing is much smaller. Delgadillas are popular in the autonomous communities of Castile and León and La Rioja, Spain. The sausage is baked in tomato sauce and served hot.

Blood Sausages in Other Spanish Speaking Countries

Blood sausages are immensely popular in Spanish speaking countries. They can be called morcilla, rellena or moronga. Moronga is found in Cuba, Puerto Rico, Central America and Mexican cuisine. Ruta, oregano, and mint, onions and chili peppers are added and then boiled in pig casings. Moronga is served in a hotter sauce than Spanish *delgadilla*, usually with red or green *chile sauce*. In Mexico morcilla is pan fried with fresh onions and jalapeño peppers and added to *gorditas* and *tacos* or served along with other sausages like *buche de costillas* and a mix of pickled onion, cilantro, and spices.

3.10.27. Fiambres.

From Spanish Food Code *(Código Alimentario Español-Decreto 2484/1967)*:

Fiambres are sausages of varied composition, containing pork, beef, back fat and other fats, poultry and their gizzards, eggs, milk, various spices, formed into blocks wrapped around with back fat sheets, cellophane or stuffed into natural or other approved casings.

Spanish fiambres:

Jamón de York. A boneless leg or shoulder of pork, skinless or not, cured with nitrite and salt, formed into a mold, covered with approved casings or canned.

Mortadela. A sausage made of finely comminuted (emulsified) pork, or pork and beef, free of fat and muscle fibers, containing cubes of back fat, stuffed in bladders, blind caps (caecum) or any approved casings, smoked and cooked in water at 90° C (194° F).

Roulada. A fiambre consisting of wrapping that holds some decorated filling or paste. The wrapping is a layer of back fat, less than 3 mm thick, the paste is the mixture of pork, beef, or pork belly with spices. The paste is decorated with tongue, poultry gizzards, eggs, blood, etc. The whole product is then cooked.

Galantinas are made from meat and offal meat of pork and beef, poultry meat and offal, including fish and seafood, milk, cream, eggs, mushrooms and vegetables.

Pastas de higado. A product made from finely ground liver of pork, beef, goose or duck, mixed with pork or poultry fat.

Chicharrones. A product made with pieces of pork skins, ears, dewlap and cracklings remaining from melting pork fat, also beef meat and tongue, *bound together with gelatin* and pressed and cooked in forming molds. Product has some rubbery texture and should not to be confused with pork chicharrones fried in oil.

Photo 2.29 Chicharrones is a fiambre.

Basically a fiambre is any kind of processed meat that is eaten cold. Fiambres are usually not stuffed but cooked in molds. Jamón de York is cooked ham that is classified as fiambre. Fiambre can be made from ground whole meat cuts or from offal meat. Meat roulade is a fiambre. Fiambre may include poultry, beef, veal, or wild game. Fiambre is stuffed in natural or synthetic casings or it can be placed in mold and baked, for example a meat loaf. The American SPAM ham has been made since the second world war from ground pork shoulder and is a good example of canned fiambre. It is known in Spain as Chopped ham *(El Chóped)*. Mortadella or American bologna is another example of fiambre. Head cheese is another example of fiambre.

Queso de Cabeza and Galantina *(Head Cheese and Meat Jelly)*

Meat jellies and head cheeses are classified as *fiambres* and are quite similar, the main difference is that head cheese is stuffed in a large diameter casing (traditionally in pork stomach) and meat jelly is allowed to cool and set in a suitable mold or dish. Meat jelly contains much more aspic than head cheese and includes ingredients (olives, bell peppers, peas, carrots) that provide an attractive visual display. The meats are precooked, the mixture is stuffed in casings or packed in molds and cooked in water or baked in oven.

Queso de cabeza (*queso* means cheese, *cabeza means* head) is Spanish name for head cheese, known in English as brawn, souse or sulz. In Mexico it is known as *queso de puerco*, in Costa Rica, Peru and Bolivia as *queso de chancho*, in Argentina and Uruguay as *queso de cerdo*, and in Colombia as *queso de cabeza*. Head cheese is very popular in Chile where it is served with bread and *pebre* (mild sauce made from vinegar, garlic, parsley and pepper).

Photo 2.30 Tongue head cheese *(fiambre)*.

Head cheese was traditionally made with pork head meat, however, it can be made with other meat cuts rich in collagen (connective tissue) as this is where the gelatin comes from. It will be unrealistic to expect that a person living in a large metropolitan city will be able to get a pork or wild boar head. What is needed is meat that is rich in connective tissue. Pig's hocks and feet are superb for producing gelatin and they taste great. Commercial gelatin is produced from skins so pork skins are usually added. The upper part of front leg, shoulder included, known as "picnic" is available in every supermarket and can be used for head cheese.

Photo 2.31 Meat jelly (*galantina-fiambre*).

Cabeza de Jabalí

Cabeza de Jabalí is a Spanish head cheese belonging to the "fiambre" group of meat products. Cabeza de Jabalí is listed in the Spanish Official Government Meat Standards Bulletin (Boletín Oficial del Estado, Real Decreto 474/2014, 13th June) as the product made from *pork* head meat. It is made from pork head meat, ears, snouts, lips, jowls, skins, tongue and is basically a head cheese (*queso de cabeza).* The Spanish word *jabalí* signifies in English "wild boar", so it may be assumed that wild boar head meat was used in the past, however, today, pork head meat is used. In Spanish supermarkets head cheese is listed as *Cabeza de Jabalí.*

Photo 2.32 Cabeza de Jabalí.

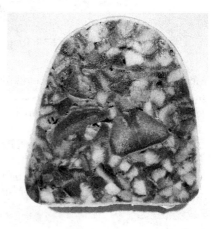

Cabeza de Jabalí has a firm texture so there is not much gelatin. It has a pleasant taste and flavor.

Other Sausages of Interest

Androlla

Androlla is one of the most popular sausages in Galicia. Androlla is a smoked dry sausage very similar to Botelo. The main material in Androlla and in Botelo are ribs and skins but the sausages differ in size as Botelo is stuffed into blind caps, stomachs or bladders which are very large casings and Androlla is stuffed into pork bungs so it has a more uniform cylindrical shape. Androlla Gallega should consists of 90% ribs and 10% skins, Botello contains 70% ribs, skins and other meats.

Ribs are cut into pieces of length 3-4 cm, salt, skins are cut into strips, then mixed for 15 minutes with all ingredients (salt, sweet and hot pimenton, garlic, oregano). The mixture is left to stand for 12 hours at 20° C (68° F) and then is stuffed into large natural or artificial casings. about 6-8 cm in diameter and 15-25 cm in length. The sausages are usually smoked with oak wood during the first 8 days of production. Drying takes place at 12° C (53° F), 75% RH humidity for 15 days. Dry Androllas were dried for 1-2 months. Androlla is always cooked before consumption.

Cooking androlla (500 g/1 lb): place whole androlla in salted water and cook for 45 minutes. Add a large diced peeled raw potato, one quartered fresh cabbage and one *salchicha* type (any cooked type) sausage. Cover the pot and simmer for additional 30 minutes. Remove ingredients from the pot and serve hot on a plate.

Photo 2.33 Androlla.

Botelo, Butelo or Botillo

A big fermented semi-dry sausage called in Galicia *botelo* or *butelo*, and in Castilla-León *botillo*. Botelo is similar to Androlla, but is a much thicker sausage owing its size to very large casings it is stuffed in.

A general recipe: ribs with attached meat (70%), spinal bones (*vertebra*) with attached meat (5%), lean pork (10%), cooked pork skins (7%), pork belly (5%), tail (2.5%), tongue (2.5%).

Meat is ground, ribs and other bones are cut into pieces ~ 4-8 cm length, salt, sweet and hot pimentón, garlic, and oregano are added and all ingredients are mixed for 15 minutes. The mixture is let to stand for 48 hours at 4-6° C (9-43° F) and then is stuffed by hand into pork blind caps (caecum), stomachs or bladders. The sausages are usually smoked with oak wood during the first 4 days of production. Drying takes place in storerooms at 10-12° C (50-53° F), 74-78% RH humidity for 15-20 days. *Dry* botelos were dried for 2-3 months.

Semi-dry botillo is always cooked before consumption. In order to remove bones easily from meat, botillo needs to be cooked from 180-240 minutes.

Photo 2.34 Botillo.

Botillo del Bierzo carries PGI (Protective Geographical Identification), 2001 classification. The El Bierzo region, made up of 38 municipalities located to the west of the province of Leon (Castile-Leon), Spain. The weight of Botillo del Bierzo averages 1 kg (2.2 lb).

Morcón

Morcón is a high quality chorizo like sausage which is fully cured and consumed raw. It follows processing steps for chorizo, but it is packed in pig blind cap (caecum), a large diameter intestine which is known in Spanish as "morcón", hence the name for the sausage. The casing is reinforced lengthwise and across with butcher twine. The sausage is popular in the regions of Andalusia, Extremadura and the province of Salamanca in Castile and León. Those three regions form boundaries with one another. Most iberian pigs are raised in Andalusia and Extremadura, so morcón produced in those provinces is made from iberian meat. Neck meat or upper shoulder (pork butt) is usually selected, the cut known as "cabacera de lomo" (loin head), although it has nothing to do with loin, except being in front of it. Secondly, loin is a lean piece, but pork butt contains about 25% of fat. However, the undeniable fact is that pork butt has a wonderful flavor and contains all classes of meat and fat. There is also a well known *Morcón de Lorca* from Murcia which is cooked and not dried. Morcón de Lorca breaks established rules for making morcón as practiced in Extremadura, Castilla-León and Andalusia and is made with different cuts of meat, without pimentón and is not dried but cooked. Occasionally Morcon can be made with blood and it is then called Black Morcon (*Morcón Negro*).

Photo 2.35 Morcón.

Chosco de Tineo is a type of morcón produced in Tineo municipality in the Asturías region in Spain. In 2011 Chosco de Tineo was granted PGI certificate (Protected Geographical Indication) which brought it the fame and recognition. Chosco de Tineo is made exclusively from cuts of pork shoulder/neck area known in Spanish as "cabecera de lomo" and tongue.

Storing Spanish Sausages

- Dry sausages are characterized by a long shelf life even at room temperature, but bear in mind that they will continue to dry out and will become very hard in time.

- For best quality it is recommended to store them at room temperature and not in a refrigerator. The ideal conditions are cool, dark and dry areas with little air flow (ventilation). If stored in a refrigerator, they should be taken out one hour before serving.

- Store them hanging or flat, but to ensure proper ventilation leave some space among them so they don't touch one another.

- Don't store sausages in plastic bags.

- Sausages will dry out faster when humidity is low, however, when humidity increases over 65% molds may appear on the surface. White is normal and can be expected. They can be easily wiped off if so desired. A touch of vinegar and a clean cloth will do the trick.

- Buy whole sausages and cut them as needed.

- Slice the sausage just before serving. The remaining part of the sausage will start to dry fast as it is not protected by the casing anymore.

- A new slice from a sausage that was cut before will be very hard and less attractive so it is often discarded.

- Large diameter sausages such as loins (*lomo embuchado*), *chorizo* and *salchichón* should be cut under angle for better visual display. They should be sliced 5 mm (1/4") or thinner.

All other sausages such as fresh or cooked should be refrigerated.

Mold

The question always arises to what to do with mold, take for example *fuet*. In home production it is stuffed into a soft delicate *natural* casing. It is not practical to fight removing it and most people will consume the mold. The same reasoning applies to small diameter dry sausages like *secallona* or *somalla*. As dry sausages are sliced thinly it is quite easy to peel off the skin. Commercially produced sausages are often stuffed into tough synthetic casings so it is best to discard the casing with mold. If you object visually to having mold on the sausage it can be easily wiped off with a piece of cloth soaked in oil or vinegar. According to a poll conducted in 2012 by the Spanish magazine La Vanguardia on preferred ways of consuming fuet:

38.5% consumers eat the sausage with mold.
55.82% consumers eat the sausage without mold.
5.68% do not care.

Chapter 3

Technology and Important Topics

Production of Spanish dry sausages consists of two major steps:

1. Meat selection, grinding, mixing, marinating (*adobo*) and holding meats (*reposo*) for 12-48 hours <8 C (F), or in refrigerator. Until the sausages are stuffed the sausage maker is fully in charge of the process.

2. Stuffing and placing sausages for around 48 hours in warmer temperatures "wakes up" lactic, color and flavor producing bacteria and forces them to start all those intricate reactions that will produce the final product. This will continue through a drying period and even in storage. The bacteria are fully in charge now, the ambient temperatures and humidity levels will significantly contribute to the quality of the finished product.

Meat Selection

Quite often we come across a statement that a particular sausage is made from low quality meats, which is not correct. There are no low quality meats, it all depends what the meat is needed for. Offal meat was not held in high esteem as it spoiled rapidly and refrigeration was not invented yet. Blood and liver had to be processed as soon as possible, but that does not mean that they are inferior material. Pork meat was rejected on religious grounds because it was often infected with *trichinais* parasites and people were getting sick consuming pork that was not fully cooked. Not knowing why it happened, we blamed the pig. Even today, any carnivore like pig, wild boar, bear, or raccoon will probably be infected with *trichinae* if its diet is not controlled. In Europe each slaughtered pig is tested for *trichinae*, in the US it is assumed that commercially raised pigs are *trichinae* free.

Nothing affects meat texture and the quality of the final product more than the selection of meat and adhering to sound production techniques. Take for example liver which is loaded with protein, nutrients and minerals. It also has a lot of cholesterol, but consuming it once a month will hardly hurt anybody.

It is taken for granted that all meats are cold, ideally spending 12-24 hours in a refrigerator before processing. Meat cuts rich in connective tissue are needed in most sausages, especially finely comminuted ones like hot dog, frankfurter or mortadella. They contain collagen which becomes gelatin when heated. Gelatin, acting like a glue, connects all meat fragments together providing a good texture.

In addition, natural gelatin tastes pleasant unlike tasteless commercial types or gums which are added to meats, fruit jellies, ice creams and other products. Ever wondered why we like spare ribs so much? Well, the bones are connected with meat rich in connective tissue which will produce a lot of gelatin and this is what our tongue and palate like. This is why rib bones are included in *androlla, botelo* or *buche de costillas*. Meat selected for Spanish dry sausages should be especially well trimmed of all all tendons, gristle, sinews and connective tissues as they will create an unpleasant experience when consuming the finished sausage. Such trimmings when emulsified can be added to cooked sausages (*salchichas, morcillas*), but should not be a part of a good dry sausage.

Best cured whole meats such as hams (*jamón*), picnics (*paleta*) or loins (*lomo*) come from pure iberian pig meat. Trimmings may end up in sausages that specifically call for pure iberian pork, but for economic reasons meat for sausages come from iberian pigs crossbred with American Duroc or from locally raised white pigs. It can, however, be safely said that all Spanish meats are of a high quality and will make great sausages.

Fat

There is no substitution for pork fat, it tastes and looks best. Hard fats such as back fat, dewlap or kidney fat are best for dry sausages because they have a higher melting point and do not smear easily. They also offer more resistance to cutting and are less prone to oxidation and rancidity. Soft fat such as belly fat are great for liver sausages, patés, salchichas or spreadable products. Beef fat has a higher melting point than pork fat, unfortunately its flavor and color are less desirable. Dry sausages need fat, this is what our tongue expects, otherwise we are not satisfied with the product. We need fat and there is nothing wrong with it, *fat is not the enemy, the calories are.* In regular type sausages, especially in emulsified ones, a substantial amount of water is added which makes products juicer and cheats our senses into believing there is fat inside. A liquid solution of water, sodium nitrite, sodium ascorbate, sodium erythorbate, phosphates and other additives is injected or added. Those ingredients together with crushed ice are added to bowl cutters where frozen blocks of meat are transformed into a paste. And phosphates bind this water so it does not leak out, at least not when the product is packed. This makes the product juicy (watery) and satisfies our senses with a pleasant feeling even if little fat was added. On a positive note, those additives are not used in home made products or in sausages that carry European certificates of origin. Those water injecting techniques cannot be applied to dry sausages as the technology behind making dry products relies on removing water from the meat and not by injecting it in. In simple terms a dry sausage is a quality product that contains meat, fat and a few ingredients whereas only the manufacturer knows what goes into his emulsified paste.

White pork fat stands out nicely when distributed within ground meat, for example in mortadella or in many blood sausages. For best visual effect, it should be partially frozen and cut with a sharp knife otherwise it smears easily. Keep in mind that a sharp knife is a much better cutting tool than a grinder's knife. By its definition the grinder "grinds" the meat, it does not cut cleanly, its advantage is the speed. You can dice partially frozen fat much cleaner with a knife. The best advice is to place it in a freezer for 45-60 minutes and then cut it. For best visual display of fat particles scald fat cubes briefly with hot water.

Do We Really Need Iberian Pork For Sausages?

Well let's see from what pigs the best Spanish hams are made from. There are 7 Spanish Hams carrying European Protected Certificates, but not all of them are made from iberian pig.

Iberian Pig: Jamón Ibérico Dehesa de Extremadura, PDO 1996
Iberian Pig: Jamón Ibérico de Guijuelo PDO, 1996
Iberian Pig: Jamón Ibérico de Huelva, PDO 1998
Iberian Pig: Jamón Ibérico Los Pedroches, PDO 2010
White Pig: Jamón de Teruel, PDO 1996
White Pig: Jamón de Trévelez, PGI 2005
White Pig: Lacón Gallego, PGI 2001(Front leg ham)

Looking at the above data we can see that selecting iberian pork for making sausages is not so crucial, after all even famous hams are made from regular European white pig. Keep in mind that there are a few quality sausages that specifically call for iberian pork: morcón, lomo (pork loin), chorizo ibérico and salchichón, however, the last two can be made from any breed of a pig.

Photo 3.1 Due to its freedom and oak acorns diet Iberian pig develops an unique texture and flavor of its meat.

Photo courtesy www.dehesa-extremadura.com

There are chorizos made with potatoes, pumpkin, pork and beef. There are butifarras made with eggs, cream, and many other sausages like salchichas which can be made with almost anything. Commercially produced sausages include chicken, turkey, flours, soy proteins plus dozens of additives and flavorings so it would be illogical and even wasteful to insist on choosing iberian pork for making regular type sausages unless the recipe requires it.

Salt

Salt plays an important role in production of dry sausages: it immediately binds free water inhibiting growth of spoilage bacteria, although lactic acid bacteria being more salt tolerant can still multiply, permit proteins to dissolve in salt and water solution during cutting/grinding what creates better binding of meat particles resulting in a firmer texture, and of course influences the flavor.

Curing

In German, Polish, or Russian terminology *curing* is treating meat with salt and *sodium nitrite*. Meat is cut into smaller sizes, mixed with nitrite cure and left in refrigerator for 24-48 hours. The spices are added later during mixing. In recent years, to save time, this curing step is skipped and the meat is ground, mixed with salt, sodium nitrite, curing accelerators and spices, stuffed *without delay* into casings, and processed. Even the marinating step (*adobo*) can be omitted when starter cultures are added.

Cured meats are usually smoked and cooked. Although the purpose of curing is to develop the desired red color, the application of nitrite offers more benefits: the meat develops "curing flavor", prevents the danger of the growth of pathogenic *Clostridium botulinum* and retards the development of fat rancidity. Nowadays, sodium nitrite is widely available and added to all sausages and it is a "must have" ingredient for commercial producers as the safety of processed meats depends on it.

In Spanish technology the word "curing" covers the entire process of making dry sausages starting from the time the casing is stuffed with meat until it is stored and consumed. This might be a month, three months or longer. The steps like fermenting, drying and maturing are often understood by "curing." Adding nitrite to meat was not as common in Spain as in north-european countries, at least with traditionally products made at home. The development of a bright red color in many sausages was achieved by adding large amounts of pimentón. Higher amounts of salt, plenty of pimentón and garlic, low drying temperatures and moderate humidity allowed production of uncooked sausages that were microbiologically stable and ready to eat even when kept at room temperature.

Today it will be hard to find any commercial plant or even a hobbyist that would manufacture sausages without sodium nitrite. The exception are the meat processors who produce meats that carry the European Certificates of Origin, so they must employ methods which have been used in the past.

If a particular sausage was always made without sodium nitrite they must continue to do so, otherwise the certificate may be revoked. It should be noted that those processors have years of experience of making the same product at the same location and under the climate conditions that remain similar each year.

American Cures

In the past potassium nitrate was used exclusively because its derivative, sodium nitrite was not discovered yet. *Sodium Nitrate (NaNO₃) does not cure meat directly* and initially not much happens when it is added to meat. After a few hours curing bacteria that is naturally present in meat begins to react with nitrate which releases *sodium nitrite* ($NaNO_2$) that will start the curing process. *If those bacteria are not present in sufficient numbers the curing process may be inhibited.* Bacteria are lethargic at low temperatures so production of nitrite will be slow, unless the curing mixture containing potassium nitrate is kept at 44-46° F (6-8° C). This however, allows spoilage bacteria to grow and shortens the shelf life of the product.

Cure #1 (also known as Instacure #1, Prague Powder #1 or Pink Cure #1). Cure #1 is a mixture of 6.25% *sodium nitrite* and 92.75% of salt. This cure does not depend on microbial action as it contains sodium nitrite which reacts with meat immediately and at refrigerator temperature. For these reasons Cure #1 is added to fast-fermented sausages.

Cure #2 (also known as Instacure #2, Prague Powder #2 or Pink Cure #2) is a mixture of 6.25% *sodium nitrite,* 4% of *sodium nitrate* and 68.75% of salt. This cure is applied to slow-fermented products, as nitrite starts an immediate reaction with meat and nitrate guarantees a steady supply of nitrite during long term drying.

Both Cure #1 and Cure #2 contain a small amount of FDA approved red coloring agent that gives them a slight pink color thus eliminating any possible confusion with common salt and that is why they are sometimes called "pink" curing salts.

There are also proprietary household cures with different proportions of salt, nitrite/nitrate, sugars and flavorings, however, to use them properly one has to follow instructions that accompany every mix.

European Cures

What counts is not the name of the cure or where it was manufactured, *but how much sodium nitrite is introduced to meat.* Most European cures contain salt and only 0.6% of sodium nitrite, so there is no danger of accidental overdose and cures are white and not colored. Such a low nitrite percentage in salt is self-regulating and it is almost impossible to apply too much nitrite to meat, as the latter will taste too salty. Following a recipe you could replace salt with European cure (0.6% sodium nitrite) altogether and the established nitrite limits will be preserved. This isn't the case with American Cure #1 which contains much more nitrite (6.5%) and we have to color it pink to avoid the danger of mistakes and poisoning.

Nitrite Safety Limits

Comminuted products (smoked and cooked sausages) - small meat pieces, meat for sausages, ground meat, poultry etc. Cure #1 was developed in such a way that if we add 4 ounces of cure # 1 to 100 pounds of meat, the quantity of nitrite added to meat will comfort to the legal limits (156 ppm) permitted by the Meat Division of the United States Department of Agriculture. That corresponds to 1 oz (28.35 g) of Cure #1 for each 25 lbs (11.33 kg) of meat or *2.5 g (1/2 tsp) per 1 kg of meat.*

Dry Cured Products

The maximum allowable sodium *nitrite* limit for Dry Cured Products (625 ppm) is four times higher than for Comminuted Products (156 ppm). The reason that there are much higher allowable nitrite limits for dry cured products is that sodium *nitrite dissipates rapidly in time and* the dry products are *dried for a long time.* Those higher limits guarantee a steady supply of nitrite in time. Adding cure #1 or #2 at 156 ppm to dry sausages will produce a product hardly containing any residual nitrite. Commercially prepared meats in the USA contain about 10 ppm of nitrite when bought in a supermarket. Sodium nitrite reacts with lean meat (myoglobin) and *not with fat.* Adding cure #1 to fat will not change its color, the fat will remain white, and the remaining nitrite will be eaten by the consumer. If the product contains a lot of fat, you may lower the amount of cure accordingly.

Curing and Meat Color

Meat color is determined largely by the amount of myoglobin (protein) a particular animal carries. The more myoglobin the darker the meat, it is that simple. Going from top to bottom, meats that contain more myoglobin are: horse, beef, lamb, veal, pork, dark poultry and light poultry. The amount of myoglobin present in meat also increases with the age of the animal. Different parts of the same animal, take the turkey legs and breast as an example, will have a different color as well. The parts that exercise frequently such as legs, wings, and the heart, need more oxygen causing them to develop more myoglobin and become darker.

This color is pretty much fixed and there is not much we can do about it unless we mix different meats together. Cured meats develop a particular pink-reddish color due to the reaction that takes place between meat myoglobin and nitrite. If an insufficient amount of nitrate/nitrite is added to the meat the cured color will suffer. This may be less noticeable in sausages where the meat is ground and stuffed but if we slice a larger piece like a ham, the poorly developed color will be easily noticeable. Some sections may be gray, some may be pink and the meat will not look appetizing.

At least 50 ppm (parts per million) of nitrite is needed to cure meat. Some of it will react with myoglobin and will fix the color, some will go into other complex biochemical reactions that develop the flavor. If we stay within Food and Drug Administration guidelines (1 oz. Cure #1 per 25 lb of meat, about 1 level teaspoon of Cure #1 for 5 lb of meat) we are applying 156 ppm of nitrite which is enough and safe at the same time. Cured meat will develop its true cured color only after submitted to cooking (boiling, steaming, baking) at 140-160° F (60-72° C). The best color is attained at 160° F (72° C).

Note: Sarasíbar et al. (1989) reported that nitrifying salts (nitrate and nitrite) decrease both the intensity and stability of the color produced by the paprika. These salts produce a yellowish discoloration of red paprika in the presence of lactic acid generated during the fermentation stage. In simple terms it means that the intense red color that was created by adding pimentón may be less vibrant. In our opinion the benefits of using sodium nitrite far outweigh any weakening of color which will be hard to notice with the naked eye anyhow.

Cutting and Grinding (*Picado*)

The size of the cut is influenced by the diameter of the casing and the visual display of texture. We do not want 25 mm meat particles in 26 mm casings. Typical sausages and grinder plate size:

Salchicha, Salchicha de Higado - 3-5 mm, or emulsified in food processor
Longaniza, Sobrasada, Chorizo de Pamplona - 3-5 mm
Salchichón, Imperial, Salami - 5-10 mm
Chorizo, Morcón, Blanco - 10-30 mm
Botelo, Butelo, Botillo, Morcón, Buche de Costillas - 20-30 mm, often by hand

The most important rule of home grinding is to use cold meat, especially the fat, which can even be partially frozen. That combined with a sharp knife will lead to a well defined particle distribution and a good texture. A dull knife will tear off fat which will smear becoming a greasy film that will envelop ingredients together. It will also clog tiny pores in the casing. As a result a barrier is created that restricts water removal from the sausage.

It is a common practice to keep the grinder with its accessories in a refrigerator before use so that the particles of meat will be defined better. Commercial processors do not worry about such details because meat cutters they use are capable of cleanly cutting whole blocks of frozen meat.

Ingredients and Spices

Sugar

Lactic acid bacteria produce lactic acid by breaking down sugar that inhibits the growth of unwanted bacteria. There are different sugars (dextrose, fructose, lactose, sucrose) and they are metabolized differently. What is important to know is that only dextrose, also known as glucose, can be metabolized immediately. Other sugars must be converted to glucose first and then they can be consumed by bacteria. This introduces a certain delay into the lactic acid production process. To avoid this delay a small amount of dextrose is usually included along with sugar.

Phosphates

Spain being a member of the European Community conforms to the same rules and phosphates are allowed. Phosphates are very effective water binders, this means that a lot of water may be introduced to emulsified sausages such as hot dog, frankfurter, mortadella and it will remain locked inside. They also contribute to maintaining acidity at prescribed levels.

Ascorbic Acid

Ascorbic acid (vitamin C) contributes to the development and maintaining of a strong red color when nitrite is added.

Herbs and Spices

Herbs and spices can be added fresh, dried or in powdered form. In addition to supplying aroma, spices like pepper, thyme, rosemary and garlic are known anti-oxidants so they are able to delay food deterioration and rancidity of fat, both problems especially important in the manufacture of dry sausages. The following herbs and spices are commonly added to Spanish sausages:

Herbs: oregano, thyme, rosemary, parsley, tarragon, onions, garlic, cilantro, ginger, fennel,

Spices: white and black pepper, pimentón, allspice, paprika, mustard seed, cinnamon, cloves, nutmeg, mace, cardamom, cumin, anise, juniper.

Truffles which are mushrooms, white and black, are often used in cooked sausages like liver sausages or *salchichas*.

White and red wine is often added, the white one in light colored sausages.

Garlic, truffles and other herbs and spices are often briefly marinated in wine for the maximum extraction of flavor. Spices lose aroma in time. Adding a large amount of spice into fresh sausage will be easy to sense, however, it will be hard to feel in a sausage that was dried for 3 months. Garlic loses aroma very fast, that is why it is added last even in general cooking.

Pimentón

After discovering America in 1492 Christopher Columbus made his first pilgrimage to Santa María Monastery of Guadalupe in Extremadura where he thanked heaven for his discovery. In 1493, on his third trip Christopher Columbus brought the first peppers to Spain which were offered to the monks of Guadalupe monastery. From there production expanded to the Monastery of Yuste in Cáceres, Extremadura, and then to Murcia, La Rioja and Andalusía. The process was held in secrecy but with time the product became known as Pimentón de La Vera.

Today Extremadura produces most and all varieties of pimentón (sweet, bitter-sweet and hot), but some sweet pimentón is also made in Murcia. There are 4 varieties of peppers (Bola, Jaranda, Jariza, Jeromín) and by selecting them properly and adjusting processing steps a sweet (*dulce*), semi-sweet (*agridulce*) or hot (*picante*) pimentón can be produced. The peppers are harvested and dried over burning oak wood in tall chambers that do not differ much from old smokehouses. The drying continues for 10-15 days. Then the seeds and stems are removed and peppers are milled into a powder.

Photo 3.2 In Extremadura there are 17 licensed companies which produce Pimentón de La Vera under own name with each container displaying Protected Designation of Origin (PDO) logo and an individual serial number on each package. When a recipe does not specify which pimentón is needed the sweet (dulce) pimentón is added. By mixing sweet (*dulce*) and hot (*picante*) pimentón together a customized solution can be produced.

Photo 3.3 Pimentón de La Vera made by Pimentón El Ángel S.L,, the company which was established in 1880.
Photo courtesy El Angel
http://www.pimentonelangel.com

Note: it is quite common to come across the definition of pimentón as smoked paprika, which is not correct. Pimentón is Spanish paprika which is usually not smoked unless the label states it is smoked. Only *Pimentón de La Vera is always smoked.* Spanish sausages such as chorizo, sobrasada and others display a unique vivid red color which is due to pimentón. Sweet paprika used for general cooking may be Hungarian, Californian, or South American but Spanish pimentón is darker and has a more intense flavor.

In order to be labelled *chorizo* the sausage *must* include pimentón, made without it the sausage becomes white chorizo (*chorizo blanco*). Many Spanish sausages, for example Chorizo Cantipalos, must include the highest quality pimentón called Pimentón de La Vera. This smoked pimentón is produced in La Vera municipality, Cáceres province in Extremadura region, where farmers harvest and dry the chiles over wood fires, creating *smoked paprika* or pimentón de La Vera. It has received European Protected Designation of Origin (PDO) in 2007. Pimentón is also produced in Murcia region of Spain and on the island of Majorca.

Unlike black pepper or other spices which are added to sausages at 0.1-0.3% per 1 kg of meat, pimentón is added to chorizos at 1-3% which is ten times more. At first it seems to be an error, as any spice such as pepper, nutmeg or cinnamon added to meat at 3% will make the product non-edible, however, pimentón fits just fine. Another benefit of pimentón is that it contains a large percentage of sugar (10%) that positively contributes to lactic acid production during fermentation.

Marinating Meat - *Adobado*

Marinating meat is a common procedure for meat or chicken which will be baked, roasted or barbecued, but not so much for sausages. In Spain, however, marinating meat plays an important part in production of dry sausages. This traditional marinating technique known as *adobado* is mixing meat with marinade paste (*adobo*) and letting it rest. This marinating period known as *reposo* is rather short and lasts from 12-24 hours for chorizos and longanizas and 24-48 hours for salchichones and salamis. During this period spices release their flavor and color, flavor and lactic acid producing bacteria increase in numbers. Meat cells release protein and juice which dissolve in salt and create exudate which is the "glue" that bins meat particles together. The sausage paste becomes firmer. After marinating the meats are stuffed and dried. Although the marinating process ends when the sausage is stuffed, nevertheless the reactions that have been triggered, for example fermenting and drying will continue until the sausage is done.

Adobo paste - salt, pimentón, garlic, oregano, spices, sometimes sugar. A little olive oil, vinegar or both. Occasionally, cumin and crushed bay leaf are included. All ingredients are mixed together and rubbed into the chopped or ground meat. Adobo paste is also applied to whole meats like pork loin (*lomo embuchado*). The meats are packed about 5 cm (2") thick in a container, and held below 8° C (46° F) or in a refrigerator for 12-48 hours.

Mixing (*Amasado*)

Mixing contributes to the release of exudate which is the solution of proteins and salt. This acts like a glue creating a bond between meat particles and forming a firm uniform texture. Add fats last as they have a tendency to smear when warm.

Water is not added to Spanish dry sausages, however, a small amount will not create a problem especially when phosphates are included. Mixing powdered starter cultures directly with meat is difficult because they are applied in small quantities (0.12-0.25 g per 1 kg of meat). It becomes practical to dissolve culture in 1-2 tablespoons of water and pour the solution over the meat.

Casings

A casing is the container that holds a sausage. It can be natural or artificial, but for dry sausages the casing must be permeable what means that it must allow the moisture or smoke to go through. Sausages packed in artificial casings dry out faster as these casings are more permeable. Sausages awarded Protected Designation of Origin (PDO) certificate must be stuffed into natural casings.

Stuffing

Dry sausages should be stuffed firmly to avoid air. Any pockets of air are invitations to bacteria as most bacteria need oxygen to survive. Even if the spoilage will not occur the little holes or discolorations will be visible in a sliced sausage. Stuffed sausages should be pricked with a needle to create an opening for the air to escape during drying. Sausages such as *chorizo*, *salchichón*, *salchicha* or *butifarra* are stuffed through a tube attached to a common manual grinder or through a separate manually cranked piston stuffer. Blood and liver sausages are soft and can be stuffed either with a stuffer or manually using a large funnel and a kitchen ladle. Large sausages such as head cheese, butelo, morcón, or any sausage stuffed into pork blind cap (caecum), stomach or bladder need to be manually stuffed on a case by case basis. Linking sausages without using butcher twine by twisting filled casings is a common procedure, but Spanish sausages are generally linked with the twine as this method is more practical for drying sausages.

There are three popular arrangements for linking dry sausages:

Atados or ristra (*atar* means "tie up", *ristra* means "string of elements", for example string of garlic heads or beads). Sausage is stuffed into the full length of a casing so it becomes one continuous rope. Then it is tied off into individual sausage links about 15 cm (6") long. After the first link is created, the twine is not cut, but continues to tie off the second link and so on until all links are connected together. *Atados, ristra* or *sarta* style sausages are shorter and of smaller diameter, making them easy to handle or separate. They end up on grills or in general cooking, for example in stews.

Photo 3.4 Sausage linked with twine-
ristra style.

Photo 3.5 Herradura (*horseshoe*) or
sarta - each sausage forms U- shaped
loop. Herradura forms a longer loop
whereas sarta is shaped more into
a ring, like in morcillas. Butcher's
twine is clipped to both ends of the
sausage forming a hanging loop 10-20
cm (4-8") long. This method is used
for 34-40 mm diameter sausages, for
example chorizo.

Fig. 3.6 Cular - one straight section
of round, but often irregular shape
sausage due to individual properties
of the casings. Pork or beef bungs
are usually employed. This method is
used for 38-50 mm diameter sausages
or for stuffed loin.

Fig. 3.7 Vela - one straight section
of the sausage, similar to "cular", but
smaller diameter around 30-40 mm
and 40 cm (16") long. The name is
derived from candle (candle is *vela* in
Spanish).

Pork bungs *(cular* or *vela)* are larger diameter and longer straight, sliced diagonally
and eaten raw. They are the best choice for dry sausages having the right thickness
and porosity for extended drying.

Photo 3.8 Pork blind caps (*ciegos*). In
addition there are traditional products
stuffed in irregular casings such
as pork blind caps (caecum), pork
stomachs, bladders or even wrapped
in caul fat (fat membrane that looks
like a net).

Spanish sausages are invariably linked or clipped with butcher twine of different colors, white, black, red, yellow or multicolored. There is no code or standard specifying what color of twine should be elected for different types of sausages. Meat plants use their own colors to distinguish different sausage types in order to avoid mix up and confusion.

A knowledgeable customer expects sausages to be packed in natural casings knowing that it usually is of a better quality than packed in synthetic casings mass produced products. Traditional production employs pork, beef and sheep casings with pork bungs having an excellent reputation for making dry sausages.

Note: Study by Roncalés et al. (1991) reported that sensory quality scores for fuet with natural casings were higher for almost all attributes except in cases of skin peeling which was scored higher for the fuet made with artificial casings.

Smoking Spanish Sausages.

Smoking technique has been commonly used during production of Spanish sausages, however, smoking was not a major processing step but rather an auxiliary step that was not really desired or highly thought of. As pigs were processed in winter in many areas of Spain, it was difficult to maintain drying temperatures of 12-16° C (53-60° F) using natural drying chambers.

The Spanish sausage maker was doing the same what his German or Lithuanian counterpart, he was burning wood to warm up his facilities. The climate in Spain is much milder than in Northern Europe so he did not need to do it on a continuous basis, just enough to be comfortable. Drawing from his experience he knew exactly when and how much wood to burn. Sausages were hung as high as possible above a slow burning fire. As burning wood produces smoke in its first stage of combustion, the meat acquires some smoke and flavor. If there was access to electrical heaters or gas burners he would not have had bothered with wood and fire, that is certain.

Generally, the smoke is applied for two reasons:

1. As a *flavoring* step to flavor the meat (hot smoking), for example frankfurter, Vienna sausage, mortadela and most salchichas. Cooked sausages receive a thick hot smoke for a short time 1-3 hours. Longer time can impart a bitter taste to the sausage. In Spain, the hot smoke temperature is assumed to be at 70-90° C (158-194° F). Smoke temperatures from 25-70° C (77-158° F) are considered medium-hot.

2. As a *drying* step to maintain temperature of the drying chamber. Most traditional air dried products like *chorizos, salchichones, sobrasadas, androlla, butelo* would be subjected to some cold smoke. Out of all sausages, *chorizo* and *longaniza* are most heavily smoked. Cold smoke is a thin smoke that can be applied for days and weeks. In Spain, the cold smoke temperature is assumed to be less than 25° C (77° F).

The dividing line which separates both methods is the temperature when meat or fish proteins start to cook. Throw an egg on a cold frying pan and start raising the heat. At a certain point the white of the egg which actually looks like a clear jelly starts changing color and becomes cooked egg white. The technical term is *coagulation of protein*, this is when the product starts to cook. In meat this usually happens at around 29° C (85° F); there is a rapid loss of moisture and the texture of the meat becomes hard. This will prevent further smoke penetration and the removal of moisture.

The sausages were hung in kitchen chimneys or over wood fired stoves where they received heat and smoke when higher temperatures were needed. If the temperature was right the sausages were hung in any suitable facility. Commercial drying chambers were heated with electric heaters. Examples of some of the arrangements follow below.

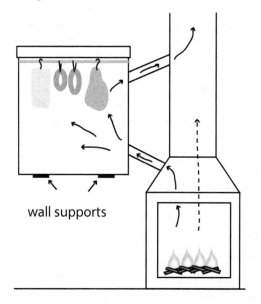

wall supports

Fig. 3.1 Box on the wall.

Fig. 3.2 Hanging meats in the chimney.

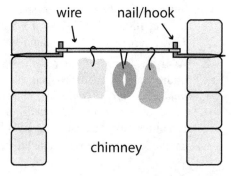

wire   nail/hook

chimney

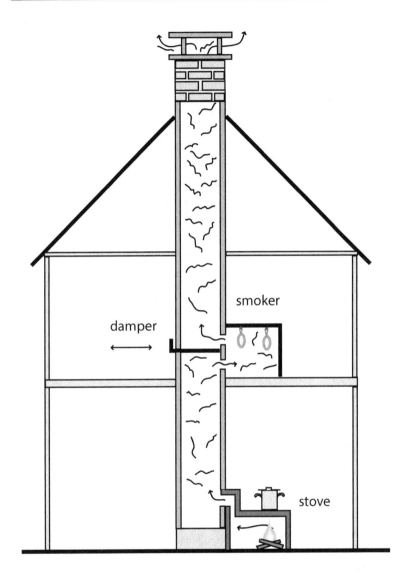

Fig. 3.3 Home chimney smoker.

A smokehouse is attached to the chimney on the second floor. Two holes were made in the chimney: one for the smoke to enter the chamber and another to allow it to escape. On the other side a flat damper was pushed in or out of the chimney allowing the smoke to go straight up or forcing it to flow into the smokehouse.

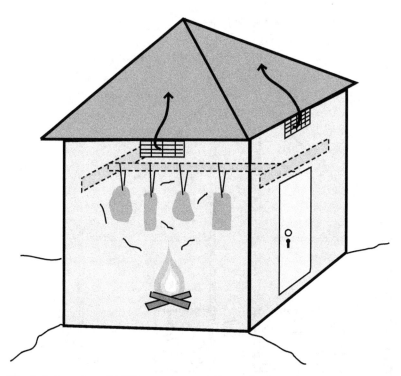

Fig. 3.4 American XVIII century smokehouse is a good example of a smoking-drying chamber. Those storerooms were popular in eastern parts of the country.

Wood for Smoking

Any hardwood is fine, but soft evergreen trees like fir, spruce, pine, or others cause problems. They contain too much resin and the finished product had a turpentine flavor to it. Wood from locally grown trees is used for smoking. If alder, oak or beech grow in the area people are not going to order cherry or pecan wood. Two types of oak trees grow in Spanish oak forests: holm oak (*encina*) and cork oak (*alcornoque*), both oaks producing acorns (*belota*) which are the staple of ibérico pigs. As the oak trees grow where the pigs feed, it is only logical to assume that oak wood is used for smoking.

We don't use wet wood for cold smoking because we want to eliminate moisture, not bring it in. D*ry wood* is used for smoking slow-fermented dry sausages. Wet chips or sawdust, seem to produce more smoke but this is not true. The extra amount of smoke is nothing else but water vapor (steam) mixed with smoke. This does make a difference when hot smoking at 105-140° F, (40-60° C) and the smoke times are short. That extra moisture prevents the sausage casings from drying out during smoking, however, wet chips are not going to be wet for very long; the heat will dry them out anyhow.

Cooking

All meats and sausages must be safe to consume which is accomplished by cooking them to 72° C (160° F) either during manufacture or before serving. It matters little whether they are boiled, fried or grilled. In most countries the majority of sausages are cooked in water at around 80° C (176° F). Baking sausages in ovens or in smokehouses takes much longer.

Fermented and dried sausages are in a separate category, they need not be cooked, however, they must develop a certain amount of acidity, lose enough moisture, or both to be considered safe. Most Spanish dry products are eaten cold, but some for example *androlla* or *butelo*, will be cooked in water and served hot with potatoes and broccoli raab also known as rapini.

Emulsified sausages like frankfurter, mortadella, smoked sausages, blood and liver sausages, head cheeses, all those products are cooked usually in water.

Cooling

Sausages cooked in water are usually cooled in water as soon as possible to prevent shrivelling and to cross the danger zone - 5 to 60° C (41 to 140° F) when bacteria grow fast. Cooling also solidifies liquid fat fast and prevents it from accumulating in one area of the sausage which results in unsightly pockets of fat so common in home made liver sausages.

Storing

Fresh and cooked sausages are stored in a refrigerator or frozen. Dry meats and sausages are hung in storage at 12-15° C (53-59° F), 60-70% humidity where they keep aging and maturing. Lower humidity does not spoil the sausage but facilitates further removal of moisture decreasing the weight of the sausage and making it hard. Very long storage negatively affects the quality of the sausage due to the fact that the fat develops rancidity which lowers the taste and flavor, although the product is safe to eat. Unfortunately keeping products refrigerated or frozen will not stop fat rancidity. To slow down rancidity sausages must be stored in a dark room. Although dry sausages can be stored at room temperature of about 15° C (53° F) or lower, storing products under refrigeration offers many benefits:

- inhibits the growth of bacteria and molds.
- retards fat rancidity which would affect the taste and the flavor of the sausage and prevents fat changing its color from white to yellowish.
- maintains the existing flavor and aroma of the sausage.

Sausages should hang and not touch each other. For longer storage the sausages can hang at 10-15° C (50-59° F) below 75% humidity in a dark and ventilated place.

Safety

Safe production of meat products at home can be achieved by Cleanliness and Common Sense. Home made sausages are subject to the ambient temperature of the kitchen and a dose of a common sense is of invaluable help:

- Take only what you need from the cooler.
- When a part of the meat is processed put it back into the cooler.
- Keep your equipment clean and cold.
- Work as fast as possible.
- Try to keep meat always refrigerated.
- Work at the lowest possible temperature.
- Wash your hands often.
- Keep processed meats refrigerated. Process only as little meat as you need.
- Use partially frozen meat and fat when grinding.
- Do not use warm equipment (last minute equipment washing).
- Work at the lowest possible temperature - set air conditioning thermostat to the lowest value. If no climate control is available, meat should be processed in the early hours of morning or in the evening.
- Consider making sausages in cooler months of the year.

It is crucial to maintain *the lowest possible temperature* during the first processing steps, such as meat selection, cutting, grinding, mixing and stuffing. During those periods, meat is hopelessly unprotected and left at the mercy of spoilage and pathogenic bacteria. Until salt and nitrite are added the only defense against meat spoilage is the low initial bacteria count of fresh meat, and the low processing temperature. Don't lower the salt amount because you are on a low sodium diet. Lowering salt levels might ruin your product and months of time investment. It may also create favorable conditions for dangerous bacteria to grow.

When making fresh or cooked sausages, one may relax some of the above recommendations and still produce a fine sausage. Most regular sausages are fully cooked which kills all bacteria and makes the sausage safe to consume. Dry sausages are raw meat sausages that are not cooked, so obviously they have to be submitted to different and more stringent rules. Making dry sausage is a serious investment in time and money. Adding too much pepper or not enough garlic will not ruin the sausage but not adding enough salt or processing meat at high temperatures surely invites disaster.

There is almost no difference between fermented and air-dried sausages as processing steps overlap and are basically the same, although more time is needed to produce a dry sausage than a fast-fermented one. Knowing the subject better one can easily manipulate the taste and the flavor of the sausage to his own liking.

Summary of Important Issues

- The length of the sausage has no influence on drying time.
- Sausages should be dried at a rate not higher than the moisture losing ability of the sausage.
- Traditionally made sausages have pH of about 5.3 and Aw about 0.88 at the end of the drying process.
- Overloading the drying chamber can impede air movement.
- Air speed - higher air speed, faster drying. The average air speed varies between 0.5 and 0.1 m/sec
- Casing type (pore size) - bigger pores, faster drying.
- Amount of fat - more fat in sausage, faster drying.
- Particle size - bigger size, faster drying.
- Sausage diameter - bigger diameter, slower drying.
- In general when pH drops rapidly the sausage dries faster. Molds will develop quicker if there is no air draft at all.
- If the outside of the sausage becomes greasy, it should be wiped off with a warm cloth otherwise it may clog the pores and inhibit drying.
- The speed of 3.6 km/h (2.2 mile/hour) corresponds to the speed of 1 meter/second which is basically a walking speed.
- The air speed of 0.5 m/sec (1.8 miles/per hour) corresponds to a slow walk.
- Often air speed is given in air changes per minute. Typical values for *fermentation* rooms are 4-6 air changes per minute, and less than 2 air changes per minute for *drying* chambers.

Sausages all over the world follow a similar pattern of basic manufacturing steps: material selection, cutting/grinding, mixing with spices and stuffing. Then depending on the type of sausage desired a more specialized procedure is applied like smoking and cooking, or fermenting/drying without cooking at all. A large number of Spanish sausages are cured in air which requires more knowledge and investment in time.

Dry sausages production cycle: Grinding (*picado*) - mixing (*amasado*) - marinating (*adobado/reposo*) - stuffing (*embutir*) - fermenting (*estufaje*) - drying and maturing (*secado* y *maduración*).
Note: when starter cultures are used the marinating period (*reposo*) may be skipped entirely.

Cooked sausages production cycle: Grinding (*picado*) - mixing (*amasado*) - stuffing (*embutir*) - smoking (*ahumado*) - cooking (*cocción*).

Basic rules are provided in this book, but for those who want to study the subject deeper a more specialized book should be consulted like the *The Art of Making Fermented Sausages.*

Are Spanish Sausages Dried, Fermented or Both?

Technically speaking fermenting is the process when lactic acid producing bacteria consume sugar and produce lactic acid. This is how most American salami, pepperoni or summer sausages are made. Meat develops enough acidity and the sausage is microbiologically safe within hours because bacteria hate acidity. Unfortunately meat also acquires a sourly taste of which not every consumer is fond of. There is some drying during the fermentation stage, but not enough to make the sausage safe. Rapid development of acidity (pH drop) is the main protection against bacteria and spoilage.

The total amount of developed acidity is proportionate to the amount of added sugar and the speed of acid production depends on temperature. However, very fast and large acid production may inhibit color and flavor forming bacteria from working resulting in less color, flavor and aroma development.

Sugar is not added to Spanish dry sausages so there should be no fermentation, right? Well it gets more complicated than that. We don't need table sugar (sucrose) to start fermentation as many ingredients that end up in meat are rich in carbohydrates (sugar). Garlic contains 1% of sugar, paprika 10%, onions 4.2%, cabbage 3.2%, nuts 4%, raw potato 4.7%, pumpkin 2.8 %, raisins 60%, wine 1-20% (from dry to sweet), instant non-fat dry milk 50%. Meat's own sugar (glycogen~1%) combined with some of the above ingredients will provide enough sugar to trigger a mild fermentation.

If a chorizo recipe is studied in detail, it can be seen that the sausage is submitted to temperatures of 18-25° C (64-77° F) for a day or two. Those temperatures combined with some sugar will start fermentation, of course providing that there is enough lactic acid bacteria present. As a result some acidity will develop that will inhibit growth of unwanted bacteria, however, such a small amount of acidity will not affect the traditional mild flavor of the sausage. To make it short and simple, Spanish dry sausages go through a weak fermentation stage but they are basically dried.

Fermenting, as explained above can be almost non-existent and can be considered the beginning of the drying stage. Technically fermenting ends when meat reaches the highest acidity level (lowest pH), however, without added sugar there is hardly any fermentation taking place to begin with.

Drying is a slow process and color and flavor producing bacteria react with proteins and fats creating internal reactions and changes in meat and the products develop wonderful texture and flavor. In Spain, this entire process is called *"curing"* although it is a combination of individual steps like fermenting, drying and aging or maturing. The products tend to develop and change also during storage.

Maturing is a part of the drying process, we cannot pinpoint when it begins or ends as it continues even in storage. This is a period when all those subtle reactions between proteins, fats and bacteria take place, some reactions occur without involvement of bacteria.

Chapter 4

Sausage Recipes

Recipe Guidelines

A significant amount of research was performed in compiling these recipes. These traditional recipes of Spanish sausages have been around for centuries, however, their manufacture is more modern. In the past instructions would simply say "dry sausages until done", today it might say "dry sausages at 12-15° C, 80-85% humidity for 30 days or until they lose 33% of original weight. Those parameters are included in each recipe and they provide valuable information for people in other countries. What cannot be duplicated is the quality of the meat, as this depends on a breed of the animal and its diet. It is unlikely that outside of Spain the sausages will be made with iberian pork so meat from locally raised animals will have to suffice.

Traditional Spanish sausage recipes, are very concise and do not usually include details about fermentation or drying temperatures. They were based on hundreds of years of empirical knowledge and they have always worked. The instructions will state "mix meats with spices and hold for 24 hours" then, "move the sausages to the drying room."Well, such technology would work for people living 100 meters above sea level, away from the shore and having temperatures that do not drop to the freezing point. Even in Spain, people living up north in the Pyrenees Mountains next to France will need to start a fire in order to keep the drying process going. And if they want it or not, those sausages will be cold smoked as the burning wood produces smoke. In areas of very high humidity the fire will be needed to warm up the room, as the air at higher temperature can hold more humidity and as a result the relative humidity in the chamber will be lowered.

How about an individual who wants to make chorizo or fuet, but lives in a tropical and humid Florida or in Philippines? Telling him to dry sausages in his kitchen makes absolutely no sense unless we provide the temperature and humidity which should be observed. He might not follow instruction to a single degree, but as long as he stays within a recommended range his sausage will be fine. At least he gets an idea of what temperature and humidity should be maintained. Instructions of the nature like "dry sausages at room temperature" might be useful for a person living in Extremadura or Andalusia but it cannot be assumed that the same sausage will be successfully produced in Alaska, Texas, Brazil, Belize or Philippines.

A proper amount of salt, adding sodium nitrite and paying attention to drying temperatures and humidity will greatly increase the odds in our favor. Almost everybody has access to the Internet, where you can buy online thermometers, humidity and pH testers, scales, sodium nitrite curing salts, spices and other ingredients. An inexpensive device known as a "line voltage controller" converts any refrigerator into a fermenting/drying chamber allowing precise control of temperature.

In the past most people did not own refrigerators and humidity meters were not commonly available. It was difficult to obtain nitrite or starter culture and an average person was not even aware of curing salts. Today we can utilize a pH tester and it will tell us how the meat is fermenting. Aw tester can tell us exactly how much moisture is still left in the sausage. This equipment is reasonably priced, widely available and constant quality dry sausages can be made in most areas of the world.

As mentioned earlier the benefits of applying nitrite are numerous: strong guaranteed color, curing flavor, preventing rancidity of fats and protection against spoilage and pathogenic bacteria.

Adding sodium nitrite (Cure #1 or Cure #2) increases the chances of a hobbyist for making products in less than ideal conditions. All manufacturers use nitrites today, the hobbyists too. The reason traditional Spanish sausage recipes, even those published by the government sources do not mention sodium nitrite is that sodium nitrite was discovered only about 100 years ago. Don't confuse sodium nitrite with potassium nitrate (saltpeter) which has been known for thousands of years.

One of the main benefits of using sodium nitrite is that it inhibits the growth of *Clostridium botulinum* known as "food poisoning", and *smoked* meats are at the highest risk. That is why the practice of adding nitrate to meat was common in countries that love smoked products. American Cure #1 or Cure #2 are stronger than European cures. As they contain more sodium nitrite they are mixed with the red colorant so they stand out and will not be mistaken with common salt. The amount of salt in Cure #1 or Cure #2 has been compensated for in all recipes by subtracting it from the total amount of salt which the recipe calls for. If you decide not to use Cure #1 (it contains 93% salt), remove it from the recipe and replace it with an equivalent amount of salt. Example:

recipe - meat 1 kg, salt **18 g**, Cure #1 **2.5 g**, pepper 2 g,
becomes - meat 1 kg, salt **20.5** g, pepper 2 g,

Adding 2.5 g of Cure #1 to 1 kg (2.2 lb) of meat introduces **156 ppm** (parts per million) of sodium nitrite which is at the upper maximum limit for a regular smoked and sausage. As dry sausages can contain more initial nitrite which will dissipate in time during drying, you are way below official limits.

Outside the USA most nitrite cures contain only 0.6% of sodium nitrite which is such a negligible amount that it can be disregarded and the total amount of salt in a recipe *can be directly substituted with curing salt (as long as the curing salt contains no more than 0.6% of sodium nitrite).* We are assuming of course that you want to introduce sodium nitrite to the recipe. For example:

recipe: meat 1 kg, **salt 20 g**, pepper 2 g,
becomes: meat 1 kg, **curing salt 20 g**, pepper 2 g,

In the above example common salt has been replaced with European curing salt (0.6% sodium nitrite) that introduced **120 ppm** of sodium nitrite which is far below 150 ppm limit for a regular smoked and cooked sausage.

Starter Cultures

Starter cultures were discovered about 1942 and they became widely accepted only about 15 years ago. Today adding cultures to food is a commonplace.

Chr-Hansen T-SPX is an ideal starter culture for slow-fermented dry sausages such as chorizo, salchichón, fuet, longaniza, sobrasada, androlla, butelo and salami. This is an aromatic culture with mild acidification which has been selected for traditional fermentation profiles applying temperatures not higher than 24° C (75° F). The culture is added at 0.12 g/kg of meat so a highly accurate digital scale is needed when making a small load of sausage. The culture should not be added to marinade (*adobo*), it should be mixed with meat just before stuffing. Such a small amount creates a distribution problem so mix the culture with 1-2 tablespoons of non-chlorinated (distilled) water about 30 minutes before application.

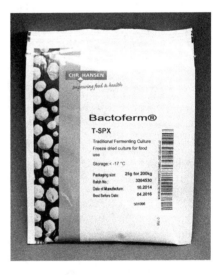

Photo 4.1 Chr-Hansen T-SPX starter culture.

Cooking

In most countries the majority of sausages are cooked in water at around 80° C (176° F). The diameter of the sausage dictates the cooking time, but the general rule of thumb says that at 80° C the sausage needs 10 minutes for 1 cm of its diameter - the sausage of 36 mm needs 36 minutes cooking time. Occasionally cooking time can be slightly readjusted, for example a sausage that was smoked at 60° C (140° F) for one hour may have an internal temperature of 35° C (95° F) already, so a few minutes less will do, however, it is better to err on a safe side (longer time). When in doubt use an instant digital thermometer, this is what it is designed for. Baking sausages in an oven or in a smokehouse takes much longer.

Pimentón

Pimentón comes as sweet and hot. When a recipe does not specify what type to use, choose sweet pimentón, however, both are included in many recipes. It is basically up to you how "hot" of a sausage you want. For chorizo a typical amount is about 25 g sweet and 2.0 g hot pimentón for 1 kg of meat.

Drying and Humidity

Pig slaughter and processing was traditionally performed in the winter. Although Spain has a moderate climate, in many areas of the country temperatures drop too low and drying chambers need to be heated.

Natural drying was performed in the kitchen, higher floors, pantries, above stoves or right in the chimney. In designated natural storerooms a slow burning fire was kept to warm up the facility.

Humidity was controlled by placing water pans inside of the room or covering inlet air openings with soaked cloth.

Such arrangements worked surprisingly well, but made the process longer than drying in modern controlled chambers. Additionally, it required a lot of experience.

Controlled drying is how we produce sausages today, these methods are not only reserved to meat plants, but everybody has access to thermometers, humidity testers, even to more specialized equipment like pH (acidity) and Aw (moisture) testers. Sausages are made in all areas of the world in all climatic zones, including humid tropics such as Florida, Louisiana, Caribbean or Philippines. They need to resort to controlled drying. Having this in mind all recipes include recommended temperatures and humidity settings which gives the reader an idea what to look for. For example, a typical range of temperatures for long term drying is 12-16° C (53-60° F), so being within this range is a safe setting. There is no reason to despair if the temperature jumped to 25° C (77° F) for an hour or so, but we must stay within the specified range.

When Sausage is Safe and Ready to Consume

This question is always present when making dry sausages, even when we employ thermometers and humidity testers. Only a water activity (Aw-moisture tester) can answer this question. They are used by meat plants and unfortunately are very expensive. It is agreed that when a sausage loses about 30-35% of its original weight it is microbiologically safe. In simple terms there is so little moisture left that bacteria can not grow. The acidity of meat also plays a significant role. A sausage that acquired more acidity can be submitted to a shorter drying period.

The simplest solution is making one or two control sausages, they do not need to be long but they must have the same diameter as the main batch of sausages. They must also be of the same type. Weigh your stuffed test sausage before processing, then weigh the sausage every few days. When you reach the point when the sausage lost 33% of its original weight it is done. The benefit of the second test sausage is that you can slice it from time to time and look at its color and texture. It will make you a better sausage maker.

Consume Raw

For example "morcón is consumed raw". This does not mean that raw meat is eaten, it means that the sausage was sufficiently cured so it can be eaten at any time without the need for cooking. In many cases it is such a high quality product that it would be a waste to use it for general cooking, for example in stews. We don't grind expensive rib eye steaks for making hamburgers, by the same token, we eat delicacies like iberian ham or morcón cold and raw.

Room Temperature

Occasionally there is a description stating that a sausage can be dried or stored at room temperature. Such temperature falls into 12-15° C (53-59° F) range, it is much lower than a typical living room temperature. Before advent of refrigeration each household had a kitchen pantry where food was stored. It had a door, no windows and was much cooler than the rest of the house. On a farm, there was similar facility called the "root cellar."

Tips and General Guidelines

Dry sausages contain more salt (2.5-3%) than other sausages. A small amount of dextrose (fast fermenting sugar) is added to *dry sausages*. The reason is that dextrose being the simplest of sugars is easily and immediately metabolized by lactic acid bacteria and a small but moderately fast pH will be immediately obtained. This will provide an extra margin of safety which is very important during the first hours of the process. Both cures (#1 and #2) contain 93.75% salt and this amount is accounted for when calculating the total amount of salt in all recipes. You may adjust the sausage recipe by adding or removing this amount of salt depending whether you add or remove cure from a recipe.

Sausage Recipe Index
A - Z

Name	Type	Spanish Region or Country	Page
Androja	cooked	Castilla y León	92
Androlla Gallega	semi-dry, smoked	Galicia	93
Androlla Maragata	semi-dry, smoked	Castilla y León	94
Baiona Curada	dry	Basque Country	95
Bisbe or Bull	dry	Catalonia	96
Bispo	semi-dry	Aragón	97
Blanco	cooked	País Valenciano	98
Blancos	cooked	Murcia	99
Blanquet de Baleares	cooked	Balearic Islands	100
Borono	blood sausage	Spain	101
Botagueña	blood sausage	Spain	102
Botelo or Butelo Gallego	semi-dry, smoked	Galicia	103
Botifarra Blanca-La Garriga	cooked	Catalonia	104
Botifarra Blanca-Lérida	cooked	Catalonia	105
Botifarra Catalana Cruda	cooked	Catalonia	106
Botifarra Catalana Trufada	cooked	Catalonia	107
Botifarra de Ceba	blood sausage	País Valenciano	108
Botifarra de Huevos (Gerona)	cooked	Catalonia	109
Botifarra Negra de Barcelona	blood sausage	Catalonia	110
Botifarra Perol	cooked	Catalonia	111
Botifarro or Blanquet	cooked	País Valenciano	112
Botillo de León	semi-dry, smoked	Castilla-León	113
Botillo del Bierzo PGI 2001	dry, smoked	Castilla-León	114
Buche de Costillas (Badajoz)	dry	Extremadura	115
Butifarra	fresh	Catalonia	116
Butifarra Blanca	cooked	Catalonia	117
Butifarra Blanca de Huevos	cooked	Catalonia	118
Butifarra Blanca Mezcla	cooked	Catalonia	119
Butifarra de Baleares	blood sausage	Balearic Islands	120
Butifarra Dulce Curada	dry	Catalonia	121
Butifarra Dulce de Gerona	fresh	Catalonia	122
Butifarra Lorquina	blood sausage	Murcia	123

Butifarra Negra	blood sausage	Catalonia	124
Butifarra Negra Mezcla	blood sausage	Catalonia	125
Butifarra Soledeña	cooked	Colombia	126
Butifarra Traidora	cooked	Catalonia	127
Butifarrón	cooked	Catalonia	128
Butifarrón de Baleares	blood sausage	Balearic Islands	129
Cabeza de Jabalí	head cheese	Spain	130
Camayot	blood sausage	Balearic Islands	131
Chanfaino or Longaniza Gallega	dry, smoked	Galicia	132
Chireta	cooked	Spain	133
Chistorra or Txistorra	dry	Navarra	134
Chistorra with Culture	dry	Navarra	135
Choriqueso	fresh	Mexico	136
Chorizo Andaluz	dry	Andalusia	137
Chorizo Antioqueño	fresh, dry	Colombia	138
Chorizo - Argentinian	fresh	Argentina	139
Chorizo Aromático	fresh	Mexico	140
Chorizo Asturiano	dry, smoked	Asturias	141
Chorizo Candelario	dry	Castilla-León	142
Chorizo Cántabro (Guriezo)	semi-dry, smoked	Cantabria	143
Chorizo Criollo Argentino	fresh	Argentina	144
Chorizo Criollo Colombiano	fresh	Colombia	145
Chorizo Cubano	fresh	Cuba	146
Chorizo Cular de Salamanca	dry	Castilla-León	147
Chorizo de Aragón	dry	Aragón	148
Chorizo de Bilbao	semi-dry	Philippines	149
Chorizo de Bofe	dry	Spain	150
Chorizo de Calabaza	dry	Spain	151
Chorizo de Cantipalos PGI 2011	dry	Castilla-León	152
Chorizo de Cebolla	dry	Galicia	154
Chorizo de Cerdo	dry	Spain	155
Chorizo de la Sierra de Aracena	dry, smoked	Andalusia	156
Chorizo de León	dry	Castilla-León	157
Chorizo de Mezcla	dry	Spain	158
Chorizo de Pamplona	dry	Navarra	159

Chorizo de Potes	dry, smoked	Cantabria	160
Chorizo de Soria	dry	Castilla-León	161
Chorizo de Villarcayo	dry, smoked	Castilla-León	162
Chorizo Extremeńo	dry	Extremadura	163
Chorizo Gallego	dry, smoked	Galicia	164
Chorizo Ibérico de Huelva	dry	Andalusia	165
Chorizo - Mexicano	fresh	Mexico	166
Chorizo Parillero	fresh	Uruguay	167
Chorizo Patatero de Monroy	dry	Extremadura	168
Chorizo Patatero Rojo	dry	Castilla La Mancha	169
Chorizo Porteńo	(fresh)	Argentina	170
Chorizo - Puerto Rican	fresh	Puerto Rico	171
Chorizo Quzande de Bandeira	dry, smoked	Galicia	172
Chorizo Riojano PGI 2010	dry	La Rioja	173
Chorizo Rojo de Teror	fresh	Canary Islands	174
Chorizo-Spanish-Fresh	(fresh)	Spain, ARGENTINA	175
Chorizo Traditional	(dry)	Spain, ARGENTINA	176
Chorizo Verde	fresh	Mexico	177
Chorizo Zamoranao	dry	Castilla-León	178
Chosco de Tineo PGI 2011	semi-dry, smoked	Asturias	179
Chosco or Choscu	dry	Asturias	180
Delgadilla	blood sausage	Spain	181
El Xolis	dry	Catalonia	182
Emberzao	blood sausage	Spain	183
Farinato	dry	Castilla-León	184
Fariñon	blood sausage	Asturias	185
Figatells	fresh	País Valenciano	186
Fuet de Barcelona	dry	Catalonia	187
Girella	cooked	Catalonia	188
Güeña	semi-dry	Castilla La Mancha	189
Imperial de Bolańos	dry	Castilla La Mancha	190
Imperial de Lorca	dry	Murcia	191
Llangonisa Rotja - Alicantina	dry	País Valenciano	192

Lomo Embuchado	dry	Spain *ARGENIA*	193
Lomo Embuchado de Huelva	dry	Andalusia	194
Lomo Embuchado de Segovia	dry	Castilla-León	195
Lomo Embuchado Ibérico	dry	Castilla-León	196
Lomo Ibérico de Bellota	dry	Andalusia	197
Lomo Ibérico Extremeño	dry	Extremadura	198
Lomo Picado	dry	Spain	199
Longanisa	fresh	Philippines	200
Longaniza	dry	Spain *ARGENIA*	201
Longaniza Andaluza	dry	Andalusia	202
Longaniza de Aragón	dry	Aragón	203
Longaniza de Mezcla	dry	Spain	204
Longaniza de Pascua	dry	País Valenciano	205
Longaniza de Payés	dry	Catalonia	206
Longaniza Dominicana	fresh	Dominican Rep.	207
Longaniza Fresca	fresh	País Valenciano	208
Longaniza Murciana	fresh	Murcia	209
Longaniza Navarra	semi-dry	Navarra	210
Longaniza Salamantina	dry	Castilla-León	211
Mondejo or Mondeju	cooked	Basque Country	212
Morcilla	blood sausage	Spain	213
Morcilla Achorizada	blood sausage	Andalusia	214
Morcilla Andaluza	blood sausage	Andalusia	215
Morcilla Asturiana	blood saus. dry	Asturias	216
Morcilla Blanca	cooked	Spain	217
Morcilla Blanca de Cazorla	cooked	Andalusia	218
Morcilla Blanca de Jaén	dry	Andalusia	219
Morcilla Blanca Provenzal	cooked	Spain	220
Morcilla de Álava	blood sausage	Basque Country	221
Morcilla de Arroz	blood sausage	Spain	222
Morcilla de Arroz (Castellón de la Plana)	blood sausage	País Valenciano	223
Morcilla de Burgos PGI 2018	blood sausage	Castilla-León	224
Morcilla de Calabaza	blood saus. dry	Spain	226
Morcilla de Calabaza de Mezcla	blood saus. dry	Spain	227
Mocilla de Cebolla	blood sausage	Spain	228

Morcilla de Cebolla de León	blood sausage	Castilla-León	229
Morcilla de Cebolla Valenciana	blood sausage	País Valenciano	230
Morcilla de Despojos	blood saus. dry	Spain	231
Morcilla de la Sierra de Huelva	blood sausage	Andalusia	232
Morcilla de Lengua	blood sausage	Spain	233
Morcilla de Pan	blood sausage	Spain	234
Morcilla de Pícaro	blood sausage	Murcia	235
Morcilla de Sangre de Oveja (Buskantza o Mondejos)	blood sausage	País Vasco	236
Morcilla de Tocino	blood sausage	Spain	237
Morcilla de Valladolid	blood sausage	Castilla-León	238
Morcilla Dulce Canaria	blood sausage	Canary Islands	239
Morcilla Dulce de Soria	blood sausage	Castilla-León	240
Morcilla Dulce Riojana	blood sausage	La Rioja	241
Morcilla Extremeńa de Badajoz	blood saus. dry	Extremadura	242
Morcilla Francesa	blood sausage	Spain	243
Morcilla Gallega (La Coruńa)	blood sausage	Galicia	244
Morcilla Lebaniega	blood sausage	Cantabria	245
Morcilla Lustre	blood sausage	Spain	246
Morcilla Lustre Malagueña	blood sausage	Andalusia	247
Morcilla Odolki - Odoloste	blood sausage	País Vasco	248
Morcilla Porteńa	blood sausage	Argentina	249
Morcilla Riojana de Arroz	blood sausage	La Rioja	250
Morcilla Rondeńa	blood sausage	Andalusia	251
Morcilla Serrana	blood saus. dry	Andalusia	252
Morcilla Toledana	blood sausage	Castilla La Mancha	253
Morcilla Vasca	blood sausage	País Vasco	254
Morcilla Vasca de Argentina	blood sausage	Argentina	255
Morcón	dry	Andalusia	256
Morcón Extremeño	dry	Extremadura	257
Morcón de Lorca	dry	Murcia	258
Morcón Gaditano	dry	Andalusia	259
Moronga	blood sausage	Puerto Rico	260
Mortadela Bolonia	cooked	Spain	261
Mortadela Cordobesa	cooked	Andalusia	262

Moscancia	blood sausage	Spain	263
Obispo de Tenancingo	fresh	Mexico	264
Paltruch-Bisbot	head cheese	Catalonia	265
Patatera	fresh	Spain	266
Perro	blood sausage	Valencia	267
Queso de Cabeza	head cheese	Argentina	268
Queso de Puerco	head cheese	Chile	269
Relleno de Huéscar	cooked	Andalusia	270
Sabadiego or Sabadeña	dry	Asturias	271
Salami Español (Spanish)	fermented, dry	Spain	272
Salchicha de Higado	liver sausage	Spain	273
Salchicha de Higado con Trufas	liver sausage	Spain	274
Salchicha de Higado con Trufas y Tomate	liver sausage	Spain	275
Salchicha de Higado de Mezcla	liver sausage	Spain	276
Salchicha de Ternera	fresh	Spain	277
Salchicha de Trufas	fresh	Spain	278
Salchicha de Turista	fresh	Spain	279
Salchicha de Zaratán	semi-dry	Castilla-León	280
Salchicha Exquisita de Higado	liver sausage	Spain	281
Salchicha Frankfurt Style	cooked, smoked	Spain	282
Salchicha Madrileña	fresh	Community of Madrid	283
Salchicha Roja	fresh	Spain	284
Salchicha Viena Style	cooked, smoked	Spain	285
Salchichón	dry	Spain	286
Salchichón de Mezcla	dry	Spain	287
Salchichón de Vic or **Llonganissa de Vic PGI 2001**	dry	Catalonia	288
Salchichón Gallego	dry	Galicia	289
Secallona-Somalla-Petador	dry	Spain	290
Sobrasada de Mallorca PGI 1996	semi-dry	Balearic Islands	291
Sobrasada de Mallorca de Cerdo Negro PGI 1996	semi-dry	Balearic Islands	292
Sobrasada Picante Casera	dry	Spain	293
Sobrasada Valenciana	dry	País Valenciano	294

Androja

Androja is a sausage that can be found in the beautiful Eastern Leon Mountain (Montaña Oriental Leonesa) region (previously known as Montaña de Riaño) in the Leon province, Castilla and León region of Spain. The sausage is made with fat and flour, a practice which is not entirely new. Russians often added a few percent of potato flour to improve binding. Portuguese Farinheira sausage consists of equal parts of wheat flour and pork belly. Androja is somewhat similar to the American Indians product known as pemmican which was made from buffalo fat, finely shredded dry meat and dry herbs and berries, however, flour was not added. If stored in a cool place Androja will keep for months so it is a good survival food.

Lard	350 g	0.77 lb
Water	45 ml	3 Tbsp
Pimentón, sweet	30 g	5 Tbsp
Pimentón, hot	25 g	4 Tbsp
Wheat flour	550 g	1.21 lb

Ingredients per 1 kg (2.2 lb) of material

Salt	6 g	1 tsp

Applying little heat, place water in a skillet, then add lard and melt it down. Add salt and pimentón and start slowly adding flour mixing continuously. Mix fat with flour until flour is well absorbed. Add more flour or fat if needed, the result is a lumpy crude mass. This is like making "roux" - a thickening agent for gravy, sauces, soups and stews, commonly used in Cajun and Creole cooking. Stuff into 60 mm diameter casings.*
Cook in water at 80° C (176° F) for 60 minutes. Cooked Androja keeps very well.

Notes
* Fresh Androja (stuffed, but not cooked) can be kept for a short time in a refrigerator or frozen for later. It can be stuffed into parchment paper, aluminum foil or a cloth bag. Then it can be cut in slices and fried with eggs for breakfast. Androja can be stuffed in cabbage leaves, laced up with twine and steamed or baked.
One teaspoon of dry herbs such as oregano, thyme or marjoram can be added.

Androlla Gallega

Androlla Gallega is a popular semi-dry sausage in Lugo and Qurense (Viana do Bolo) province situated in Galicia region of Spain. Galician Androlla includes rib bones, however, in Androlla Maragata the bones are removed. Maragatería is a historic region in León, Spain.

Pork spare ribs with attached meat	900 g	1.98 lb
Pork skins	100 g	0.22 lb

Ingredients per 1 kg (2.2 lb) of meat

Salt	24 g	4 tsp
Cure #2	2.5 g	1/2 tsp
Pimentón, sweet	25 g	4 Tbsp
Pimentón, hot	3.0 g	1 tsp
Garlic	7.0 g	2 cloves
Oregano, ground	2.0	1 tsp
White dry wine	60 ml	2 oz fl

Chop ribs into ¾" (2 cm) long pieces. The bones are not removed. Cut skins into smaller strips.

Mix wine, salt, cure #2 and spices together. Add ribs and skins and mix all together. Place in refrigerator for 48 hours.

Stuff firmly into 50 mm natural casing. Make links 20 cm (8") long.

Smoke/dry for 8-10 days by hanging sausages above the kitchen stove. Move the sausages to a different area of the kitchen and dry them for 1-2 months.*

Notes

Androlla is always cooked in water before consumption. It is usually served with boiled potatoes and turnip greens, known in UK as *rapini* and in US as *broccoli raab or broccoli rabe*. Pieces of rib bones are easy to spot and separate from meat.

The sausage exhibits an intense red color.

The texture is rather loose and varied unlike in dry, smoked or emulsified sausages.

The average weight of the sausage is about 1/2 kg (1 pound).

The flavor of the sausage is strongly influenced by the quality of the meat that comes from locally grown and free roaming "celta" pigs.

* traditional method of smoking known as "la campana de Lareira." Today, the process will be shorter:

Apply a thin smoke at 18° C (64° F) for 10 hours.
Dry at 12-15° C (53-59° F) for 30-40 days.
Store at 10-12° C (50-53° F), <70% humidity or refrigerate.

Androlla Maragata

Androlla Maragata is a popular sausage in communities of el Bierzo and la Maragatería in Castilla y León region of Spain. The sausage is similar to Galician Androlla as both sausages are made with pork ribs, however, in Androlla Maragata *the bones are removed and only the meat is processed.* Due to the high content of connective tissue (ribs, skins and jowls) the sausage contains a lot of collagen which gels upon heating and provides a pleasant experience upon eating.

Jowls	500 g	1.10 lb
Spare rib meat (no bones)	400 g	0.88 lb
Back fat, skins	100 g	0.22 lb

Ingredients per 1 kg (2.2 lb) of meat

Salt	24 g	4 tsp
Cure #2	2.5 g	1/2 tsp
Pimentón, sweet	25 g	4 Tbsp
Pimentón, hot	3.0 g	1 tsp
Oregano, rubbed	2.0 g	3 tsp
White dry wine	60 ml	2 oz fl

Cut rib meat and jowls into 20 mm (3/4") pieces. Cut skins into smaller strips. Mix salt, cure #2, spices, meat and skins together. Place in refrigerator for 48 hours.
Stuff firmly into a 50 mm casing. Make links 20 cm (8") long.
Smoke/dry for 8-10 days by hanging sausages above the kitchen stove. Move the sausages to a different area of the kitchen and dry them for 1-2 months.*

Notes
Androlla is always slow cooked in water before consumption. Add soup greens to water for best results. It is usually served with boiled potatoes and turnip greens, known in UK as *rapini* and in US as *broccoli raab or broccoli rabe*. The sausage exhibits an intense red color.
The average weight of the sausage is about ½ kg (1 pound).

* traditional method of smoking known as "la campana de Lareira." Today, the process will be shorter:

Apply a thin smoke at 18° C (64° F) for 24 hours.
Dry at 12-15° C (53-59° F) for 30-40 days.
Store at 10-12° C (50-53° F), <70% humidity or refrigerate.

Baiona Curada

Baiona curada, also known as little ham (*jamoncito*) is made with boneless pork butt (*paletilla*) which is the upper part of a shoulder. It is somewhat similar to lomo embuchado in that both products are made from whole cuts of meat and they are stuffed in casings and dried. Baiona is most popular in the Spanish Basque country.

Pork butt, boneless	2-3 kg	4.4-6.6 lb

Ingredients per 1 kg (2.2 lb) of meat

Coarse salt for salting loin, *as needed.*

Cure #2	5.0 g	1 tsp
Pepper	2.0 g	1 tsp
Sugar	3.0 g	1/2 tsp
Oregano, ground	2.0 g	1 tsp
Cumin, ground	1.0 g	1/2 tsp
White wine or vinegar	30 ml	2 Tbsp

Trim off the skin from the butt. Using force rub in a generous amount of coarse salt (as needed) all over butt. The butt should rest in a suitable container on a layer of salt and be well covered with salt all around leaving no exposed areas. Hold in refrigerator for 24 hours.

Brush off the salt, wash briefly in running water and pat dry with paper towels. Mix all ingredients with wine to form the marinade paste. Remainder: *multiply the above ingredients per weight of butt.* No more salt is needed.

Apply the paste all around the butt. Hold in refrigerator for 48 hours.

Stuff the butt into pork bungs that will tightly accommodate the piece.

Ferment/dry at 22-24° C (72-75° F), 85-90% humidity, for 2 days.

Dry at 15→12° C (59-53° F), 85→75% humidity for 2 months. The butt should lose about 35% of its original weight.

Store at 10-12° C (°F), <75% humidity.

Bisbe or Bull

Bisbe also known as bull is a Catalan cooked sausage. Bisbe is made from cooked pork meat, fat, tongue, occasionally stomach, and seasoned with salt, pepper and spices. It is a large diameter sausage usually stuffed in pork blind cap (caecum), occasionally in bladders. Bisbe is popular all over Catalonia, including Balearic Islands, and as there are many counties so there are countless variations of the sausage; it can be made with heart, kidney, spleen, brains, tongue, liver, bread, eggs, rice, onions or some blood. The basic seasoning is salt and pepper, cinnamon and nutmeg are often included, sometimes saffron is added for yellow color. Occasionally, mushrooms, peppers or pistachios are added.

Lean pork	400 g	0.88 lb
Pork shoulder	150 g	0.33 lb
Pork tongue	200 g	0.44 lb
Pork belly	200 g	0.44 lb
Pork skins	50 g	0.11 lb

Ingredients per 1 kg (2.2 lb) of meat

Salt	18 g	3 tsp
White pepper	2.0 g	1 tsp
Cinnamon	0.5 g	1/4 tsp
Nutmeg	0.5 g	1/4 tsp

Place all meats in water* and cook below boiling point until soft. Save 1 cup of meat stock and filter it through a paper towel.
Dice tongue into 12 mm (1/2") cubes.
Grind meats through 8 mm (3/8") plate.
Grind skins through 3 mm (1/8") plate.
Mix all meats with salt and spices. Add 45 ml (3 Tablespoons) of meat stock.
Stuff into pork blind cap (caecum).
Cook in water at 85° C (185° F) for 2 hours.
Immerse in cold water for 15 minutes.
Hang in air to cool and to evaporate moisture.
Refrigerate.

Notes

* for a better flavor you can add some soup greens to water.
Bisbe is consumed fresh, added to salads or sliced and eaten on bread.

Bispo

Bisbo is a large cooked sausage popular in Pyrenees valleys of Aragón in northeastern Spain. It is made from pork head meat, pork mask (face), including the tongue and cuts of lean pork. Meats are ground, mixed with spices, stuffed in pork blind cap (caecum) and dried.

Pork head meat, tails, tongue,
ribs with attached meat   1000 g   2.2 lb

Ingredients per 1 kg (2.2 lb) of meat

Salt	30 g	5 tsp
Cure #1	2.5 g	1/2 tsp
Pimentón, sweet	25 g	4 Tbsp
Pimentón, hot	2.0 g	1 tsp
Oregano, ground	1.0 g	1/2 tsp
Garlic, smashed	7.0 g	2 cloves

Chop ribs and tails into smaller pieces. Do not remove bones.
Chop other meats.
Mix salt with all spices adding a little water to create a paste.
Mix meats with the paste and hold for 24 hours in refrigerator.
Stuff firmly into pork blind cap (caecum) or large diameter casing.
Using oak wood apply cold smoke at 18° C (64° F) 3-4 days. Try to deliver smoke at least 8 hours each day.
Dry at 12-15° C (53-59° F), 65-75% humidity, for at least 3-4 days.
Refrigerate.

Notes
Cook in water (below the boiling point) for about 2 hours before serving, it is usually served with potatoes and vegetables.

Blanco

Blanco, sometimes called "blanc" is a cooked sausage popular in eastern regions of Spain: Alicante in País Valenciano, Murcia and Balearic Islands. Blanco, like Blanquet is a white short sausage, with a large proportion of fat that creates a light colored sausage somewhat similar to white morcilla, or butifarra, but shorter. Technically speaking, it is a cooked sausage (salchicha cocida). The typical spices are pepper, cinnamon and cloves, occasionally star anise and beaten egg are included.

Lean pork	500 g	1.10 lb
Dewlap	500 g	1.10 lb

Ingredients per 1 kg (2.2 lb) of meat

Salt	21 g	3.5 tsp
Black pepper	2.0 g	1 tsp
Cinnamon	1.0 g	1/2 tsp
Cloves, ground	0.3 g	1/8 tsp

Grind meats through 6 mm (1/4") plate.
Mix with all ingredients.
Stuff into 20-30 mm pork or veal casings. Tie off into 10-15 cm (4-6") units, each weighing approximately 120-140 grams (4-5 oz).
Cook in water at 80° C (176° F) for 20-30 minutes.
Cool in air. Refrigerate.

Notes
Consume raw or cooked.
Blanco is often served with stews, rice or with bread.
In the past the sausage was kept for 1 month at room temperature (12-15° C/53-59° F), <75% humidity).

Blancos

Blancos is a popular sausage in eastern regions of Spain: Murcia, Valencia ("blanc") and Balearic Islands ("blanquet").

Lean pork	250 g	0.55 lb
Pork head meat, cooked	250 g	0.55 lb
Pork belly	500 g	1.10 lb

Ingredients per 1 kg (2.2 lb) of meat

Salt	18 g	3 tsp
White pepper	2.0 g	1 tsp
Pimentón, sweet	4.0 g	2 tsp
Cinnamon	0.5 g	½ tsp
Aniseed, ground	0.3 g	1/8 tsp
Eggs	1 egg	1

Cook split heads in water at 95° C (203° F) until meat separates from bones. Recover the meat when the heads are still warm.

Cut all meats manually or grind through 8 mm (3/8") plate.

Beat the egg and mix with meat and all ingredients. Hold in refrigerator for 24 hours.

Stuff into 30-40 mm calf casings forming 5-6 cm (2-3") long links.

Cook in water at 80° C (176° F) for 45 minutes.

Cool in air.

Notes

The sausage can be stored at room temperature in a dry ventilated area for up to 2 weeks.

It is often stored in oil with pimentón.

Consume raw.

Blanquet de Baleares

Blanquet is a short cooked pork sausage popular in Balearic Islands (Mallorca, Menorca, Ibiza, Formentera) and eastern regions (Valencia, Murcia) of Spain. The sausage is often added to stews or served with rice.

Lean pork and pork belly	300 g	0.66 lb
Pork head meat	500 g	1.10 lb
Back fat	200 g	0.44 lb

Ingredients per 1 kg (2.2 lb) of meat

Salt	22 g	2.5 tsp
Cure #1	2.5 g	1/2 tsp
Cinnamon	2.0 g	1 tsp
White pepper	6.0 g	3 tsp
Cloves, ground	0.3 g	1/8 tsp
Nutmeg	0.5 g	¼ tsp
Pine nuts	28 g	1 oz

Cook split heads in water at 95° C (203° F) until meat separates from bones. Recover the meat when the heads are still warm.
Grind meat and fat together through 6 mm (1/4") plate.
Mix all meat and fat with spices and nuts. Hold for 24 hours in refrigerator.
Stuff into 20-40 mm natural casings forming links 20 cm (8") long.
Cook in water at 80° C (176° F) for 30 minutes. Cool in air.
Refrigerate.

Notes
Serve cold, fried or grilled.

Borono

Borono is a cooked product made with salt, pork fat, suet, onions, blood, corn or wheat flour and parsley. Technically speaking borono is not a sausage as it is not stuffed into casings. However, it is an interesting type of a "blood sausage" which has the shape of an American elongated football. The sausage is popular in northern regions of Spain; Asturias, Cantabria and north of Palencia in Castilla-León.

Pork fat or lard	200 g	0.44 lb
Blood	250 ml	250 ml
Onions, diced	350 g	0.77 lb
Corn flour	100 g	0.22 lb
Wheat flour	50 g	0.11 lb
Water	50 ml	1.66 oz fl

Ingredients per 1 kg (2.2 lb) of meat

Salt	12 g	2 tsp
Pepper, black	2.0 g	1 tsp
Parsley, chopped	1 bunch	4 Tbsp

Take a mixing bowl and fill with blood, water, fat, chopped onions and parsley. Mix all together and start adding flours slowly until a dough like texture is obtained. Let it rest for one hour.

Place some fat in the center and shape the mass into an elongated oval ball. Immerse borono in boiling water and cook for 90-120 minutes depending on size. At first the sausage will sink to the bottom, then it will rise to the surface. Drain and cool in air.

Refrigerate.

Notes

Borono is usually served for breakfast; it is sliced, fried in hot oil and served with cold milk. It is also served as a snack at any time, often served with sugar or with fried potatoes.

Beef suet or a combination of suet and pork fat may be used.

Botagueña

Botagueña, also known as *tarángana* in Castilla la Vieja, *güeña* in La Nueva, *virica* in Navarra, is a blood sausage made with *encallado* (pieces of lungs, heart or stomach) which is also called offal meat. Botagueña, unlike typical blood sausages, *is not cooked* after stuffing. The sausage is smoked, dried and stored in a cool well ventilated room and is characterized by its long shelf life.

Pork fat, fat trimmings	300 g	0.66 lb
Pork lungs, heart, stomach	550 g	1.21 lb
Pork blood	150 ml	5 oz fl

Ingredients per 1 kg (2.2 lb) of meat

Salt	28 g	4.5 tsp
Cure #1	2.5 g	1/2 tsp
Pimentón, sweet	25 g	4 Tbsp
Pimentón, hot	2.0 g	1 tsp
Red pepper or cayenne	1.0 g	1/2 tsp
Cinnamon	0.5 g	1/4 tsp
Anise	0.3 g	1/8 tsp
Cilantro, ground	0.5 g	1/4 tsp
Oregano, ground	1.0 g	1/2 tsp

Cook lungs, heart and stomach until soft. Cool and grind through 5 mm (1/4") plate.

Grind fat through 5 mm (1/4") plate.

Mix meat, fat and all ingredients together. Hold for 24 hours in refrigerator.

Stuff into 32 mm pork casings.

Apply a thin cold smoke 18° C (64° F) for 10 days. Traditionally, the sausage was hung above the wood fired kitchen stove where it acquired different flavors and smoke from everyday cooking.

Dry at 12-15° C (53-59° F), 75-85% humidity for 2 weeks.

Store in cool, not humid and well ventilated place. The sausages keep well for up to 6 months.

Botelo or Butelo Gallego

Butelo also known as butelo or botillo is a popular sausage in Lugo province situated in Galicia region of Spain. Botelo is especially popular in el Barco de Valdeorras; a municipality in Ourense in the Galicia region. The sausage is similar to Androlla, however, it is stuffed into a larger casing.

Pork spare ribs	700 g	1.54 lb
Pork skin	100 g	0.22 lb
Meat trimmings*	150 g	0.33 lb
Back fat, belly,		
fat trimmings	50 g	0.11 lb

Ingredients per 1 kg (2.2 lb) of meat

Salt	25 g	4 tsp
Cure #2	2.5 g	1/2 tsp
Sugar	5.0 g	1 tsp
Pimentón, sweet	20 g	3.5 Tbsp
Pimentón, hot	2.0 g	1 tsp
Garlic, diced	10 g	3 cloves
Oregano, ground	2.0 g	1 tsp
White dry wine	60 ml	2 oz fl

Chop ribs into 3/4" (2 cm) long pieces. The rib bones are not removed. Chop other bones with attached meat. Cut skins into smaller strips.
Mix wine, salt and spices together. Add ribs, meat and skins and mix all together. Place in refrigerator for 48 hours.
Stuff firmly into a large diameter casing like pork caecum, stomachs or bladders. The casings are not uniform so the shape of the sausage will vary – caecum being long and oval, round and bag-shaped for bladders and stomachs.
Apply a thin cold smoke 18° C (64° F) for 8-10 days. Traditionally the sausage was hung above the wood fired kitchen stove or in chimneys where it acquired different flavors and smoke from everyday cooking.
Dry at 12-15° C (53-59° F) for 2-3 months.
Store in a cool, well ventilated and dark room or refrigerate.

Notes
Botelo is cooked before serving.
The sausage exhibits an intense red color.
The texture is rather loose and different meat cuts are easy to distinguish.
* Meat trimmings attached to skeleton and bones, shoulder, head meat. Bones may be included. Botelo is always cooked before consumption. It is usually served with boiled potatoes and turnip greens, known in UK as *rapini* and in US as *broccoli raab or broccoli rabe.*

Botifarra Blanca - La Garriga

Botifarra blanca is a cooked sausage which can be found in eastern regions
of Spain: Catalonia, Valencia and Murcia. La Garriga is a municipality in the
province of Barcelona and autonomous region of Catalonia, Spain. Different cuts
of meats are employed in different regions, aromatic spices (cinnamon, nutmeg,
cloves, anise) are often added, what is peculiar is that instead of pimentón
botifarras are made with black or white pepper. La Garriga is very popular
botifarra in the olive-growing district of La Garriga near Lleida, about 40 km
(25 miles) north of Barcelona. La Garriga is made with pork dewlap (double
chin), lean pork and pork stomach (tripe). La Garriga is a white-colored sausage.

Skinless dewlap* or fat trimmings	600 g	1.32 lb
Pork, lean	300 g	0.66 lb
Pork stomach	100 g	0.22 lb

Ingredients per 1 kg (2 lb) of meat

Salt	22 g	3.5 tsp
White pepper	3.0 g	1.5 tsp
Cinnamon	0.5 g	1/4 tsp
Nutmeg	0.5 g	1/4 tsp
White wine	15 ml	1 Tbsp

Cook stomach in water (below boiling point) until soft. Drain and cool.
Grind all meats through 6 mm (1/4") plate.
Dice one third of fat into 6 - 10 mm (1/4-3/8") cubes. Grind remaining fat
through 6 mm (1/4") plate.
Mix meats and fats with all ingredients. Hold for 24 hours in refrigerator.
Stuff the mixture into 32-34 mm pork casings. Make rings about 40 cm (16")
long and tie the ends together.
Cook in water at 75-80° C (167-176° F) for 30-40 minutes.
Cool in cold water to solidify fats and distribute them uniformly all over the
sausage.
Refrigerate.

Notes
* Dewlap is a fatty double chin of the pig.
Consume raw.

Botifarra Blanca - Lérida

This version of botifarra sausage is popular in a city of Lérida (Lleida in Catalan) which is located in the western part of Catalan region of Spain. The sausage contains perishable meat cuts (offal meat) that are used for making head cheese and which would be hard to sell in a common store. It is called "white botifarra" (*blanca*) because no blood is added.

Pork dewlap	200 g	0.44 lb
Pork head meat, lean	100 g	0.22 lb
Snouts, head meat, dewlap, skins	100 g	0.22 lb
Meat trimmings, fat included	450 g	0.99 lb
Tongue	100 g	0.22 lb
Heart	50 g	0.11 lb

Ingredients per 1 kg (2.2 lb) of meat

Salt	20 g	3.5 tsp
Black pepper	5.0 g	2.5 tsp

Place snouts, dewlap, skins, head meat trimmings in pot, add 1 bay leaf, 1 allspice berry and 1 clove (per 1 kg of meats) and simmer until done. Drain and spread on the table.
Cut tongue and heart into smaller pieces.
Grind tongue, heart and cooked meats through 8-10 mm (3/8") plate.
Mix all with salt and pepper.
Stuff into 30-40 mm pork casings. Form horseshoe loops about 50 cm (20") long.
Cook in water at 85° C (185° F) for 30 minutes or until the sausage reaches 72° C (160° F) internal temperature.
Cool with running water or place in cold water for 10-15 minutes.
Allow the moisture to evaporate and refrigerate.

Notes
Sausage can be consumed cold or cooked.

Botifarra Catalana Cruda

Botifarra Catalana Cruda is a simple fresh sausage from Barcelona, Spain. The sausage must be refrigerated and fully cooked before serving.

Pork, lean	600 g	1.32 lb
Pork belly, skinless	400 g	0.88 lb

Ingredients per 1 kg (2.2 lb) of meat

Salt	18 g	3 tsp
Pepper, white	4.0 g	2 tsp

Grind lean pork through 6 mm (1/4") plate.
Grind pork belly through 6 mm (1/4") plate.
Mix ground lean pork with salt adding a little water until sausage mass feels sticky.
Add ground pork belly and pepper and mix all together.
Stuff into 28-30 mm pork casings forming rings about 25 cm (10") long.
Refrigerate.

Notes
Cook fully before serving by frying, grilling or cooking in water.

Botifarra Catalana Trufada

Botifarra Catalana Trufada is made with black truffle of the Pyrenees mountain range that separates the Iberian Peninsula from the rest of Europe forming the natural border between France and Spain. This truffle which is underground growing mushroom is intensely aromatic and is nicknamed "the black gold of Pyrenees." The sausage is especially popular in the province of Lérida in the region of Catalonia.

Pork, lean	750 g	1.65 lb
Pork trimmings with		
attached fat, pork belly	250 g	0.55 lb

Ingredients per 1 kg (2.2 lb) of meat

Salt	20 g	3.5 tsp
Pepper	5.0 g	3 tsp
Sugar	5.0 g	1 tsp
Nutmeg	0.5 g	1/4 tsp
Truffles	30 g	1.0 oz

Cut lean pork into 30-40 mm (1-1.5") pieces. Mix with 15 g salt and 4 g sugar. Hold in refrigerator for 2 days.
Cut pork belly into 10 x 40 mm strips. Mix with 5 g salt and 1 g sugar. Hold in refrigerator for 2 days.
Grind lean pork through 6 mm (1/4") plate and mix with nutmeg and chopped truffles.
Grind pork belly through 3 mm (1/8") plate and mix with ground lean pork.
Stuff into 40-60 mm pork bungs about 50 cm (20") long.
Cook in water at 80° C (176° F) for 60-90 minutes depending on the diameter of the sausage.
Keep refrigerated.

Notes
Consume cold.

Botifarra de Ceba

Botifarra de Ceba ("ceba" means onion in Castilan and Valenciano), also known as Morcilla de Cebolla is a popular blood sausage in municipality of Alicante in region of País Valenciano in Spain.

Onions	650 g	1.32 lb
Back fat and hard fat trimmings	300 g	0.55 lb
Blood	50 ml	1.66 oz fl

Ingredients per 1 kg (2.2 lb) of materials

Salt	12 g	2 tsp
Pepper	2.0 g	1 tsp
Pimentón	8.0 g	4 tsp
Oregano	2.5 g	4 tsp
Cloves, ground	0.5 g	¼ tsp

Peel onions and cook in water for 60 minutes. Drain, cut in half and let cool.
Grind meat, fat and onions through 6 mm (1/4") plate.
Mix all materials with salt, spices and blood together.
Stuff into 32-34 mm beef or pork casings. Make rings about 35-40 cm (13-16") long or form links about 10 cm (4") long.
Cook in water at 80° C (176° F) for 30 minutes.
Cool in air and refrigerate.

Notes
The sausage is ready to eat, but it can be served by frying, grilling or heating in water.
Allowable range of materials: onions at 50-75%, back fat and fat trimmings at 20-30%, blood at 3-5%.

Botifarra de Huevos (Gerona)

As the name implies Botifarra de Huevos is a sausage made with eggs ("huevo" means an egg). Mixing one egg with ground meat to improve binding is a common culinary practice and many German sausages employ this technique, however, in botifarra de huevos eggs are added in a large number, usually 2-5 eggs per 1 kg of meat. The sausage is very popular in Gerona (in Catalan language Girona) which is the city and municipality in region of Catalonia.

Pork tongue, lungs, heart, stomach	750 g	1.65 lb
Dewlap and pork belly	250 g	0.55 lb

Ingredients per 1 kg (2.2 lb) of meat

Salt	18 g	3 tsp
Pepper	5.0 g	2.5 tsp
Eggs	4	4

Place tongue, lungs, heart and stomach in a boiling water and cook at 95-100° C (203-212° F) for 30-45 minutes.

Place dewlap and pork belly in a boiling water and cook at 95-100° C (203-212° F) for 5-10 minutes.

Drain meats, cool so they can be handled and grind through 6 mm (1/4") plate.

Beat the eggs and mix them with spices and ground meats.

Stuff into natural casings:

thin botifarra - 20-30 mm, form rings,

thick botifarra - 30-40 mm, form rings or leave in straight sections. Make rings and straight sections about 20-30 cm (8-12") long.

Cook in water at 80° C (176° F) for 30 minutes.

Store in refrigerator.

Notes

The sausage is ready to eat.

Botifarra Negra de Barcelona

Botifarra Negra de Barcelona is a Spanish blood sausage, similar to morcilla, which is very popular around Barcelona area in the Catalonia region of Spain.

Back fat	350 g	0.77 lb
Lungs	150 g	0.33 lb
Pork skins	250 g	0.55 lb
Blood	250 ml	0.55 lb

Ingredients per 1 kg (2.2 lb) of meat

Salt	12 g	2 tsp
Black pepper	2.0 g	1 tsp
Nutmeg	0.5 g	¼ tsp
Cinnamon	0.5 g	1/4 tsp

Place lungs and skins in boiling water and cook at 95-100° C (203-212° F) for 45 minutes. Cool and grind through 5 mm (1/4") plate.

Place skins in a boiling water and cook at 95-100° C (203-212° F) until soft. Grind skins when still warm through 5 mm (1/4") plate.

Grind back fat through 10 mm (3/8") plate.

Mix ground meat, fat, blood and spices together.

Stuff into 34-38 mm pork casings linking sausages every 35-40 cm (14-16").

Cook in water at 80° C (176° F) for 45-60 minutes.

Keep refrigerated. The sausage is ready to eat without cooking, however, it is often fried.

Botifarra Perol

Botifarra Perol originated in Gerona (in Catalan language Girona) which is the city and municipality in region of Catalonia, but it has become popular in other Catalan provinces. In traditionally produced botifarra all meats were cooked in a pot called "perol" which is a type of a Dutch oven and this is how the sausage acquired its name.

Pork head meat, lungs, skins, heart, tongue, stomach	750 g	1.65 lb
Dewlap (or jowls)*	250 g	0.55 lb

Ingredients per 1 kg (2.2 lb) of meat

Salt	18 g	3 tsp
Pepper	4.0 g	2 tsp
Cinnamon	0.5 g	1/4 tsp
Nutmeg	0.3 g	1/8 tsp
Cloves, ground	0.3 g	1/8 tsp

Place all meats in boiling water and cook at 95-100° C (203-212° F) for 60 minutes. Drain and cool.

Grind through 3 mm (1/8") plate.

Mix ground meats with all spices.

Stuff into natural casings: thin botifarra - 20-30 mm, thick botifarra - 30-40 mm, form rings or leave in straight sections about 20-30 cm (8-12") long.

Cook in water at 80° C (176° F) for 30 minutes.

Cool in air at 8-12° C (46-53° F).

Store in refrigerator.

Notes

* dewlap is pork double chin, you can substitute with jowls (cheeks).

Serve the sausage cold, grilled or use in stews.

Botifarro or Blanquet

This Botifarro or Blanquet sausage is very popular in the municipality of Alicante in the region of País Valenciano in Spain.

Pork, butt	700 g	1.54 lb
Skins	300 g	0.66 lb

Ingredients per 1 kg (2.2 lb) of meat

Salt	20 g	3.5 tsp
White pepper	4.0 g	2 tsp
Pimentón, sweet	6.0 g	3 tsp
Cinnamon	1.0 g	1/2 tsp
Cloves, ground	0.3 g	1/8 tsp
Pine nuts	28 g	1 oz
Egg	2	2

Cook skins at 95° C (203° F) for 1-2 hours until soft.
Grind meat and skins through 6 mm (1/4") plate.
Mix meats with salt, spices, nuts and beaten eggs.
Stuff into 30-40 mm ox or hog casings. Form links about 15 cm (6") long.
Cook in water at 80° C (176° F) for 30-40 minutes.
Cool in air. Refrigerate.

Notes
Consume cold or cooked.

Botillo de León

This is a large sausage from Castlla- León region of Spain, weighing 1-1.5 kg and stuffed into pork blind cap (caecum) or stomach. It is called botelo or butelo in Galicia, but in Castlla- León its name is "botillo."

Pork tails, ribs and jaws with attached meat	1000 g	2.2 lb

Ingredients per 1 kg (2.2 lb) of meat

Salt	30 g	5 tsp
Cure #1	2.5 g	1/2 tsp
Pimentón, sweet	15 g	7 tsp
Pimentón, hot	10 g	5 tsp
Oregano, dry, rubbed	1.0 g	1 tsp
Garlic, smashed	7.0 g	2 cloves

Cut meats into 50-60 mm (2") long pieces.

Mix salt with all spices adding a little water to create a paste.

Mix meats with the paste and hold for 24 hours in refrigerator.

Stuff firmly into pork blind cap (caecum).

Using oak wood apply cold smoke at 18° C (64° F) 3-4 days. Try to deliver smoke at least for 8 hours each day.

Dry at 12-15° C (53-59° F), 65-75% humidity, from 3-4 days to 15-20 days for a drier sausage.

Notes

Serve by cooking in water (below the boiling point) for about 2 hours. Botillo de León is usually served with potatoes and vegetables.

Botillo del Bierzo

Botillo del Bierzo is a type of semi-dry smoked sausage which is stuffed into pig's cap (caecup), a large diameter pouch which is the beginning of a large intestine. The weight of Botillo del Bierzo averages 1 kg (2.2 lb).The El Bierzo region, made up of 38 municipalities located to the west of the province of Leon (Castile-Leon), Spain. Botillo del Bierzo carries PGI (Protective Geographical Identification), 2001 classification. The Botillo del Bierzo Regulatory Council, established in 2000, takes care of all matters related to Botillo del Bierzo: records, issuance of numbered certificates, licensing producers authorized to manufacture the sausage, control over materials and spices that are allowed to be used, production and quality guidelines, promotion and marketing, cooking recipes and more.

Pork rib meat	700 g	1.54 lb
Bone-in tails	100 g	0.22 lb
Meat trimmings: tongue,		
jowls, spine meat, shoulder	200 g	0.44 lb

Ingredients per 1 kg (2.2 lb) of meat

Salt	25 g	4 tsp
Cure # 1	2.5 g	1/2 tsp
Pimentón, sweet	15 g	3.5 Tbsp
Pimentón, hot	10 g	2.5 Tbsp
Oregano, rubbed	2.0 g	2 tsp
Garlic, minced	10 g	3 cloves

Chop ribs and tails into smaller pieces. Do not remove bones.
Chop other meats.
Mix meats with salt, cure and all ingredients. Place in refrigerator for 24 hours.
Stuff firmly into a large diameter casing like pork cap or bung.
Using oak wood apply cold smoke at 18° C (64° F) for 4 days (one day being the minimum).
Dry at 16-12° C (60-54° F) for 9 days.
Store at 12° C (60° F), <65% humidity or refrigerate.

Notes
The required amount of ribs 65-90%
The required amount of tail meat 10-20%
Trimmings from the following parts may also be incorporated: tongue, jowls, shoulder, backbone meat, no more than 20% total and none of the trimmings should account for more than half of this 20%.
Weight - 500-1600 g
Botillo del Bierzo is usually served in the form of a stew which is made by boiling botillo with cabbage, potatoes and a few fresh chorizos, a task that requires from 2 -2-1/2 hours.

Buche de Costillas (Badajoz)

Buche de Costillas originates in Badajoz, the capital of the province of Badajoz in the region of Extremadura, Spain. The sausage is made from pieces of spare ribs, tails, snouts, tongues plus lean pork and fat. The mix is spiced, stuffed into pork stomachs, dried and aged. The buche sausage was produced and consumed in the winter. The sausage was stored in stone jars filled with lard. Buche sausage was served by cooking it in large Dutch ovens over open fire. About 2 hours were needed to cook buche weighing 1 kg (2.2 lb). Chorizo sausage, pork shoulder, whole garlic cloves and red peppers were usually added and cooked in the same pot. Cabbage was always added to pot during the last 30 minutes of cooking. Next the meats and vegetables were removed and rice was cooked in the remaining meat stock. Then all was presented on a plate and served with red wine. Eating Buche in Extremadura was a social gathering, it was a party.

Lean pork	500 g	1.10 lb
Back fat	250 g	0.55 lb
Tails	50 g	0.11 lb
Tongues	50 g	0.11 lb
Spare ribs	50 g	0.11 lb
Pig mask*	100 g	0.22 lb

Ingredients per 1 kg (2.2 lb) of meat

Salt	30 g	5 tsp
Cure #2	3.0 g	1/2 tsp
Dextrose	5.0 g	1 tsp
Pimentón	25 g	4 Tbsp
Garlic, smashed	15 g	4 cloves

Cut all lean pork, fat, tails, tongues, spare ribs and face meats into smaller (finger length) pieces.
Mix meats with salt and spices. Hold for 24 hours in refrigerator.
Stuff into pork stomachs.
Dry at 20° C (68° F) for 20 days.
Dry at 15-10° C (59-50° F) for 1-2 months depending on the size of a stomach.

Notes
* pig mask is the face of the pig (cheeks, snout, ear) - skin with attached meat and small bones. It will not be easy to obtain in metropolitan areas so use dewlap (chin) or jowls (cheeks).
Consume sausage raw or cooked.

Butifarra

Butifarra sausage is one of the most important dishes of the Catalan cuisine. They are also popular in South America, especially in Colombia (Botifarra Soledeña).

| Beef | 700 g | 1.54 lb |
| Pork jowls, pork belly | 300 g | 0.66 lb |

Ingredients per 1 kg (2.2 lb) of meat

Salt	18 g	3 tsp
Pepper	1.0 g	1/2 tsp
Garlic powder	1.0 g	1/2 tsp
Cinnamon	0.5 g	1/4 tsp
Cayenne	0.5 g	1/4 tsp
Red wine	60 ml	2 oz fl

Grind beef through 1/4" (5 mm) plate.
Grind pork through 3/8" (10 mm) plate.
Mix/knead beef with salt until sticky. Add wine and spices and remix. Add ground jowls and mix all together.
Stuff into 36 mm hog casings, leave in one coil.
Refrigerate. Cook before serving.

Butifarra Blanca

Butifarra blanca translates in Spanish into a "white sausage." There are versions with rice, in many cases whole eggs are included. Many countries have similar sausages, for example Boudin Blanc in France or White Pudding in England.

Pork lean, butt	700 g	1.54 lb
Dewlap, jowls, fat trimmings	100 g	0.22 lb
Pork belly	200 g	0.44 lb

Ingredients per 1 kg (2.2 lb) of meat

Salt	18 g	3 tsp
White pepper	2.0 g	1 tsp
Cinnamon	1.0 g	1/2 tsp
Nutmeg	0.5 g	1/4 tsp

Dice 1/3 part of fat into 6 mm (1/4") cubes.

Grind remaining 2/3 fat through 6 mm (1/4") plate.

Grind meats through 6 mm (1/4") plate.

Mix ground meat, fat, and all ingredients. Hold for 24 hours in refrigerator.

Stuff into into 36 mm hog casings.

Cook in water at 80° C (176° F) for 40 minutes.

Cool the sausages for 10 minutes in cold water.

Drain and place on a table to evaporate the moisture.

Refrigerate.

Butifarra Blanca de Huevos

Butifarra de Huevos is a simple to make white sausage with eggs (*huevo* means an *egg* in Spanish).

Lean pork, rear leg (ham cut)	700 g	1.54 lb
Dewlap, jowls	100 g	0.22 lb
Back fat or hard fat trimmings	200 g	0.44 lb

Ingredients per 1 kg (2.2 lb) of meat

Salt	18 g	3 tsp
White pepper	4.0 g	2 tsp
Eggs, whole	2 eggs	2
Nutmeg	0.5 g	1/4 tsp

Grind meats through 1/4" (6 mm) plate.
Mix ground meat with all ingredients.
Stuff into 36 mm hog casings.
Cook in water at 80° C (176° F) for 35 minutes.
Cool the sausages in cold water.
Drain, briefly dry and refrigerate.

Butifarra Blanca Mezcla

Butifarra like Butifarrón can be made not only from pure pork, but from pork and beef as well.

Lean pork	250 g	0.55 lb
Lean beef	300 g	0.66 lb
Skins	100 g	0.22 lb
Back fat, belly fat or fat trimmings	350 g	0.77 lb

Ingredients per 1 kg (2.2 lb) of meat

Salt	22 g	3.5 tsp
White pepper	2.0 g	1 tsp
Cinnamon	1.0 g	1/2 tsp
Nutmeg	1.0 g	1/2 tsp
White wine	15 ml	1 Tbsp

Cook skins in water (below the boiling point) for 60 minutes.
Dice 1/3 part of fat into 6 mm (1/4") cubes.
Grind remaining 2/3 fat through 6 mm (1/4") plate.
Grind meats through 6 mm (1/4") plate.
Mix ground meat, fat, and all ingredients. Hold for 24 hours in refrigerator.
Stuff into into 32 mm hog casings or 40-45 mm beef middles forming 20 cm (8") rings. Tie the ends together.
Cook in water at 80° C (176° F) for 40 minutes.
Cool the sausages for 10 minutes in cold water.
Drain and place on a table to evaporate the moisture.
Refrigerate.

Butifarra de Baleares

This butifarra is popular in Balearic Island and is made with lean pork, dewlap, back fat and a little blood so its texture is not as black as in other Spanish blood sausages such as Butifarra Negra, Blanquet, Paltruch or in morcillas.

Dewlap*	720 g	1.58 lb
Pork, lean	120 g	0.26 lb
Back fat	120 g	0.26 lb
Pork blood	40 ml	1.33 oz fl

Ingredients per 1 kg (2.2 lb) of meat

Salt	20 g	3.5 tsp
Black pepper	5.0 g	2.5 tsp
Pimentón	2.0 g	1 tsp

Grind meats and fat through 10 mm (3/8") plate.
Mix ground meat with spices and blood.
Stuff into 20 mm sheep casings forming 10-12 cm (4-5") long links.
Cook in water at 80° (176° F) for 30 minutes.

Notes
Consume cold, cooked or grilled.
* can be substituted with jowls.

Butifarra Dulce Curada

Sweet Butifarra is a traditional Spanish sausage that is presented fresh or dried, like a salami. The sausage is popular in the Catalonia region of Spain, especially in Gorona which is North of Barcelona. It is said that this sausage was one of the favorite dishes of the painter Salvador Dali. This is a dry version of Sweet Butifarra.

Pork, lean	700 g	1.54 lb
Pork back fat or		
hard fat trimmings	300 g	0.66 lb

Ingredients per 1 kg (2.2 lb) of meat

Salt	28 g	5 tsp
Cure #1	2.5 g	1/2 tsp
Dextrose	3.0 g	1/2 tsp
Honey	20 g	1 Tbsp
Pimentón, sweet	4.0 g	2 tsp
Lemon zest, grated	1/2 lemon	
Cinnamon	2.0 g	1 tsp

Grind meat and fat through 1/4" (6 mm) plate.

Mix all ingredients with ground meat and fat. Hold for 24 hours in refrigerator.

Stuff firmly into 32 mm hog casings. Make 24" (60 cm) long links.

Ferment/dry at 25° C (77° F) for 24 hours, 90-85% humidity.

Dry at 16-12° C (60-54° F), 85-80% humidity for 14 days. Store sausages at 10-12° C (50-54° F), <75% humidity or refrigerate.

Notes

Dry sweet butifarra can be served like fresh sweet butifarra (with apples):

Butiffara sausage, 2
Sugar, 2 Tbsp
Lemon peel, 1 lemon
Golden apples, 4
Cinnamon stick, 1
Water, 120 ml (1/2 cup)
Sweet wine or grape juice, 60 ml (1/4 cup)
Sweet butter, 20 g (1 oz)

Peel the apples, remove the core and cut into wedges. Put everything in a skillet, less apples, and cook uncovered for 10 minutes. Prick the sausages with a fork and add with apples to the skillet. Cook for additional 10 minutes.

Butifarra Dulce de Gerona

Sweet (*dulce*) Butifarra is popular in the Catalonia region of Spain, especially in Gerona which is north of Barcelona. It is a traditional sausage that is presented fresh or dried, like a salami. It is said that this sausage was one of the favorite dishes of the painter Salvador Dali.

Pork	1000 g	2.2 lb

Ingredients per 1 kg (2.2 lb) of meat

Salt	18 g	3 tsp
Pepper	2.0 g	1 tsp
Pimentón, sweet	4.0 g	2 tsp
Cinnamon	3.0 g	1.5 tsp
Honey	20 g	1 Tbsp
Lemon zest, grated	1/2 lemon	
Sherry	30 ml	1 oz fl
Cream	30 ml	1 oz fl

Grind meat through 1/4" (6 mm) plate.
Using a mixer blend sherry, cream, salt and spices together.
Stuff into 32 mm hog casings.
Refrigerate. Cook before serving.

Notes
Sweet butifarra is usually served with apples:

Butifarra sausage, 2
Sugar, 2 Tbsp
Lemon peel, 1 lemon
Golden apples, 4
Cinnamon stick, 1
Water, 120 ml (1/2 cup)
Sweet wine or grape juice, 60 ml (1/4 cup)
Sweet butter, 20 g (1 oz)

Peel the apples, remove the core and cut into wedges. Put everything in a skillet, less apples, and cook uncovered for 10 minutes. Prick the sausages with a fork and add with apples to the skillet. Cook for additional 10 minutes.

Butifarra Lorquina

Butifarra Lorquina is a Spanish blood sausage popular in regions of Murcia and Valencia. Lorca is a municipality and city in the autonomous community of Murcia in southeastern Spain, and this is where the sausage name – Butifarra "Lorquina" comes from.

Back fat	420 g	0.92 lb
Pork skins	200 g	0.44 lb
Head meat, jowls (cheeks)	300 g	0.66 lb
Blood	80 ml	2.66 oz fl

Ingredients per 1 kg (2.2 lb) of meat

Salt	18 g	3 tsp
Black pepper	2.0 g	1 tsp
Cinnamon	1.0 g	½ tsp
Aniseed, ground	0.3 g	1/8 tsp
Cloves	0.3 g	1/8 tsp

Cook skins and split heads (if used) in water at 95° C (203° F) until meat separates from bones. Spread on the table, cool and when still warm but comfortable to handle, separate meat from bones. Break or cut into smaller pieces.
Dice back fat into 6 mm (1/4") cubes.
Mix all materials with salt, spices and blood.
Stuff into 50-70 mm pork bungs forming 50 cm (20") closed loops.
Cook at 85° C (185° F) for 45-75 minutes depending on the diameter of the sausage.
Store in refrigerator.

Notes
The sausage can be eaten cold, cooked or grilled.

Butifarra Negra

Butifarra Negra (*Black Butifarra*) is a Spanish blood sausage from Catalonia. Depending on production style butifarra can be a fresh, cooked or even dry sausage. Some butifarras are sweet (*Butifarra Dulce*) and are of light color, others contain blood (*Butifarra Negra*) and are dark.

Pork butt, heart, pork trimmings	400 g	1.32 lb
Pork jowl, belly	200 g	0.44 lb
Pork back fat	100 g	0.22 lb
Pork liver	50 g	0.11 lb
Pork skins	100 g	0.22 lb
Pork blood	150 ml	5 oz fl

Ingredients per 1 kg (2.2 lb) of meat

Salt	18 g	3 tsp
Pepper	2.0 g	1 tsp
Cinnamon	1.0 g	1/2 tsp
Nutmeg	1.0 g	1/2 tsp
Cloves, ground	0.3 g	1/8 tsp
Onion, chopped	40 g	1/2 onion

Chop onion finely and fry in a little oil until glassy but not browned.
Cut back fat into 1/4" (6 mm) cubes.
Cook the skins in a little water (below the boiling point) until soft. Drain and cool.
Grind the skins through 1/8" (3 mm) plate.
Grind all meats through 3/8" (10 mm) plate.
Mix all meats, fat, spices and blood together.
Stuff into 36 mm hog casings forming 12" (30 cm) long loops.
Cook in water at 80° C (176° F) for 35 minutes.
Cool in cold water for 10 minutes. Cool in air to evaporate moisture and refrigerate.

Butifarra Negra Mezcla

Butifarra Negra is a Catalan blood sausage usually made from pork. This particular butifarra is a mixture (*mezcla* means mixture in Spanish) of pork and beef.

Back fat	250 g	0.55 lb
Fat trimmings with attached meat or pork belly	350 g	0.77 lb
Beef, semi-fat	200 g	0.44 lb
Blood	200 ml	0.44 lb

Ingredients per 1 kg (2.2 lb) of meat

Salt	25 g	4 tsp
Black pepper	1.0 g	1/2 tsp
Cilantro, ground	0.5 g	1/4 tsp
Oregano, ground	0.5 g	1/4 tsp
Cloves, ground	0.3 g	1/8 tsp

Dice back fat and fat trimmings into small pieces.
Grind beef through 6 mm (1/4") plate.
Mix beef, pork fat, blood and all ingredients.
Stuff into small 32-36 mm beef or pork casings.
Cook in water at 80° C (176° F) for 40 minutes. Prick the sausage with a needle and if the blood is not visible, the sausage is cooked.
Cool in cold water for 10 minutes. Cool in air to evaporate moisture and refrigerate.

Butifarra Soledeña

Butifarra Soledeña is an extremely attractive little sausage made in the municipality of Soledad which lies next to the large city of Barranquilla on the Atlantic coast of Colombia. It looks like a long string of pearls which are basically little meat balls connected together. The sausage is popular with street vendors as the vendor can cut off any number of sausages depending on the order. It is usually made from pork, however, many recipes call for a combination of pork and beef. It contains a few standard spices, the beauty of the sausage lies in its looks and the presentation.

| Pork meat | 700 g | 1.54 lb |
| Back fat or belly | 300 g | 0.66 lb |

Ingredients per 1 kg (2.2 lb) of meat

Salt	15 g	2-1/2 tsp
Pepper	2.0 g	1 tsp
Garlic	4.0 g	1 clove
Water	30 ml	2 Tbsp

Grind lean meat through 6 mm (1/4") plate.
Grind fat through 6 mm (1/4") plate.
Dissolve salt and spices in water.
Pour the mixture over ground lean meat and mix/knead until sticky. Add more water if needed. Add ground fat and mix all together well.
Stuff firmly into 32 mm hog casings forming one continuous coil.
Take a section of the coil (do not cut), slightly flatten and tie the knots with twine every 5 cm (2"). Form the balls. The knots will separate the balls.
Cook in water at 80° C (176° F) for 10 minutes.
Remove the string of sausages, place flat on the table and prickle each sausage with a needle. This releases some of the pressure and liquid fat so the customer will not get dirty when biting into the sausage.
Return to hot water and cook additional 20 minutes.
Place for 2 minutes in cold water then hang and cool in the air.
Refrigerate.

Notes
The size of the sausage ball is up to you, so is the selection of spices. For example nutmeg, cumin and ginger.

Butifarra Traidora

This butifarra is nicknamed "treacherous" (*traidora*) as it is made with tongue and we all know the saying: loose lips sink ships. The sausage is popular in north-western parts of Catalonia in Pyrenees mountains. This rather greasy sausage was made from offal meat, fat and leftover meat trimmings. It is slightly darker than a typical butifarra.

Pork head meat, liver, skins (<10%), kidneys, lungs, skins, meat trimmings	400 g	0.88 lb
Pork tongue	100 g	0.22 lb
Fat, fat trimmings	400 g	0.88 lb
Wheat flour	40 g	1.41 oz
Onion, finely chopped	30 g	1.0 oz
Water or meat stock	30 ml	2 Tbsp

Ingredients per 1 kg (2.2 lb) of meat

Salt	12 g	2 tsp
White pepper	2.0 g	1 tap
Cilantro, finely chopped	10 g	2 Tbsp
Cumin	1.0 g	1/2 tsp
Nutmeg	1.0 g	1/2 tsp
Garlic, smashed	10 g	3 cloves

Cook all meats (except liver) until soft. Remove meat from bones and cut into smaller pieces.

Scald liver in hot water for 5 minutes. Cool in cold water.

Grind meats, fat and liver with 5 mm (1/4") plate.

Mix meats with water (or meat stock from boiling meats) all ingredients and flour.

Stuff into 40-50 mm pork or beef middles.

Cook in water at 80° C (176° F) for 40-50 minutes.

Cool in cold water for 5 minutes. Hang briefly to cool.

Refrigerate.

Butifarrón

Butifarrón, a cooked sausage popular in Catalonia is very similar to butifarra. It is made from lean pork, hard pork fat and often from pork and beef. Hard fat is usually diced in little cubes which become visible show pieces once the sausage is sliced.

Lean pork	600 g	1.32 lb
Lean beef	200 g	0.44 lb
Back fat or		
hard fat trimmings	200 g	0.44 lb

Ingredients per 1 kg (2.2 lb) of meat

Salt	18 g	3 tsp
Cure #1	2.5 g	1/2 tsp
Pepper	2.0 g	1 tsp
Coriander	0.5 g	1/4 tsp
Nutmeg	1.0 g	1/2 tsp
Cloves, ground	0.3 g	1/8 tsp
Garlic, diced	3.0 g	1 clove

Dice back fat into 6 mm (1/4") cubes.
Grind pork through 5 mm (1/4") plate.
Grind beef through 5 mm (1/4") plate.
Mix beef and pork with all ingredients. Add cubed fat and mix again.
Stuff into 40-50 mm beef middles, make sections 30-40 cm (12-14") long.
Hold overnight in refrigerator or for 4 hours at room temperature.
Optional step: smoke at 60° C (140° F) for two hours.
Cook in water at 80° C (176° F) for 60 minutes.
Cool in cold water for 10 minutes. Cool in air to evaporate moisture and refrigerate.

Butifarrón de Baleares

Butifarrón is a cooked sausage from Balearic Islands (Mallorca, Menorca, Ibiza, Formentera) which is made with pork meat, pork offal (liver, lungs), pork belly and a little blood.

Pork, lean	500 g	1.10 lb
Skins	150 g	0.33 lb
Lungs, liver	150 g	0.33 lb
Back fat	100 g	0.22 lb
Blood	50 ml	1.76 oz fl
Fried pork belly or pork skins with attached meat	50 g	0.11 lb

Ingredients per 1 kg (2.2 lb) of meat

Salt	30 g	5 tsp
Black pepper	5.0 g	2.5 tsp
Cinnamon	1.0 g	½ tsp
Nutmeg	0.5 g	¼ tsp
Cloves, ground	0.3 g	1/8 tsp
Star anise, ground	0.3 g	1/8 tsp
Fennel, ground	0.2 g	1/8 tsp

Boil lungs (if used) for 1-2 hours. Boil skins for 1-2 hours.
Grind lungs, liver and skins through 3 mm (1/8").
Grind all other meats and fat through 5 mm (1/4") plate.
Mix all meats and fats with blood and spices.
Stuff into 34-36 mm pork casings forming links 10-12 cm (4-5") long.
Cook in water at 80° C (176° F) for 45 minutes.

Notes
Consume cold, cooked or grilled.

Cabeza de Jabalí

The Spanish word *jabalí* signifies in English "wild boar", so it is probably how it was made in the past, however, today pork head meat is used. Cabeza de Jabalí is listed in the Spanish Official Government Meat Standards Bulletin (Boletín Oficial del Estado, Real Decreto 474/2014, 13th June) as the product made from *pork* head meat. Cabeza de Jabalí is a Spanish head cheese belonging to the "fiambre" group of meat products. It is made from pork head meat, ears, snouts, lips, jowls, skins, tongue and is basically a head cheese (*queso de cabeza*). When sliced or formed in mold as meat jelly, it offers a wonderful display of different meat cuts which are held together by a natural aspic (jelly). Of course it can be and often is made with a commercial gelatin, but this would be an inferior product due to gelatin's neutral flavor. By selecting meats of different color and including decorative items such as red bell pepper, olives, sliced lemon or pistachios an attractive product can be created.

Pork head meat*	400 g	0.88 lb	*Ingredients per 1 kg of meat*		
Pork jowls	300 g	0.66 lb	Salt	18 g	3 tsp
Meat trimmings,			Pepper, white	4.0 g	2 tsp
ears, snouts	200 g	0.44 lb	Cumin	2.0 g	1 tsp
Pork skins	100 g	0.22 lb	Garlic, diced	3.5 g	1 clove
			Meat stock	100 ml	3.3 oz fl

Cook meats in a small amount of water: pork heads at 85°C (185°F), and pork skins at 95°C (203°F) until soft. Add soup greens for better flavor.
Spread meats on a flat surface to cool. *Save* meat stock. Separate meat from bones when still warm.
Cut meat into smaller pieces, cut skins into short strips. Mix all meats with spices adding 10% of meat stock in relation to the weight of pork heads with bones. The meat stock is the result of boiling meats.
Stuff mixture loosely into pork stomachs or beef bungs about 12" (30 cm) long. Cook in water at 82°C (180°F) for 90-150 min (depending on size) until the internal temperature of the meat reaches 154-158°F (68-70°C). Remove air with a needle from pieces that swim up to the surface.
Spread head cheeses on a flat surface at 2-6°C (35-43°F) and let the steam out. Place sausages between two boards and place a heavy weight on top. Leave undisturbed for 12 hours at cool temperature. After cooling clean head cheeses of any fat and aspic that accumulated on the surface. Store in refrigerator.

Notes
* Head cheese was traditionally made with pork head meat, however, a person in a city will find it hard to get a pork or wild boar head. What is needed is meat that is rich in connective tissue; picnic (front leg), hocks, feet, skin are great gelatin producers.

Camayot

Camayot is a large original sausage from Balearic Islands that looks like a large blood sausage or blood head cheese. In traditional home production the sausage mix is stuffed into a large sack made from the skin that remains after trimming ham or shoulder. The skin is accordingly cut and sewn to make a large casing. After stuffing the neck is sewn tightly to prevent loss of meat juices during cooking.

Dewlap *	720 g	1.58 lb
Pork, lean	110 g	0.24 lb
Back fat	110 g	0.24 lb
Liver	30 g	1.05 oz
Pork blood	30 ml	1 oz fl

Ingredients per 1 kg (2.2 lb) of meat

Salt	30 g	5 tsp
Black pepper	5.0 g	2.5 tsp
Pimentón, sweet	1.0 g	½ tsp
Cinnamon	1.0 g	½ tsp
Nutmeg	0.5 g	¼ tsp
Cloves	0.3 g	1/8 tsp

Cut all meats and fat into 18 mm (3/4") pieces.
Mix with blood and all ingredients.
Stuff into pork stomachs or bladders.
Cook in water at 80-90° C (176-194° F) for 2-3 hours.

Notes
* dewlap (double chin) can be substituted with jowls.
Camayot was traditionally stuffed into ham (rear leg) or shoulder skins that were sewn after stuffing.
Consume cold or grilled.

Chanfaino or Longaniza Gallega

Chanfaino or *chanfaina*, also known as *Longaniza Gallega* originates in Lugo province of Galicia region. The sausage is made with pork heart, lungs, fat and typical galician spices such as pimentón, garlic, oregano and onions. It might as well be called *sabadeña* or *sabadiego* which are made in Galicia and in other parts of the country. The sausage is smoked, dried and served hot with boiled potatoes, turnips and other vegetables.

Pork, semi-fat, shoulder .... 200 g   0.44 lb
Pork offal meat (heart, lungs,
spleen, stomach diaphragm) ....   800 g   1.76 lb

Ingredients per 1 kg (2.2 lb) of meat

Salt	24 g	4 tsp
Cure #1	2.5 g	1/2 tsp
Pimentón, sweet	25.0 g	4 Tbsp
Pimentón, hot	5.0 g	1 Tbsp
Garlic	10 g	3 cloves
Oregano, rubbed	2.0 g	2 tsp

Grind pork meat with 10 mm (3/8") plate.
Chop offal meat into smaller pieces.
Mix meats with all other ingredients and hold in refrigerator for 24 hours.
Stuff firmly into 32 mm hog casing forming links or rings.
Smoke at 18° C (64° F) with oak wood for 2-3 days. The smoking process may be interrupted as long as the temperature stays below 18° C (64° F).
Dry at 12-15° C (53-5°9 F) for 21 days.
Store at 12° C (53° F), <65% humidity.

Chireta

Chireta is an Aragonese sausage made with pork belly, sheep offal meat
(intestines, heart, lungs, liver), rice, parsley and spices. It is stuffed into sheep
stomach. The sausage is similar to Catalonian Girella (*Gireta*).

Sheep offal meat		
(heart, tripe, lungs, liver)	300 g	0,66 lb
Pork meat	200 g	0.44 lb
Pork belly, fat trimmings	300 g	0.66 lb
Rice	200 g	0.44 lb

Ingredients per 1 kg (2.2 lb) of material

Salt	15 g	2.5 tsp
Black pepper	2.0 g	1 tsp
Sweet pimentón	10 g	2 tsp
Garlic, smashed	7.0 g	2 cloves
Parsley	1 bunch	2 Tbsp
Cinnamon	1.0 g	1/2 tsp

Cook rice, but don't overcook.
Cook offal meats for 15 minutes, Cut into smaller pieces.
Grind all other meat through 5 mm (1/4") plate.
Mix meats with all ingredients and rice.
Prepare sheep stomach. The stomach is cleaned with white vinegar then rinsed
very well before filling The stomach is cut with scissors into smaller sheets.
Each sheet is filled with sausage mix, folded over and sewn with twine. Fill
casing loosely as the rice will expand a little.
Cook in water at 80° C (176° F) for 30-40 minutes depending on the diameter of
the bag.
Refrigerate.

Notes
Chiretas can be cooked in water and served immediately. For better flavor add
soup greens such as carrot, parsley root, celery, turnip, onion and piece of ham
or a sausage.
Chiretas are usually served hot as a main dish. They are also sliced, dipped in an
egg-flour batter, and fried to a golden color.

Chistorra or Txistorra

Chistorra also known as Txistorra is a popular sausage in Navarra region of Spain. Similar to chorizo, but shorter and stuffed into narrower casings, Chistorra has high fat content, usually around 50%, sometimes even more. The sausage is shortly dried and looks like a meat stick.

Pork, lean	250 g	0.55 lb
Beef	250 g	0.55 lb
Back fat	250 g	0.55 lb
Pork belly	250 g	0.55 lb

Ingredients per 1 kg (2.2 lb) of meat

Salt	28 g	5 tsp
Cure #1	2.5 g	1/2 tsp
Dextrose	2.0 g	1/2 tsp
Sugar	3.0 g	1/2 tsp
Pimentón, sweet	25 g	4 Tbsp
Pimentón, hot	2.0 g	1 tsp
Garlic	3.5 g	1 clove

Cut meats into 25 mm (1") pieces. Mix with all ingredients.
Hold in refrigerator for 24 hours.
Grind meats through 8 mm (3/8") plate.
Stuff into 20-24 mm sheep casings, forming 15 cm (6") straight links.
Ferment/dry at 22-24° C (72-75° F), 85-90% humidly for 48 hours.
Dry at 15-12° C (59-53° F), 80-85% humidity for 6-25 days (depending on size).
Hold semi-dry sausage in refrigerator. Drying sausage for 25 days or more will produce a ready to eat dry sausage.

Notes
Chistorra can be made from all pork (replace beef with pork shoulder).
The sausage is usually fried or added to stews.

Chistorra with Culture

Chistorra is a type of a dry sausage from Aragon, the Basque Country, and Navarre, Spain.

Lean pork	700 g	1.54 lb
Back fat, jowls, hard fat trimmings	300 g	0.66 lb

Ingredients per 1 kg (2.2 lb) of meat

Salt	28 g	5 tsp
Cure #1	2.5 g	1/2 tsp
Dextrose	2.0 g	1/2 tsp
Sugar	3.0 g	1/2 tsp
Pimentón, sweet	25 g	3.5 Tbsp
Pimentón, hot	2.0 g	1 tsp
Garlic	3.5 g	1 clove
T-SPX culture	0.12 g	use scale

Grind pork and fat through 8 mm (3/8") plate.

30 min before applying, mix culture with 15 ml (1 Tbsp) de-chlorinated water.

Mix all ingredients with ground pork.

Stuff firmly into 24 mm sheep casings. Make 24" (60 cm) long links.

Ferment at 20° C (68° F) for 72 hours, 90-85% humidity.

Dry at 15-12° C (59-53° F), 85-80% humidity for 3 weeks.

Store sausages at 10-12° C (50-53° F), 65-70% humidity or refrigerate.

Choriqueso

Mexican fresh sausage with cheese.

Pork shoulder	700 g	1.54 lb
Oaxaca or		
Monterey Jack cheese ...... 300 g		0.66 lb

Ingredients per 1 kg (2.2 lb) of material

Salt	12 g	2 tsp
Chili powder	2.0 g	1 tsp
Cayenne	1.0 g	1/2 tsp
Jalapenos, diced	10 g	1 Tbsp
Corn flour	20 g	1 Tbsp
Vinegar	30 ml	1 oz fl

Grind pork through 10 mm (3/8") plate.
Cut cheese into 12 mm (1/2") cubes.
Mix ground pork with spices. Add cheese and mix again.
Stuff into 36 mm hog casings.
Refrigerate.
Cook before serving.

Notes

Oaxaca cheese is a white, semi-hard cheese from Mexico, similar to American Monterey Jack. It is named after the state of Oaxaca in southern Mexico, where it was first made.

Chorizo Andaluz

Chorizo Andaluz originates in southern region of Spain known as Andalusia.

Pork, semi-fat	1000 g	2.2 lb

Ingredients per 1 kg (2.2 lb) of meat

Salt	25 g	4 tsp
Cure #2	2.5 g	1/2 tsp
Pimentón, sweet	25 g	4 Tbsp
Pimentón, hot	2.0 g	1 tsp
Pepper, black	1.0 g	1/2 tsp
Garlic, smashed	3.5 g	1 clove
Water	30 ml	1 oz fl

Grind meat through 6 mm (1/4") plate.

Mix meat with all ingredients. Hold for 24 hours in refrigerator.

Stuff into 36 mm pork or beef casings.

Apply a thin smoke at 20-24° C (68-75° F) (smoking step is optional) or ferment/ dry sausages at 20-24° C (68-75° F) for 24-48 hours.

Dry at 15-12° C (59-54° F), 75-80% humidity for 15 days.

Store sausages at 10-12° C (50-53° F), 65-70% humidity or refrigerate.

Chorizo Antioqueño

A popular fresh chorizo sausage from Colombia. It is also made as a dry sausage.

Pork shoulder	700 g	1.54 lb
Pork fat	300 g	0.66 lb

Ingredients per 1 kg (2.2 lb) of meat

Salt	18 g	3 tsp
Pepper	2.0 g	1 tsp
Paprika	4.0 g	2 tsp
Cumin	2.0 g	1 tsp
Oregano	2.0 g	1 tsp
Garlic	3.5 g	1 clove
Water	30 ml	2 Tbsp

Grind meat and fat through 10 mm (3/8") plate.
Mix meat, fat and all ingredients.
Stuff into 36 mm hog casings forming 10 cm (4") long links.
Refrigerate. Cook before serving.

To make a dry sausage:

Salt	28 g	5 tsp
Cure #2	2.5 g	1/2 tsp
Dextrose	2.0 g	1/2 tsp
Sugar	3.0 g	1/2 tsp
Pepper	2.0 g	1 tsp
Paprika, sweet	12 g	6 tsp
Paprika, hot	2.0 g	1 tsp
Cumin	2.0 g	1 tsp
Oregano	2.0 g	1 tsp
Garlic	3.5 g	1 clove
Water	30 ml	2 Tbsp

Grind meat and fat through 10 mm (3/8") plate.
Mix meat, fat and all ingredients. Hold for 24 hours in refrigerator.
Stuff into 36 mm hog casings forming 10 cm (4") long links.
Dry/ferment at 22-24° C (72-75° F), 80-90% humidity for 48 hours.
Dry at 12-15° C (53-59° C), 75-80% humidity for 21 days or until the sausage loses about 33% of its original weight.
Store at 10-12° C (50-53° F), <75% humidity or refrigerate.

Notes
For better color and flavor replace paprika with "pimentón".

Chorizo - Argentinian

Argentinian chorizo is a fresh sausage and although it is similar to sausages made in Chile, Uruguay, Paraguay, Peru or Bolivia, it has its distinctive character. When sold on street corners or soccer stadiums they are served on a long French roll. When served this way they go by the name of Choripan which is a combination of two words: Chori-zo (sausage) and pan (bread). The roll is cut lengthwise on one side and the sausage is placed on one of its halves. The second half is always covered with chimichurri which is Argentinian steak sauce. Sometimes the sausage is split lengthwise which is known as butterfly (mariposa) style.

In Uruguay it will be served with mayonnaise and ketchup. South American sausages often include beef. Fresh sausages are usually grilled. South American chorizos contain more hot spices and are often seasoned with nutmeg, fennel and cloves. Another difference is that South American chorizos are made with wine or in the case of Mexican chorizo with vinegar which makes them much moister.

Beef	250 g	0.55 lb
Lean pork	500 g	1.10 lb
Pork back fat, bacon or fat trimmings	250 g	0.55 lb

Ingredients per 1 kg (2.2) of meat

Salt	~~18 g~~	3 tsp ✻ try 16 g salt
Pepper	3.0 g	1½ tsp
Paprika or sweet pimentón	10.0 g	5 tsp
Garlic	7.0 g	2 cloves
Red wine	125 ml	½ cup Use half as much wine

Grind pork meat and fat through 8 mm (3/8") plate.
Grind beef through 3 mm (1/8") plate.
Smash garlic cloves and mix with a little amount of wine.
Mix meat, garlic, salt and all ingredients together. Hold for 24 hours in refrigerator.
Stuff into hog casings, 32-36 mm and form 6" (15 cm) links.
Keep in a refrigerator. Cook before serving.

Chorizo Aromático

Chorizo Aromático is a Mexican fresh sausage.

Pork shoulder, pork trimmings   1000 g   2.2 lb

Ingredients per 1 kg (2.2 lb) of meat

Salt	18 g	3 tsp
Red chili powder	4.0 g	2 tsp
Paprika	4.0 g	2 tsp
Cayenne	0.5 g	1/4 tsp
Oregano, rubbed	4.0 g	4 tsp
Thyme, rubbed	2.0 g	2 tsp
Cumin	2.0 g	1 tsp
Cinnamon	0.5 g	1/4 tsp
Cloves, ground	0.3 g	1/8 tsp
Garlic, smashed	7.0 g	2 cloves
Vinegar	125 ml	1/2 cup

Grind pork through 6 mm (1/4") plate.

Mix all ingredients with vinegar. Pour over the meat and mix all together.

Stuff into 36 mm hog casings.

Refrigerate. Cook before serving.

Chorizo Asturiano

Chorizo Asturiano is produced in Asturias province in north-west Spain where a large number of sausage types are produced. Asturian sausages are often smoked.

Lean pork	600 g	1.32 lb
Back fat and meat		
trimmings with attached fat	400 g	0.88 lb

Ingredients per 1 kg (2.2 lb) of meat

Salt	22 g	3.5 tsp
Cure #2	2.5 g	1/2 tsp
Sugar	3.0 g	1/2 tsp
Pimentón, sweet	20 g	5 tsp
Pimentón, hot	5.0 g	5 tsp
Oregano, rubbed	2.0 g	2 tsp
Garlic, minced	7.0 g	2 cloves

Grind pork and fat through 8 mm (3/8") plate.

Mix all ingredients with ground meat. Hold for 24 hours in refrigerator.

Stuff into 32-34 mm pork casings forming 30 cm (12") loops OR into 50-60 mm pork bungs making straight sections.

Ferment/dry at 25-30° C (77-86° F) 2-3 days, 80-85% humidity. Apply a thin cold smoke at <25° C (77° F) during this step.

Dry 32-34 mm sausages at 12-15° C (53-59° F), 70-75% humidity for 14 days OR pork bungs for 2 months.

Store sausages at 10-12° C (50-53° F), 65-70% humidity.

Notes
Consume cold or cooked.

Chorizo Candelario

Chorizo Candelario originates in the municipality of Candelaria in Salamanca province of Castilla y León region of Spain. It is made from lean pork, pork fat and is always seasoned with pimentón, oregano and garlic. The sausage is stuffed into straight or U-shaped casings. The same area produces another well known chorizo called "White Chorizo Candelario" (*Chorizo Blanco Candelario)* which is made without pimentón. All other ingredients and processing steps remain the same as in Chorizo Candelario.

Lean pork: head, loin, shoulder, legs	1000 g	2.2 lb

Ingredients per 1 kg (2.2 lb) of meat

Salt	28 g	4.5 tsp
Cure #2	2.5 g	1/2 tsp
Dextrose	2.0 g	1/2 tsp
Sugar	2.0 g	1/2 tsp
Black pepper	1.0 g	1/2 tsp
Pimentón, sweet	20 g	10 tsp
Pimentón, hot	2.0 g	1 tsp
Oregano, ground	2.0 g	1 tsp
Garlic	3.5 g	1 clove
Wine	15 ml	1 Tbsp
Water, as needed	30 ml	1 oz fl

Smash garlic and using a mortar and pestle grind it with wine into a paste.
Lean cuts from pork head, loin, shoulder, legs. Remove all membranes, sinews, gristles etc.
Grind meat through 8 mm (3/8") plate.
Mix ground meat with all ingredients adding as little water as needed for proper texture of the meat mass. Hold in refrigerator for 48 hours.
Stuff into 40-55 mm pork middles, tying off 8-10 cm (4") links or into 50-90 mm pork bung. Prick each sausage with a needle, especially in visible air pockets.
Ferment/dry at 22-24° C (72-75° F) for 48 hours, 90-85% humidity.
Dry sausages for 30 days at 12-15° C (53-59° F), 75-80% humidity. Dry pork bungs longer, depending on diameter, until the sausage loses 33% of its original weight.
Store at 10° C (53° F) in a cool and ventilated area or refrigerate.

Chorizo Cántabro (Guriezo)

Chorizo Cántabro is a Basque chorizo popular in Cantabria, an autonomous region on Spain's north coast. The sausage is made with the "choricero pepper" (pimiento choricero), a variety of sweet red pepper (a variant of the species *Capsicum annuum)* that is usually air dried in strings to preserve it better. Chorizo Cántabro is also known as Chorizo de Guriezo. Guriezo is a municipality located in the autonomous community of Cantabria, Spain.

Pork, lean	600 g	1.32 lb
Pork belly	400 g	0.88 lb

Ingredients per 1 kg (2.2 lb) of meat

Salt	21 g	3.5 tsp
Cure #1	2.5 g	½ tsp
Dextrose	2.0 g	1/2 tsp
Sugar	2.0 g	1/2 tsp
Chorizo pepper (choricero)*	15 g	7 tsp
Pimentón, hot	2.0 g	1 tsp
Garlic	7.0 g	2 cloves

Grind meat and belly through 10 mm (3/8") plate.
Mix with all spices. Hold the mixture for 12 hours in refrigerator.
Stuff into 32-36 mm hog casings forming links, Tie the ends together.
Apply a thin cold smoke and dry at 18° C (64° F) for 2 days. Cold smoking does not have to be a continuous process.
Dry sausages for 14 days at 12-15° C (53-59° F), 75-80% humidity.

Notes
Sausage can be consumed raw, fried or cooked in white wine or cider.
* In US the chorizo pepper (*Choricero*) can be ordered from Edwards Greenhouse, Boise, ID
https://www.edwardsgreenhouse.com
It is a common practice in northern Spain to cook (simmer) chorizos in white wine. Cook them whole or cut into 7-10 cm (3-4") pieces and heat in wine for 30 minutes. Fat will leak into the wine, pimentón will color the liquid red and the sausage is enjoyed with bread soaked in wine.

Chorizo Criollo Argentino

It is logical to assume that Chorizo Criollo originates in Spain, however, this
sausage comes from Argentina. It is also popular in Uruguay which sits on the
northern side of Río de la Plata river which forms the natural border between
Argentina and Uruguay. The sausage is also popular in North America and can
be found in Spain as well. This is a fresh sausage that is usually barbecued or
grilled. Argentina is all about beef so it is not surprising that this is the main
ingredient in the sausage. What differentiates Chorizo Criollo from Spanish
sausages is that it does not include pimentón and is not cured. Chorizo Criollo is
a fresh sausage which is grilled or barbecued.

Beef	700 g	1.54 lb
Pork, semi-fat	300 g	0.66 lb

Ingredients per 1 kg (2.2 lb) of meat

Salt	18 g	3 tsp
Pepper	2.0 g	1 tsp
Chili powder	4.0 g	2 tsp
Nutmeg	1.0 g	1/2 tsp
Oregano, rubbed	4.0 g	4 tsp
Garlic, diced	12 g	4 cloves
Fennel seed, whole	2.0 g	1 tsp
Red wine	60 ml	4 Tbs

Grind pork through 8 mm (3/8") plate.
Grind beef through 5 mm (1/4") plate.
Mix wine with all ingredients. Pour over ground meat and mix. Hold in
refrigerator over night.
Stuff into 36 mm pork casings making 15 cm (6") links.
Refrigerate. Cook fully before serving.

Chorizo Criollo Colombiano

Chorizo Criollo Colombiano is a fresh Columbian sausage.

Beef	400 g	0.88 lb
Pork, lean	400 g	0.88 lb
Back fat, pork belly or fat trimmings	200 g	0.44 lb

Ingredients per 1 kg (2.2 lb) of meat

Salt	18 g	3 tsp
Pepper	2.0 g	1 tsp
Chopped onion	30 g	1/2 small
Oregano, rubbed	1.0 g	1 tsp
Bay leaf, crushed	1	1
Nutmeg	1.0 g	1/2 tsp
Garlic, crushed	7.0 g	2 cloves
Lime juice	30 ml	2 Tbsp
Dry red wine	15 ml	1 Tbsp
Water	30 ml	2 Tbsp

Grind pork meat and fat through 10 mm (3/8") plate.
Grind beef through 3 mm (1/8") plate.
Mix beef and lean pork with salt and water until sticky. Add spices, lime, wine and mix. Finally add fat and mix all together.
Stuff into 36 mm pig casings forming 20 cm (8") links.
Refrigerate.
Fry or grill before serving.

Chorizo Cubano

Cuban chorizo, unlike Spanish dry chorizo is a fresh sausage and must be cooked before serving.

Pork shoulder or		
70/30 (lean/fat) pork trimmings	1000 g	2.2 lb

Ingredients per 1kg (2.2 lb) of meat

Salt	18 g	3 tsp
Paprika, sweet	6.0 g	3 tsp
Cumin	2.0 g	1 tsp
Cilantro, chopped	10 g	3 Tbsp
Garlic, smashed	10 g	3 cloves
Cider vinegar	60 ml	2 oz fl

Grind pork through 8 mm (3/8") plate.
Mix ground meat with all ingredients.
Stuff firmly into 32 mm hog casings forming 4-6" (10-15 cm) long links.
Refrigerate. Cook before serving.

Chorizo Cular (Salamanca)

Chorizo cular is a very popular sausage in Salamanca and de la de Ávila provinces of the Castilla and León region of Spain. This is a large chorizo sausage, 45-70 mm in diameter, 50-60 cm (20-24") in length, weighing about 850 grams (1.87 lb). In traditional home production methods sausages are suspended below the kitchen range hood for 2-3 days. Old kitchen stoves were wood fired and had removable top plates. Removing the plate allowed to smoke/dry products hanging above. As an additional bonus the sausages acquired different flavors from foods which were being cooked on the stove. Chorizo derives its name from the pork casing it is stuffed in - tripa "cular" which is a pork bung (the last section of casing).

Lean pork*	800 g	1.76 lb
Back fat	200 g	0.44 lb

Ingredients per 1 kg (2.2 lb) of meat

Salt	30 g	5 tsp
Cure #2	2.5 g	1/2 tsp
Sugar	2.5 g	1/2 tsp
Pimentón, sweet	20 g	3.5 Tbsp
Pimentón, hot	4.0 g	2 tsp
Oregano, dry	3.0 g	3 tsp
Garlic	10 g	3 cloves
Cinnamon	1.0 g	½ tsp
Nutmeg	0.5 g	¼ tsp
Cloves	0.3 g	1/8 tsp
Ginger	0.3 g	1/8 tsp
White wine	30 ml	2 Tbsp
Olive oil	30 ml	2 Tbsp

Grind meat through 8 mm (3/8") plate. For better particle definition manually cut partially frozen fat into 6-10 mm cubes.
Mix meat, fat and all other ingredients and hold in refrigerator for 48 hours.
Stuff into 40-60 mm pork bungs (*"tripa cular"*) forming 50-60 cm (20-24") straight sections.
Dry/ferment for 24 hours at 24° C (75° F), 85-90% humidity.
Dry at 12-14° C (53-57° F), 70-80% humidity for 2 months.
Store at 10-12° C (50-53° F), <75% humidity or refrigerate.

Notes
* preferably from Iberian pig. In traditional home production the stuffed sausages were hung for 2-3 days below kitchen range hood ("campana de cocina") and then dried in natural homemade drying chambers for 3-4 months. Consume raw. Sliced sausage should display visible marbling with a larger proportion of lean to fat and the sausage should exhibit a vivid red color.

Chorizo de Aragón

Chorizo de Aragón is a Spanish semi-dry sausage popular in the region of Aragón, especially around its capital Zaragoza. The sausage is made with lean pork, fatty pork cuts like pork belly, dewlap and classical Spanish chorizo spice combination: pimentón paprika, oregano and garlic.

Pork, lean	700 g	1.54 lb
Pork belly, dewlap or back fat	300 g	0.66 lb

Ingredients per 1 kg (2.2 lb) of meat

Salt	30 g	5 tsp
Cure #1	2.5 g	1/2 tsp
Pepper	2.0 g	1 tsp
Pimentón, sweet	24 g	4 Tbsp
Pimentón, hot	2.0 g	1 tsp
Oregano, ground	2.0 g	1 tsp
Nutmeg	0.5 g	¼ tsp
Garlic, smashed	7.0 g	2 cloves

Grind lean meat through 8 mm (3/8") plate.

Grind fat cuts through 8 mm (3/8") plate. You can manually cut partially frozen fat into 8 mm pieces for better particle definition.

Mix ground meat with all spices, then add ground fat and mix again. Pack the mixture in container and place for 24-36 hours in refrigerator.

Stuff into 28-32 mm pork or sheep casings forming 10 cm (4") long links.

Dry/ferment at 22-24° C (72-75° F), 85-90% humidity for 24 hours.

Dry for 48 hours at 15-18° C (59-64° F), 70-80% humidity.

Dry at 12-15° C (53-59° F) for 48 hours. At this point Chorizo de Aragón can be classified a semi-dry sausage which is served fried or cooked.

Notes

To make a dry sausage continue drying at 12-14° C (53-57° F), 75-80% humidity until the sausage loses 33% of its original weight. The dry sausage can be consumed raw.

Nowadays commercial producers stuff sausage into horseshoe loops about 40 cm (16") long.

Chorizo De Bilbao

Chorizo de Bilbao is a spicy semi-dry sausage popular in the Philippines.

Beef, lean	500 g	1.10 lb
Pork, lean	300 g	0.66 lb
Pork back fat	200 g	0.44 lb

Ingredients per 1 kg (2.2 lb) of meat

Salt	28 g	5 tsp
Cure #1	2.5 g	1/2 tsp
Dextrose	2.0 g	1/2 tsp
Sugar	3.0 g	1/2 tsp
Pimentón, sweet	20 g	3.5 Tbsp
Pimentón, hot	3.0 g	1.5 tsp
Cumin	2.0 g	1 tsp
Oregano, ground	2.0 g	1 tsp
Garlic	7.0 g	2 cloves

Grind beef through 6 mm (1/4") plate. Grind pork through 8 mm (3/8") plate.
Dice partially frozen fat into 6 mm (1/4") cubes.
Mix ground meats, fat and all ingredients together. Hold in refrigerator for 24 hours.
Stuff firmly into 36 mm casings forming 6" (15 cm) long links.
Ferment for 24 hours at room temperature, 90-85% humidity.
Refrigerate.
Cook before serving.

Notes
After fermenting instead of refrigerating, the sausages may be submitted to the drying process:
Dry at 15-12° C (59-54° F), 75-80% humidity for 3 weeks. (Larger diameter casings will require longer drying times). The sausage is dried until around 30-35% in weight is lost.
Store dried sausages at 10-12° C (50-53° F), 70% humidity or in refrigerator.
If making dry sausage TSPX starter culture (0.12 g per 1 kg meat) can be added just before stuffing for better control of the process.

Chorizo de Bofe

Chorizo de bofe (*bofe* means lungs) is made with offal meat (lungs, spleen, stomach), skins and other meat by products which will be hard to obtain in metropolitan areas, however, in rural areas such meats and blood are usually processed first for sausages. The sausage is also known as *sabadeño* in Castilla, *sabadiego* in León and *bofeños* in Extremadura.

Lean pork	300 g	0.66 lb
Beef, semi-fat	200 g	0.44 lb
Lungs, spleen, stomach, skins	400 g	0.88 lb
Trimmings rich in connective tissue, skins ..	100 g	0.22 lb

Ingredients per 1 kg (2.2 lb) of meat

Salt	24 g	4 tsp
Cure #1	2.5 g	1/2 tsp
Pimentón, sweet	30 g	5 Tbsp
Pimentón, hot	5.0 g	1 tsp
Oregano, ground	1.0 g	1/2 tsp
Nutmeg	1.0 g	1/2 tsp
Garlic, smashed	7.0 g	2 cloves
Wine	60 ml	2 oz fl

Take heart, lungs, stomach, skins and trimmings and cook in water (below boiling point) until soft. Drain and cool.
Grind beef and pork through 8 mm (3/8") plate. Grind cooked meats through 3 mm (1/8") plate.
Mix meats and all ingredients together. Hold for 12 hours in refrigerator.
Stuff into 40-50 mm pork or beef middles.
Ferment/dry at 22-24° C (72-75° F), 90% humidity for 48 hours.
Dry at 14-15° C (57-59° F), 70% humidity for 30 days.
Store at 10-12° C (50-52 F), 60-65% humidity or refrigerate.

Chorizo de Calabaza

Pumpkin is used in Spanish sausage known as Chorizo de Calabaza or in Portuguese Chouriço de Abóbora de Barroso-Montalegre which carries the prestigious PGI award.

Pork butt	500 g	1.10 lb
Pumpkin	500 g	1.10 lb

Ingredients per 1 kg (2.2 lb) of material

Salt	25 g	4 tsp
Cure #1	2.5 g	1/2 tsp
Dextrose	1.0 g	1/4 tsp
Sugar	2.0 g	1/2 tsp
Allspice	0.5 g	1/2 tsp
Bay leaf, crushed	1 leaf	1 leaf
Pimentón, sweet	10.0 g	5 tsp
Nutmeg	1.0 g	1/2 tsp
Cinnamon	2.0 g	1 tsp
Cloves, ground	0.3 g	1/8 tsp
Ginger, ground	0.5 g	1/4 tsp
Sherry wine	30 ml	1 oz fl

Cut meat into small pieces and marinate with salt, cure #1, bay leaf, all spices and wine.

Scrape the flesh of the pumpkin, discard the seeds. Mash the flesh with a potato masher. Wrap with a cheese cloth, place in a colander, add some weight on top and let it drain overnight.

Mix meat, pumpkin and all ingredients together. Hold for 24 hours in refrigerator.

Stuff into 36 mm hog casings.

Ferment at 20° C (68° F) for 72 hours, 90-85% humidity.

Dry at 16-12° C (60-54° F), 85-80% humidity for 30 days. The sausage is dried until around 30% in weight is lost.

Store sausages at 10-12° C (50-53° F), <75% humidity or refrigerate.

Notes

To make 1 kg of cooked pumpkin you need about 4 kg of raw pumpkin.

Pumpkin puree: cut pumpkin into smaller sections, remove seeds and fiber. Cook pumpkin for 25 minutes in water, 15 minutes in steam or bake for 30 minutes at 176° C (350° F). Remove the skin (it peels off easily) and cut the pieces into smaller parts. Place the pumpkin flesh in a food processor and emulsify it into the puree. Don't add any water as pumpkin has plenty of it. Place pumpkin puree in a draining bag, place some weight on top and let it drain overnight.

Chorizo de Cantipalos

This classic, dry chorizo originates in the municipality of Cantipalos in the province of Segovia of the autonomous region de Castilla y León in the middle of Spain.

For hundreds of years the area of Cantipalos was highly regarded for making sausages, but 1900 is the date which is credited as the official beginning of the sausage making industry in Cantipalos. By 1928 the sausages from Cantipalos were regularly shipped (packed in cans) to Mexico and other countries. From 2011 Chorizo de Cantipalos carries protective geographical indication certificate (PGI). Chorizo de Cantimpalos is a cured sausage product made from fresh fatty pork, with salt and pimentón as basic ingredients to which garlic and oregano may also be added and subjected to a drying and maturing process.

Since 2008 all matters related to Chorizo de Cantipalos are handled by Regulatory Council of Cantipalos (Consejo Regulador) in the province of Segovia in Castilla y León region of Spain. For example it is required that: all pigs chosen for Chorizos de Cantipalos be marked since birth with CS symbol, only white pigs are used, in their last 3 months of life their diet must consists of at least 75% of wheat and barley, they must be 7-10 months old and weigh 115-160 kg when slaughtered, each chorizo must have its own etiquette and serial number, the ends of the sausage must be connected with twine having 3-color threads (white, red and black).

Meat composition: lean pork 70-80%, fat 20-30%. No previously frozen meat is permitted.

Pimentón - applied at 15-25 g per 1 kg of meat and at least 50% of Pimentón de La Vera must be used.

Salt - Fine sea salt is added at 15-22 g per 1 kg of meat.

Garlic - added at no more than 4 g per 1 kg of meat.

Oregano - dry oregano at no more than 0.2 g per 1 kg of meat.

Sugar - permitted only for chorizo stuffed into pork bungs.

Phosphates - are allowed.

Anti-oxidants - ascorbic acid or citric acid are allowed.

Proteins - only non-fat dry milk is allowed.

Nitrite/nitrate - not allowed.

Lean pork	700 g	1.54 lb
Back fat or		
hard fat trimmings	300 g	0.66 lb

Ingredients per 1 kg (2.2 lb)

Sea salt, finely ground	22 g	4 tsp
Pimentón de la Vera, sweet	20 g	3.5 Tbsp
Pimentón de la Vera, hot	2.0 g	1 tsp
Oregano, rubbed	0.2 g	1/4 tsp
Garlic, diced	4.0 g	1.5 cloves

For chorizos *sarta* and *achorizado* style grind meat through 10-16 mm (3/8-1/2") plate.

For chorizos c*ular* style grind meat through 18-26 mm (3/4-1") plate.

Mix salt, spices and meats together. Hold for 12-36 hours in refrigerator.

Stuff into natural casings:

- 34-40 mm pork ring shaped casings (**sarta** style), the ends tied together.
- a string of several chorizo sausages (**achorizado** ristra style) about 12 cm (5") long, 36-50 mm in diameter, tied or wired together with ends connected together with twine forming a long U-shaped loop.
- pork bungs (**cular** style) of more than 38 mm in diameter, an irregular cylindrical shape straight sections.

Dry at 6-16° C (43-60° F), 60-85% humidity for 1/2 of the total drying time.

Dry at 12-15° C (57-59° F), 60-80% humidity for the remaining drying time.

- *sarta* style - total drying time 21 days.
- *achorizado* ristra style - total drying time 24 days.
- *cular* - total drying time up to 40 days.

Store at 10-12° C (50-52° F), 60-70% humidity.

Notes

The sausage develops a thin white mold.

The sausage is finished when it loses about 30% of its original weight.

Chorizo de Cebolla

Chorizo de cebolla (*cebolla* means onion) is a popular dry sausage from Galicia region of Spain.

Pork belly, jowls	400 g	0.88 lb
Offal meat: diaphragm muscle, lungs, heart, skins	300 g	0.66 lb
Diced onions, cooked	300 g	0.66 lb

Ingredients per 1 kg (2.2 lb) of material

Salt	25 g	4 tsp
Cure # 1	2.5 g	1/2 tsp
Sweet pimentón	20 g	3.5 Tbsp
Hot pimentón	2.0 g	1 tsp
Garlic, diced	3.5 g	1 clove
Oregano, ground	2.0 g	2 tsp
Parsley, dry	1.0 g	1 tsp
Bay leaf, crushed	1 leaf	1

Remove tendons, sinews, and hard connective tissue from offal meats, then cook the meats in water (below boiling point) until soft. Drain and cool.

Chop the onions and cook in water for 45 minutes. Drain and let the moisture evaporate.

Grind meats through 6 mm (1/4") plate and mix with all spices. Hold for 24 hours in refrigerator.

Mix the sausage mix with cooked onions and stuff without delay into 40 mm pig casings forming links ~ 15 cm (6") long.

Apply cold smoke at 15-18° C (53-64° F) for 7-10 days. Smoking need not to be continuous.

Dry at 15-12° C (59-53° F), 75-80% humidity for 45 days.

Store sausages at 10-12° C (50-53° F), 65-70% humidity or refrigerate.

Notes

For home production it is recommended to cook the onions as that will eliminate much of the moisture, otherwise drying will be prolonged and unsafe.

Sodium nitrite/nitrate and sugars are not added in the traditional manufacturing process.

Chorizo de Cerdo

This is a typical example of chorizo making technology which can l
most chorizo sausages. The quality chorizo is made from well trimmed lean cuts
of pork and *hard* fat, the preferred cut being the back fat. Salt, pimentón and
garlic are main ingredients, the rest is following proper processing.

Lean pork	750 g	1.65 lb
Hard fat (back fat) or		
hard fat trimmings	250 g	0.55 lb

Ingredients per 1 kg (2.2 lb) of meat

Salt	25 g	4 tsp
Cure #2	2.5 g	1/2 tsp
Pimentón, sweet	25 g	4 Tbsp
Pimentón, hot	5.0 g	1 tsp
Oregano, ground	1.0 g	1/2 tsp
Garlic, smashed	3.0 g	1 clove

Grind meat through 8 mm (3/8") plate.
Grind fat through 8 mm (3/8") plate.
Mix meat with all ingredients. Hold for 24 hours in refrigerator.
Stuff into 36 mm pork or beef casings.
Apply a thin smoke at 22-24° C (72-75° F) (smoking step optional) or dry/
ferment sausages at 22-24° C (72-75° F) for 24-48 hours.
Dry at 15-12° C (59-53° F), 75-80% humidity for 15 days.
Store sausages at 10-12° C (50-53° F), 65-70% humidity or refrigerate.

Chorizo de la Sierra de Aracena

Chorizo de la Sierra de Aracena owes its name to Sierra de Aracena and Picos de Aroche Natural Park, a protected area in the Sierra de Aracena range, part of the Sierra Morena mountain system which lies in Huelva province in Andalusia region of southwestern Spain. This mountain range and national park abounds with many oak forests ("dehesas") where Iberian pigs roam free on and feed between December and April on oak acorns ("bellota").

Lean Iberian pork	600 g	1.32 lb
Pork belly and dewlap (chin)	400 g	0.88 lb

Ingredients per 1 kg (2.2 lb) of meat

Salt	28 g	4.5 tsp
Cure #1	2.5 g	1/2 tsp
Pimentón, sweet	25 g	4 Tbsp
Pimentón, hot	2.0 g	1 tsp
Garlic, diced	3.5 g	1 clove

Grind meats into 8 mm (3/8") pieces.

Mix meats with salt and spices. Marinate for 24 hours in refrigerator.

Stuff into 40-45 mm beef middles forming small 15 cm (6") rings. Tie the ends together.

Apply a thin smoke at 22-24° C (72-75° F) and dry/ferment sausages at 22-24° C (72-75° F) for 24-48 hours.

Dry at 15-12° C (59-53° F), 75-80% humidity for 30 days.

Store sausages at 10-12° C (50-53° F), 65-70% humidity or refrigerate.

Notes

Consume raw, cooked, fried or grilled.

Chorizo de León

Chorizo de León is a dry sausage from León region of Spain. This is a rather fat sausage which is heavily smoked during fermentation. The sausage is made from white pig quality meats such as pork shoulder, rear leg (ham) trimmings, pork belly, dewlap and back fat.

Pork, lean	750 g	1.54 lb
Pork back fat, belly	250 g	0.55 lb

Ingredients per 1 kg (2.2 lb) of meat

Salt	25 g	4 tsp
Cure #2	2.5 g	1/2 tsp
Dextrose	3.0 g	1/2 tsp
Pimentón, sweet	20 g	3.5 Tbsp
Pimentón, hot	2.0 g	1 tsp
Oregano, ground	2.0 g	1 tsp
Garlic, diced	3.5 g	1 clove

Grind meat and pork fat through 10 mm (3/8") plate.

Mix meats with spices and hold for 24 hours in refrigerator.

Stuff into 36 mm pork casings forming U-shaped loops with ends tied together. In other locations apply cold smoke at <18° C (64° F) and dry sausages at 12-15° C (53-59° F), 85-75% humidity.

Apply a thin smoke at 22-24° C (72-75° F) and dry/ferment sausages at 22-24° C (72-75° F) for 24-48 hours.

Dry at 15-12° C (59-53° F), 75-80% humidity for 30 days. The temperature in León can reach low levels so a slow burning fire is started to warm up the drying chamber. This means that the sausages are additionally cold smoked during the drying stage .

Store sausages at 10-12° C (50-53° F), 65-70% humidity or refrigerate.

Notes

Sodium nitrite/nitrate and sugars are not added in the traditional manufacturing process.

Chorizo de Mezcla

Most chorizos are made with pork, but occasionally other meat is combined with pork together, usually beef.

Pork meat	300 g	0.44 lb
Pork fat	300 g	0.66 lb
Beef	400 g	0.88 lb

Ingredients per 1 kg (2.2 lb) of meat

Salt	25 g	4 tsp
Cure #2	2.5 g	1/2 tsp
Pimentón, sweet	25 g	4 Tbsp
Pimentón, hot	5.0 g	2 tsp
Oregano, ground	1.0 g	1/2 tsp
Garlic, smashed	7.0 g	2 cloves
Red wine	60 ml	2 oz fl

Grind pork through 6 mm (1/4") plate.
Dice fat into 6 mm (1/4") cubes.
Grind beef through 3-5 mm (1/8") plate.
Mix ground meats, fat and spices together. Hold for 24 hours in refrigerator.
Stuff into 36 mm pork or beef casings.
Apply a thin smoke at 22-24° C (72-75° F) (smoking step optional) or dry/ ferment sausages at 22-24° C (72-75° F) for 24-48 hours.
Dry at 15-12° C (59-54° F), 75-80% humidity for 15 days.
Store sausages at 10-12° C (50-53° F), 65-70% humidity or refrigerate.

Chorizo de Pamplona

Chorizo de Pamplona is a large dry sausage which is very popular not only in Navarra region of Spain where it originates from, but everywhere else in Europe as well as in the USA. It is a large diameter (min 40 mm), one piece sausage, about 30-40 cm (12-15") long weighing around 1.5 kg (3.3 lbs). The sausage is made with pork and beef, or pork only (80/20 lean/fat). In difference to other chorizos, meats in Chorizo de Pamplona are finely ground.

Pork	450 g	0.99 lb
Beef	200 g	0.44 lb
Back fat	350 g	0.77 lb

Ingredients per 1 kg (2.2 lb) of meat

Salt	28 g	4.5 tsp
Cure #1	2.5 g	1/2 tsp
Dextrose	3.0 g	1/2 tsp
Pimentón, sweet	25 g	4 Tbsp
Pimentón, hot	5.0 g	2 tsp
Garlic	3.5 g	1 clove

Grind pork and beef through 3 mm (1/8") plate.

Dice partially frozen back fat 3-5 mm (1/8-1/4") cubes.

Mix ground meats with all spices. Add ground fat and mix all together. Hold for 24 hours in refrigerator.

Stuff into 55-80 mm natural or artificial permeable (allowing liquids or gases to pass through) casings. Make straight links ~20 cm (8") long. Prick with needle to remove air.

Dry/ferment sausages at 22-24° C (72-75° F) for 48 hours.

Dry for 45-60 days at 15→12° C (59→53° F), 65-85% humidity. You can apply old smoke (<18° C/64° F) during this step. Cold smoking is performed with a thin smoke and the process is usually interrupted at night time and resumed in the morning, however, cold smoking can be interrupted at any time.

Store sausages at 10-12° C (50-53° F), 65-70% humidity or refrigerate.

Notes

Cold smoking is not required, it is usually introduced when the temperatures are dropping below 12° C (53° F).

Chorizo de Potes

Chorizo de Potes is a well-known smoked and dried sausage from Cantabria region of Spain. What differs Chorizo de Potes from the majority of Spanish chorizos is that in addition to pimentón it also contains regular pepper. Using thyme is another characteristic of the sausages.

Pork, lean	500 g	1.10 lb
Pork belly	500 g	1.10 lb

Ingredients per 1 kg (2.2 lb) of meat

Salt	25 g	4 tsp
Cure #1	2.5 g	1/2 tsp
Pepper	2.0 g	1 tsp
Pimentón, sweet	24 g	4 Tbsp
Pimentón, hot	2.0 g	1 tsp
Garlic	3.5 g	1 clove
Oregano, dry	2.0 g	3 tsp
Thyme, dry	2.0 g	3 tsp

Grind meat and belly through 10 mm (3/8") plate.

Mix with all ingredients and hold in refrigerator for 12 hours.

Stuff into 36 mm hog casings and form links using one continuous string of butcher twine.

Smoke and dry with oak wood at 15-18° C (59-64° F), 70-80% humidity for 25 days. The smoking process can be interrupted, so it is smoking-drying-smoking-drying etc. Usually drying at night and smoking by day. As the process continues start lowering slowly temperature.

Notes

The sausage is served in many forms; sliced and consumed raw, in sandwiches, or in bean stews.

Chorizo de Soria

Soria is the city in north-central Spain, the capital of the province of Soria in the region of Castile and León. The sausage is made of lean pork and fat, although adding some beef is permitted. Just a few spices - salt, pimentón and garlic are added and the sausage is stuffed into large diameter pork or beef casings and dried.

Lean pork	700 g	1.43 lb
Back fat, pork belly	300 g	0.55 lb

Ingredients per 1 kg (2.2 lb) of meat

Salt	28 g	4.5 tsp
Cure #2	2.5 g	1/2 tsp
Dextrose	2.0 g	1/2 tsp
Sugar	3.0 g	1/2 tsp
Pimentón	25 g	4 Tbsp
Garlic, smashed	3.5 g	1 clove

Dice a half of the partially frozen fat (150 g) into 6-8 mm (1/4-3/8") cubes.
Grind pork meat and remaining fat (150 g) through 10 mm (3/8") plate.
Mix meat, all fat with ll ingredients. Hold in refrigerator for 24 hours.
Stuff into 26-80 mm pork or beef casings. Thin sausages were linked with butcher twine (*rastra* style) or formed into rings with ends tied together (*herradura* style), and the thick ones left in straight sections (*vela* style).
Dry/ferment sausages at 22-24° C (72-75° F) for 48 hours.
Dry at 15-12° C (59-53° F), 70-80% humidity, for 30-50 days depending on diameter. The sausages are considered dry when they lose about 33% of their original weight.

Notes

In traditional home production climatic conditions established parameters of drying (temperature and humidity). The sausages were dried at 10-28° C (50-82° F), 40-90% humidity, for 16-50 days, depending on time of the year and the diameter of the sausage. When the temperature dropped low a small wood burning fire was started to warm up the drying facility.
The sausage was stuffed into pork or beef casings of different diameters - 26-80 mm. Nowadays, large diameter synthetic protein-lined fibrous casings can be used.
Chorizo de Soria can be made with the following combination of meats: lean pork-60-70%, beef-0-15%, back fat, pork belly or both – 25-28%.

Chorizo de Villarcayo

As the name implies Chorizo de Villarcayo originates in Villarcayo, a municipality in Burgos province of Castilla y León region of Spain. It is situated about 75 km from Burgos, the capital of the province and 79 km from Bilbao, the port in Bay of Biscay in Atlantic. The sausage is made from pork and the principal spices are pimentón and garlic.

Lean pork	800 g	1.96 lb
Pork belly or lean meat trimmings with attached fat	200 g	0.44 lb

Ingredients per 1 kg (2.2 lb) of meat

Salt	28 g	4.5 tsp
Cure #2	2.5 g	1/2 tsp
Pimentón	20 g	10 tsp
Oregano	1.0 g	1 tsp
Cinnamon	0.5 g	¼ tsp
Cloves	0.3 g	1/8 tsp
Garlic	3.5 g	1 clove

Cut meat and fat into 30 mm (1.3") pieces.
Mix meat and fat with salt and spices. Hold for 24 hours in refrigerator.
Stuff into 40-60 mm pork bungs (tripa *cular*) or beef bungs (tripa *roscal*) forming 50-60 cm (20-24") straight sections (*vela*) or make loops with ends tied together (*herradura*).
Dry/ferment with a thin oak smoke at 22-24° C (72-77° F) for 48 hours.
Dry at 15-12° C (59-53° F), 60-80% humidity, for 40-60 days, depending on the diameter of the sausage until it loses about 33% of its original weight.
Store sausages at 10-12° C (50-53° F), 65-70% humidity or refrigerate.

Notes
Consume raw or cooked.

Chorizo Extremeño

Chorizo Extremeño is a dry sausage made from Iberian meat, oregano, garlic, white wine and pimentón. Extremadura, an autonomous region of western Iberian Peninsula is an important area for wildlife, particularly with the major reserve at Monfragüe, which was designated a National Park in 2007, and the International Tagus River Natural Park (Parque Natural Tajo Internacional). Wild black Iberian pigs roam in the area and feed on acorns in oak forests known as *dehesas*.

Lean Iberian pork	800 g	1.76 lb
Back fat, belly	200 g	0.44 lb

Ingredients per 1 kg (2.2 lb) of meat

Salt	22 g	3.5 tsp
Cure #2	2.5 g	1 tsp
Pimentón, sweet	25 g	4 Tbsp
Pimentón, hot	5.0 g	1 Tbsp
Oregano, dry	2.0 g	2 tsp
Garlic, diced	7.0 g	2 cloves
Dry sherry	30 ml	2 Tbsp
Water	60 ml	2 oz fl

Grind lean pork and fat through 5-8 mm (1/4") plate.

Mix meats with all ingredients. Hold in refrigerator for 48 hours.

Stuff into 40-50 mm hog casings. Form 5-10 cm (3-4") links or 45 cm (18") straight sections or 45 cm (18") rings.

Dry/ferment at 12-15° C (53-59° F), 80-85% humidity, for 2-3 days.

Dry at 12-15° C (53-59° F), 80% humidity for 1-2 months depending on the diameter of the sausage.

Store sausages at 10-12° C (50-53° F), 65-70% humidity or refrigerate.

Notes

Pimentón brand "de la Vera" recommended.

Consume raw, cooked, fried or grilled.

Chorizo Gallego

Chorizo Gallego is the most popular sausage in Galicia. The sausage is produced by commercial meat plants and hobbyists at home from quality meats: lean pork (70-80%) and back fat (20-30%). It is characterized by a dark red color and visible and generous distribution of fat pieces. Sausage is safe to eat after losing 30% of its original weight. Chorizo Gallego is consumed raw, fried, grilled or becomes an ingredient in many dishes.

Pork, lean (shoulder or ham)	700 g	1.54 lb
Pork back fat, belly or		
fat trimmings	300 g	0.66 lb

Ingredients per 1 kg (2.2 lb) of meat

Salt	22 g	3.5 tsp
Cure #2	2.5 g	1 tsp
Pimentón, sweet	20 g	3 Tbsp
Pimentón, hot	5.0 g	1 Tbsp
Garlic	7.0 g	2 cloves

Cut or grind meat and fat into 8 mm (3/8") pieces.
Mix salt, cure #1 and spices together. Mix with meats.
Hold for 24 hours in refrigerator.
Stuff firmly into 36 mm pork casing forming 15 cm (6") links.
Smoke at 18° C (64° F) with oak wood for 12-48 hours.
Dry at 12-15° C (53-5°9 F) for 30-45 days.
Store in a dark place at 12° C or less, <65% humidity.

Notes
Chorizo Gallego was traditionally smoked in home chimneys.
The sausage was traditionally preserved by keeping it in oil or in lard.
The sausage can be consumed raw, cooked, fried or grilled, but is usually served with boiled potatoes and turnip greens, known in UK as *rapini* and in US as *broccoli raab or broccoli rabe*.
It is also added to bean stew. There are local variants of the sausage, often onion is added (chorizo de cebolla or "ceboleira"), sometimes pumpkin (chorizo de calabaza).

Chorizo Ibérico de Huelva

Chorizo Ibérico de Huelva originates in Huelva, an old port city, in southwestern Spain, the capital of the province of Huelva in the autonomous region of Andalusia. To the north of the city there is a number of mountain ranges and national parks with oak forests ("dehesas") where Iberian pigs roam free and feed between December and April on oak acorns. During that time an average Iberian pig (Pata Negra) consumes 10 kg (22 lbs) of acorns each day. This diet influences the flavor and the texture of its meat and fat.

Lean Iberian pork	800 g	1.76 lb
Back fat	200 g	0.44 lb

Ingredients per 1 kg (2.2 lb) of meat

Salt	28 g	4.5 tsp
Cure #1	2.5 g	1/2 tsp
Pimentón, sweet	25 g	4 Tbsp
Pimentón, hot	2.0 g	1 tsp
Garlic, diced	3.5 g	1 clove

Cut chilled lean pork into 35 mm (1.5") pieces.
Dice partially frozen fat into 12 mm (1/2") cubes.
Mix meats with salt and spices. Marinate for 24 hours in refrigerator.
Stuff into 50-55 mm pork bungs or beef middles, about 40-50 cm (16-20") long.
Dry/ferment at 22-24° C (72-77° F), 80-85% humidity, for 48 hours.
Dry at 12-15° C (53-59° F), 80% humidity, for about 45 days. When temperatures were dropping low a slow burning fire provided heat in a chamber.
Store sausages at 10-12° C (50-53° F), 65-70% humidity or refrigerate.

Notes
Consume raw.

Chorizo Mexicano

Original Spanish chorizo is made from coarsely chopped pork and seasoned with paprika and garlic. Most South American chorizos are of a fresh type which is fried for breakfast or grilled on a fire. Mexican Chorizo is a fresh sausage made from ground pork and seasoned with chili peppers, garlic and vinegar. It is moister and much hotter than the Spanish chorizo.

Pork butt (shoulder)   1000 g   2.20 lb

Ingredients per 1 kg (2.2 lb) of meat

Salt	18 g	3 tsp
Pepper	2.0 g	1 tsp
Paprika, sweet	4.0 g	2 tsp
Cayenne pepper	2.0 g	1 tsp
Oregano, rubbed	2.0 g	2 tsp
Garlic, smashed	7.0 g	2 cloves
White vinegar	50 ml	1/5 cup
Cold water	50 ml	1/5 cup

Grind meat through 12 mm (1/2") plate.
Mix meat, all ingredients, vinegar and water together.
Stuff into 32-36 mm hog casings and make 8" long links.
Keep in a refrigerator.
Cook before serving.

Notes
Chorizo with eggs is often served for breakfast: mix pieces of chorizo with scrambled eggs.

Chorizo Parillero

A basic Uruguayan fresh sausage for the grill.

Pork, lean	700 g	1.54 lb
Back fat, dewlap, fat trimmings	300 g	0.66 lb

Ingredients per 1 kg (2.2 lb) of meat

Salt	18 g	3 tsp
Pepper, black	2.0 g	1 tsp
Paprika, sweet	4.0 g	2 tsp
Garlic, smashed	3.5 g	1 clove
Oregano, rubbed	2.0 g	2 tsp
Cumin	1.0 g	1/2 tsp
Water ~~WINE~~	30 ml	2 Tbsp → ARGENTINIAN → USE WINE

Grind lean pork through 8 mm (3/8") plate.
Grind fat through 8 mm (3/8") plate.
Mix lean pork with salt until sticky. As you mix, start adding water and spices.
Add fat and mix all together.
Stuff into 32-34 mm pork casings.
Refrigerate.

Notes
Pork shoulder contains about 25% of fat so you may just grind it whole through 8-10 mm (3/8") plate and the sausage will be great.
Beef is often added.

Chorizo Patatero de Monroy

Chorizo Patatero ("patata" means potato in English) originates in Monroy, a municipality in Cáceres province, in the autonomous community of Extremadura, Spain. The meat and fat come from Iberian pig and the main ingredient are boiled potatoes. The typical spices are salt, pimentón and garlic, however, chopped parsley and a little wine are occasionally included too.

Lean pork and pork belly	100 g	0.22 lb
Hard fat trimmings (various)	400 g	0.88 lb
Boiled potatoes	500 g	1.10 lb

Ingredients per 1 kg (2.2 lb) of material

Salt	25 g	4 tsp
Pimentón, sweet	25 g	4 Tbsp
Pimentón, hot	2.0 g	1 tsp
Garlic, diced	7.0 g	2 cloves

Grind meat and pork belly through 8 mm (3/8") plate.

Dice partially frozen hard fat into 6-8 mm (1/4-3/8") cubes.

Mix meats, fat, potatoes and spices together. Hold for 6 hours in refrigerator.

Stuff into 45-50 mm beef middles forming 20 cm (8") links.

Dry at 10-12° C (50-53° F), 80% humidity, for 35 days.

Dry at room temperature (below 15° C/59° F) until fully cured which will take about 60 days total, depending on the diameter of the sausage and drying conditions.

Notes

Meat and fat should come from Iberian pig.

Pimentón de la Vera is recommended.

Chorizo Patatero Rojo

Chorizo Patatero Rojo is a well-known sausage in Ciudad Real province of Castilla-La Mancha region in Spain. The composition of this chorizo differs from others mainly in that that this sausage is made with a touch of blood and potatoes.

Lean pork	250 g	0.55 lb
Back fat	490 g	1.08 lb
Potatoes, cooked	250 g	0.55 lb
Blood	10 ml	2 tsp

Ingredients per 1 kg (2.2 lb) of material

Salt	21 g	3.5 tsp
Pimentón, sweet	25 g	4 Tbsp
Pimentón, hot	2.0 g	1 tsp
Garlic, smashed	7.0 g	2 cloves

Boil potatoes until cooked, but do not overcook. Drain and cool.
Cut potatoes, lean pork and fat into 6-8 mm (1/4-3/8") cubes.
Mix the mixture with salt, blood and spices. Hold for 24 hours in refrigerator.
Stuff into 28-40 mm natural casings forming links or loops 15-20 cm (6-5") long.
Dry at 14-16° C (57-60° F), 75% humidity, for 10-15 days, depending on the diameter of the sausage.
Store at 10-12° C (50-53° F), <65% humidity or in refrigerator.

Notes
Adjust the hotness of the sausage by changing the proportion of sweet and hot pimentón. Consume raw or grilled.

Chorizo Porteño

Argentinian fresh chorizo sausage popular in the capital. Porteño is a resident of Buenos Aires.

Beef	400 g	0.88 lb
Pork shoulder	400 g	0.88 lb
Pork jowls, fat trimmings	200 g	0.44 lb

Ingredients per 1 kg (2.2 lb) of meat

Salt	18 g	3 tsp
Pepper	2.0 g	1 tsp
Red pepper	1.0 g	1/2 tsp
Oregano, rubbed	2.0 g	2 tsp
Coriander	1.0 g	1/2 tsp
Nutmeg	0.3 g	1/8 tsp
Garlic	3.5 g	1 clove
Red vermouth	60 ml	2 oz fl

Grind beef through 3 mm (1/8") plate.
Separately grind pork meat and jowls through 10 mm (3/8") plate.
Mix beef with salt, then add pork and mix until sticky.
Mix spices with wine and pour over the meat paste. Add ground jowls and mix all together.
Stuff into 36 mm hog casings forming 4" (10 cm) long links.
Refrigerate.
Fry or grill before serving.

Chorizo - Puerto Rican

Puerto Rican chorizo is a smoked, well-seasoned sausage.

Pork shoulder or
70/30 lean/fat meat cuts   1000 g   2.2 lb

Ingredients per 1 kg (2.2 lb) of meat

Salt	18 g	3 tsp
Cure #1	2.5 g	1/2 tsp
Pepper	2.0 g	1 tsp
Paprika, sweet	4.0 g	2 tsp
Cayenne	1.0 g	1/2 tsp
Annatto, ground	2.0 g	1 tsp
Cumin	2.0 g	1 tsp
Oregano, rubbed	6.0 g	6 tsp
Garlic, smashed	7.0 g	2 cloves
Water	30 ml	2 Tbsp

Grind pork through 8 mm (3/8") plate.
Mix/knead ground meat with salt, cure #1, and water until sticky. Add all remaining ingredients and mix well together.
Stuff firmly into 36 mm hog casings forming 8" (20 cm) long links.
Hang at room temperature for 30 minutes.
Smoke at 48-60° C (120-140° F) for 60 minutes.
Refrigerate. Cook before serving.

Chorizo Quzande de Bandeira

Chorizo Quzande de Bandeira Chorizo Quzande de Bandeira is a short pork sausage popular in La Estrada, in Pontevedra province in Galicia. The sausage is made with lean pork, back fat and a classical Galician spice combination: pimentón and garlic.

Pork, lean	700 g	1.54 lb
Back fat	300 g	0.66 lb

Ingredients per 1 kg (2.2 lb) of meat

Salt	24 g	4.5 tsp
Cure #1	2.5 g	1/2 tsp
Pimentón, sweet	25.0 g	4 Tbsp
Pimentón, hot	4.0 g	2 tsp
Garlic, smashed	7.0 g	2 cloves
Oregano, ground	2.0 g	1 tsp
Red dry wine	60 ml	2 oz fl

Grind meat with 10 mm (3/8") plate.

Mix with all ingredients and place in refrigerator for 24 hours.

Stuff into 32-34 mm hog casings linking sausages every 10 cm (4").

Apply a thin smoke at 22-24° C (72-75° F) and dry/ferment sausages at 22-24° C (72-75° F), 80-85% humidity for 48 hours.

Dry at 15-12° C (59-54° F), 75-80% humidity for 21 days.

Store sausages at 10-12° C (50-53° F), 65-70% humidity or refrigerate.

Notes

Consume raw, cooked or fried.

Quzande de Bandeira was stored in the past in lard in clay jars.

Chorizo Riojano

Chorizo Riojano (*Chorizo de la Rioja*) is made in the
autonomous community of La Rioja in Spain. The
sausage carries Protective Geographical Indication
(PGI 2010) award.

This recipe is for PGI certified product which is made by six licensed
manufacturers, all located in La Rioja. There are other versions of Chorizo
Riojano, some stuffed into 26-28 mm loops, others into 40-50 mm pork or beef
middles straight sections. Proportion of meat/fat can vary from 20-40% fat and
60-80% lean, but the spices remain the same: salt, pimentón and garlic.

Lean pork	700 g	1.54 lb
Pork belly or meat trimmings with attached fat	300 g	0.66 lb

Ingredients per 1 kg (2.2 lb) of meat

Salt	28 g	5 tsp
Pimentón, sweet	25 g	4 Tbsp
Pimentón, hot	2.0 g	1 tsp
Garlic, minced	7.0 g	2 cloves

Grind all meat through 3/8" plate (10 mm).
Mix meat with all ingredients.
Hold the sausage mass for 24 hours in refrigerator.
Stuff into 30-40 mm pork casings making 30 cm (12") rings (*sarta*) or U-shaped
loops (*herradura*) style, about 300 g in weight.
Dry/ferment at 22-24° C (72-75° F), 80-85% for 2-4 days. In home production
the temperature of the chamber was controlled by burning oak wood.
Dry at 14-16° C (57-60° F), 75-80% humidity for 15-20 days.
Store sausages at 10-12° C (50-53° F), 65-70% humidity or refrigerate.

Notes
Consume raw or on sandwiches.
For your own version of the sausage you can add Cure #1 (2.5 g, 1 tsp) and
sugar (5.0 g, 1 tsp).

Chorizo Rojo de Teror

The characteristic of the Teror sausage is its soft texture, almost a paste, in order to be easily spread on a roll or bread. To obtain soft texture the sausage is made with soft fats such as pork belly, dewlap or jowls. Chorizo de Teror comes in two varieties: red colored chorizo rojo made with pimentón and less popular light colored chorizo blanco made without it. In northern European countries such a sausage will be classified as a fermented spreadable sausage, for example Polish Metka or German Mettwurst, although European sausages will be briefly cold smoked. Teror is a town and a municipality in the northern part of the island of Gran Canaria in the Province of Las Palmas in the Canary Islands.

Lean pork	450 g	0.99 lb
Pork belly	100 g	0.22 lb
Fat	450 g	0.99 lb

Ingredients per 1 kg (2.2 lb) of meat

Salt	20 g	3.5 tsp
Cure #1	2.5 g	1/2 tsp
Pimentón	20 g	3 Tbsp
Oregano, ground	2.0 g	1 tsp
Garlic, smashed	7.0 g	2 cloves
Cinnamon	0.5 g	¼ tsp
Nutmeg	0.3 g	1/8 tsp
Cloves	0.3 g	1/8 tsp
Ginger	0.3 g	1/8 tsp
White wine	45 ml	3 Tbsp

Grind meat and fat through 3 mm (1/8") plate.
Mix ground meats with salt, wine and all spices. Hold for 12 hours in refrigerator.
Stuff into 30-40 mm pork or beef casings. Form links about 7-10 cm (3-4") long. The sausage is also stuffed into cellulose or other synthetic casings.
Keep refrigerated.

Notes
The sausage which is a meat paste is served raw, usually spread on sandwiches.

Chorizo-Spanish-Fresh   *A CHORIZO COLORADO IN ARGEN*

Spanish chorizo is a dry sausage, however, in recent years a fresh variety is gaining popularity as grills become commonplace.

Pork, semi-fat (shoulder)   1000 g   2.20 lb

Ingredients per 1 kg (2.2 lb) of meat

Salt	18 g	3 tsp
Pimentón, sweet	10.0 g	3 tsp
Pimentón, hot	5.0 g	3 tsp
Oregano	2.0 g	2 tsp
Garlic, smashed	3.0 g	1 clove
White wine, dry	60 ml	2 oz fl

Grind pork through 10 mm (3/8") plate.
Combine spices with wine.
Mix meat with all ingredients.
Stuff into 36 mm hog casings forming 6" (15 cm) links.
Refrigerate.
Cook before serving.

Chorizo Traditional

This is a traditional recipe for pure Spanish chorizo. Spanish chorizo is a dry sausage made from pork, pimentón, oregano and garlic. Pork is coarsely chopped and seasoned with oregano, garlic and *pimentón* which gives the sausage its deep red color.

Lean pork, ham or butt	750 g	1.65 lb
Back fat or hard fat trimmings	250 g	0.55 lb

Ingredients per 1 kg (2.2 lb) of meat

Salt	25 g	4 tsp
Cure #2	2.5 g	1/2 tsp
Pimentón, sweet	28 g	4.5 Tbsp
Pimentón, hot	5.0 g	1 Tbsp
Oregano, ground	2.0 g	1 tsp.
Garlic, diced	3.5 g	1 clove

Grind meat and fat through 8 mm (3/8") plate.

Mix all ingredients with meat. Hold in refrigerator for 24 hours.

Stuff firmly into 32-36 mm hog casings, form 6" long links.

Ferment/dry at 22-24° C (72-75° F) for 48 hours, 90-85% humidity. A thin smoke at 22-24° C (72-75° F) can be applied during this step.

Dry for 6-8 weeks at 16-12° C (60-54° F), gradually decreasing humidity from 85 to 75%.

Store sausages at 10-12° C (50-53° F), <75% humidity or refrigerate.

Notes

In the past chorizo was made without cure (#2 or #1) as most people were not aware of them.

Chorizo Verde

Chorizo Verde (Green Chorizo) is a specialty sausage in the area of Toluca, Mexico. Fresh chorizos are more popular in South American countries where the recipes are varied and do not necessarily follow the composition and processing steps of chorizos made in Spain.

Pork shoulder	1000 g	2.2 lb

Ingredients per 1 kg (2.2 lb) of materials

Salt	12 g	2 tsp
Pepper	1.0 g	1/2 tsp
Poblano chile	200 g	0.44 lb
Tomatillos	200 g	0.44 lb
Serrano chile	15 g	1 pepper
Chipotle chile, dried	10 g	3 peppers
Cayenne	3.0 g	1-1/2 tsp
Cilantro, fresh	90 g	3 oz
Garlic, smashed	10 g	3 cloves
Coriander	4.0 g	2 tsp
Cumin	2.0 g	1 tsp
Vinegar	90 ml	3 oz fl

Roast poblano and serrano chile over a gas flame. Put them in a plastic bag to steam for about 20 minutes, as this will make removing the skins much easier. Remove the charred skins and chop the chile finely.
Tear the dried chipotle and soak them in a little water.
Stem and chop cilantro and tomatillos.
Place vinegar and all ingredients in food processor and emulsify into a paste.
Grind pork through 1/4" (5 mm) plate.
Mix ground pork with emulsified paste.
Stuff into 32-36 mm hog casings.
Hold in refrigerator for 24 hours for the flavors to develop.
Fry or grill before serving.

Notes
Tomatillo (*little tomato*) also known as husk tomato or tomate verde (green tomato) are native to Central America and Mexico.
Poblano is a mild chili pepper originating in the state of Puebla, Mexico. Dried, it is called ancho or chile ancho.
Chipotle is a smoke-dried jalapeño.
The serrano pepper is a type of chili pepper that originated in the mountainous regions of the Mexican states of Puebla and Hidalgo. Serrano is typically eaten raw and is much hotter than the jalapeño pepper.

Chorizo Zamorano

Chorizo Zamorano is a dry pork sausage popular in Zamora province of the Castilla-León region of Spain. The sausage is usually covered with a light white mold. The color is intense red with visible particles of fat. The sausage is stuffed in different casings so it acquires different shapes: straight links, continuous links, horseshoe loops or cylindrical straight sections when pork bungs are used (tripa *cular*).

Lean pork	800 g	1.76 lb
Back fat	200 g	0.44 lb

Ingredients per 1 kg (2.2 lb) of meat

Salt	28 g	4.5 tsp
Cure #1	2.5 g	1/2 tsp
Pimentón, sweet	25 g	4 Tbsp
Pimentón, hot	2.0 g	1 tsp
Oregano, ground	3.0 g	1.5 tsp
Garlic	7.0 g	2 cloves

Grind meat through 8 mm (3/8") plate.

Dice fat into 8 mm (3/8") cubes.

Mix meat and fat with salt and spices. Hold in refrigerator for 12 hours.

Stuff into 20-25 mm sheep casings forming rings about 30 cm (1 foot) long OR into 50-60 mm pork bungs or beef casings forming straight sections.

Dry/ferment at 18-20° C (64-67° F), 85-90% humidity for 3 days.

Dry for 4-8 weeks, depending on diameter, at 15-12° C (59-53° F), gradually decreasing humidity from 85 to 75%.

Store sausages at 10-12° C (50-53° F), <75% humidity or refrigerate.

Notes

The sausage is ready to eat raw or cooked.

Pimentón de la Vera is required.

The development of a thin white mold is natural and accepted.

Chosco de Tineo

Chosco de Tineo is produced in Tineo municipality in the Asturías region in Spain. In 2011 Chosco de Tineo was granted PGI certificate (Protected Geographical Indication) which brought it the fame and recognition. Chosco de Tineo is made exclusively from cuts of pork shoulder/neck area known in Spanish as "cabecera de lomo" and tongue.

The meats are seasoned, packed by hand into pork blind cap (*caecum*), smoked and dried, giving it characteristics that differ from those of other types of sausage. When cut, the different pieces of meat used are clearly visible. The meat must not be minced. It is a large (weighing 500 g - 2 kg) special sausage made with high quality cuts, which is reserved to a great extent for special occasions.

Pork butt (boneless), at least 80%	800 g	1.76 lb
Pork tongue, at least 15%	200 g	0.44 lb

Ingredients per 1 kg (2.2 lb) of meat

Salt	28 g	4.5 tsp
Pimentón, sweet	25 g	4 Tbsp
Pimentón, hot	2.0 g	1 tsp
Garlic	3.5 g	1 clove

Cut butt (*cabecera*) into 2-3 pieces. Trim off tendons, skin, membrane. Cut tongue into 25 mm (1") pieces.

Mix meats with all ingredients and hold in refrigerator for 48 hours.

Stuff firmly into pork blind cap (caecum).

Apply a thin cold smoke at 18° C (64° F) for at least 8 days. Use oak, beech or chestnut wood.

Dry at 15-12° C (59-53° F), 75-80% humidity for minimum of 8 days.

Store at 10-12° C (50-53° F), <75% humidity.

Notes

Instead of drying there is an option of cooking smoked Chosco in water at 80-100° C (176-212° F). To eliminate the possibility of rupturing the sausage it is recommended to cook at 80° C (176° F). This will take at least 2 hours, until the sausage reaches 72° C (160° F) internal temperature. Cooked Chosco de Tineo must be kept in refrigerator.

Chosco or Choscu

Chosco is a large diameter sausage very popular in Asturías. This recipe is for a fully cured version of chosco. The sausage is made from chunks of pork tongue, lean pork or pork loin and dewlap (double chin). Pimentón delivers characteristic red color. Chosco is a fully cured sausage that is ready to eat at any time, however, if the same Chosco sausage is only lightly cured it becomes Choscu and must be refrigerated, and of course cooked before serving. In other words both sausages include the same ingredients, but due to different drying times they carry different names. It would be simpler to use just one name and add semi-dry or dry at the end. Fully cured (dried) chosco can be consumed raw or added to other dishes, but partially dried choscu must be cooked, usually in water before serving. The sausage is usually served with cut boiled potatoes (*cachelos*) or added to the famed Spanish bean stew (*fabada asturiana*).

Pork tongue	500 g	1.10 lb
Lean pork or loin	350 g	0.77 lb
Dewlap or jowls	150 g	0.33 lb

Ingredients per 1 kg (2.2 lb) of meat

Salt	28 g	4.5 tsp
Cure #2	2.5 g	1/2 tsp
Pimentón	25 g	4 Tbsp
Garlic	7.0 g	2 cloves

Cut all meats into smaller chunks.

Mix meats with all ingredients and hold in refrigerator for 2 days.

Stuff firmly into pork blind cap (caecum), 60-70 mm pork middles, or 70-90 mm pork bungs.

Dry at 15-12° C (59-53° F), 75-80% humidity in a dark, well ventilated rom for 2-3 months. Sausage is done when it loses 30% of its original weight.

Store sausages at 10-12° C (50-53° F), <75% humidity or refrigerate.

Delgadilla

Delgadilla ("delgado" means *thin* in Spanish) is a slim Spanish blood sausage (*morcilla*) stuffed into sheep casings, popular around Miranda de Ebro, a city on the Ebro river in the province of Burgos in the autonomous community of Castile and León, Spain. The sausage is also popular in the autonomous community of La Rioja which lies to the northeast.

Rice, cooked	500 g	1.1 lb
Lard or fat trimmings	350 g	0.77 lb
Blood	150 ml	5 oz fl

Ingredients per 1 kg (2.2 lb) of material)

Salt	12 g	2 tsp
Black pepper	4.0 g	2 tsp
Nutmeg	2.0 g	1 tsp
Cloves, ground	1.0 g	1/2 tsp
Cumin	2.0 g	1 tsp
Cinnamon	2.0 g	1 tsp

Cook rice, but do not overcook.
Grind fat or lard through 3 mm (1/8") plate.
Mix rice, blood, fat and spices together.
Stuff into 22-26 mm sheep casings forming long loops.
Cook delgadillas in hot tomato sauce for 15 minutes. Serve hot with bread and poached or fried eggs, noodles or potatoes.

Notes
* If not planning to eat delgadillas soon, cook the sausages in water at 75-80° C (167-176° F) for 20 minutes. Refrigerate. Serve with hot tomato sauce.

Tomato sauce

Tomatoes	1 kg	2.2 lb
1 onion	100 g	0.22 lb
Garlic	7.0 g	2 cloves
Pimentón, sweet	2.0 g	1 tsp
Sugar	5.0 g	1 tsp
Olive oil	60 ml (2 oz fl, as needed)	

Peel tomatoes, remove the seeds and dice into cubes.
Dice onions and garlic and fry in oil until golden. Add tomatoes and spices and slow-cook for 30 minutes, stirring once in a while.
Add delgadillas and cook for 15 minutes.
Serve hot with bread and poached or fried eggs, noodles or potatoes.

El Xolis

El Xolis is a quality dry sausage made from lean pork, fat and spices that is related to salchichón and fuet. The sausage has been produced for many years in the Pallars area, in the Pyrenees in north western Catalonia. The sausage is made in December-January and cured in natural chambers. The area sits at around 1300 meters high so the winter temperatures are cold and the air is pure.

Lean pork from rear leg (ham), loin or butt (shoulder) meat	750 g	1.55 lb
Pork back fat or dewlap	250 g	0.55 lb

Ingredients per 1 kg (2.2 lb) of meat

Salt	25 g	4 tsp
Cure #2	2.5 g	1/2 tsp
Dextrose	2.0 g	1/2 tsp
Sugar	3.0 g	1/2 tsp
Black pepper	3.0 g	1.5 tsp
Black pepper, whole	1.0 g	1 tsp

Grind meat and fat through 6-8 mm (1/4-3/8") plate.
Mix meat with spices and stuff into pork bungs or large diameter casings. Leave both ends open for now.
Hold for 24 hours in refrigerator. Tie off the ends with twine.
Hang for 4 days at 8-10° C (48-50° F).
Place on a flat surface, place a suitable board with a weight on it (wooden planks were normally used) and flatten for 24 hours, of course at low temperature.
El Xolis is a flattened sausage, often "8" shaped. The top groove was usually created manually with fingers.
Hang at 12-15° C (53-59° F), 80-85% humidity, for 2-3 months.
Store at 10-12° C, <75% humidity.

Notes
Traditional El Xolis was made without cure #2 and sugar.

Emberzao

Emberzao is an original Spanish sausage which is stuffed into cabbage leaves, and then cooked. The practice of stuffing meat into unusual wrappings is quite common, for example Nham fermented semi-dry Thai sausage packed in banana leaves, Korean sausage stuffed into squid body or Italian Zampone stuffed into pork's front trotter (leg).

Back fat	300 g	0.66 lb
Onions	150 g	0.33 lb
Blood	275 ml	0.60 lb
Corn flour	225 g	0.49 lb
Wheat flour	50 g	0.11 lb

Ingredients per 1 kg (2.2 lb) of material

Salt	12 g	2 tsp
Pimentón, sweet	10 g	5 tsp
Pimentón, hot	2.0 g	1 tsp
Parsley, chopped	1 bunch	2 Tbsp

Cook cabbage in water until leaves can be separated. This makes them soft and pliable.
Grind back fat through 3 mm (1/8") plate.
In a mixing bowl place fat, chopped onions, parsley, spices and flours. Mix all together and start adding blood slowly until a dough like texture is obtained.
Shape the sausage mass into balls. Then wrap the cabbage leaf around the ball.
Lace the stuffed sausage with twine all around.
Immerse sausages in a boiling water and cook for 90-120 minutes depending on size. Drain and cool in air.
Refrigerate.

Notes
Serve by cutting the sausage into discs and frying in hot oil.

Farinato

Farinato is a sausage which contains no meat, just lard, flour and pimentón. The sausage is popular in provinces of Salamanca, Zamora and León in Castlla-León region of Spain. There is a similar Portuguese sausage called Farinheira ("farinha" denotes flour in Portuguese). Originally, thought to be the food of poor people, Farinato has gained widespread acceptance to such a degree that a native of Ciudad Rodrigo (*Rodrigo City*) is nicknamed "farinato."

White wheat bread, without crust	450 g	0.99 lb
Vegetable oil	230 ml	7.66 oz fl
Lard	230 g	0.50 lb
Flour	90 g	0.20 lb

Ingredients per 1 kg (2.2 lb) of material

Salt	12 g	2 tsp
Pimentón, sweet	16 g	8 tsp
Onion	90 g	1 medium

Cook onion in water for 45 minutes. Drain.
Grind onion, bread and lard together.
Mix the ground mixture with all other ingredients.
Stuff into 34-36 mm pork casings. Form 40 cm (16") loops with ends tied together.
Dry sausages at 18° C (64° F) for three days. In traditional production the sausages were hung in the kitchen above the wood fired stove for 3 days.
Move sausage to a drying chamber and dry them at 12-14° C (53 -57° F), 75% humidity, for 15 days.

Notes
The sausage is ready to eat – serve raw or fried.
Often used: pumpkin, aniseed and aguardiente (aniseed flavored liqueur).

Fariñon

Fariñón also known as *fariña* is large thick blood sausage very popular in Candás, in Asturias region of Spain.

Pork back fat	300 g	0.66 lb
Onions	300 g	0.66 lb
Pork blood	250 ml	1 cup
Corn flour	150 g	0.33 lb

Ingredients per 1 kg (2.2 lb) of material

Salt	12 g	2 tsp
Black pepper	2.0 g	1 tsp
Pimentón	10 g	5 tsp
Oregano, rubbed	3.0 g	3 tsp
Parsley, chopped	1 bunch	3 Tbsp
Nutmeg	1.0 g	1/2 tsp
Cloves, ground	0.3 g	1/8 tsp

Cut back fat into 8-10 mm (3/8") pieces.

Mix fat, chopped onion, oregano and chopped parsley together. Add blood and flour and mix again.

Stuff into 50 mm pork or 60 mm beef middles.

Cook in water at 80° C (176° F) for 90-120 minutes.

To serve, cut into slices and fry until crispy.

Figatells

Figatells is a fresh Spanish sausage made of pork meat, pork liver and kidneys. The sausage is popular in the regions of Valencia and Aragon. It is a type of hamburger which is wrapped in caul fat membrane and then fried or grilled.

Semi-fat pork		
(70/30, lean to fat)	400 g	0.88 lb
Pork liver	300 g	0.66 lb
Pork kidneys	300 g	0.66 lb

Ingredients per 1 kg (2.2 lb) of meat

Salt	18 g	3 tsp
Black pepper	2.0 g	1 tsp
Nutmeg	1.0 g	1/2 tsp
Chopped parsley	1 bunch	3 Tbsp

Rinse kidneys well in water, drain and cut in halves. Remove any veins and connective tissues. Immerse in cold water for 1 hour. Change water and soak again for 2 hours. Repeat the procedure until the water becomes clear.
Scald liver in hot water for 5 minutes.
Grind all meats with 5 mm (1/4") plate.
Mix meat with all ingredients. Form meat balls.
Wrap each meat ball with a sheet of caul fat. Flatten into meat patty shape. Refrigerate.
Cook before serving. Figatells are usually fried or grilled and served with potatoes and vegetables or on toasted bread, often with fried onions.

Notes
Caul fat is a type of fat netting that separated abdomen from intestines. It is a white and very firm membrane that can be purchased already cleaned and scalded. Used often in making fancy products like French crépinette, Swiss atriau, or roulades and pâtés.
Occasionally garlic and pine nuts are added.

Fuet de Barcelona

Fuet is a Spanish pork sausage, dry cured, like salami. It is a smaller version of salchichón. Fuet sausage is frequently found in Catalonia, Spain. Unlike the Butifarra, another in the family of Catalan sausages, fuet is dry cured. The name fuet means whip (*látigo*) in the Catalan language. Fuet de Barcelona is closely related to much smaller Secallona, Sumaya (Somalla) or Espatec. The main difference is that fuet is covered with mold and the small sausages mentioned above are not.

Lean pork	600 g	1.32 lb
Skinless pork belly	400 g	0.88 lb

Ingredients per 1 kg (2.2 lb) of meat

Salt	25 g	4 tsp
Cure #1	2.5 g	1/2 tsp
White pepper	3.0 g	1.5 tsp
Sugar	5.0 g	1 tsp

Grind lean pork and pork belly through 6-8 mm (1/4") plate.
Mix all ingredients with meat.
Stuff into 34-36 mm pork casings making straight links.
Dry at 14-15° C (54-59° F), 75-80% humidity for 12 days.
Store sausages at 10-12° C (50-53° F), <75% humidity or refrigerate.

Notes
Fuet is covered with white mold.

Girella

Girella and Chireta are similar, the sausage is called Girella in Catalonia and
Chireta in Aragón. The main ingredients are lamb offal meat (heart, lungs, tripe,
liver, head meat) and rice. Girella is very similar to Butifarra Blanca.

Lamb hearts, lungs, head meat	400 g	0.88 lb
Pork ham (leg)	100 g	0.22 lb
Pork belly, pork trimmings	100 g	0.22 lb
Rice	350 g	0.77 lb
Bread crumbs or dry white bread	50 g	0.11 lb

Ingredients per 1 kg (2.2 lb) of meat

Salt	12 g	2 tsp
Pepper, white	2.0 g	1 tsp
Garlic, smashed	7.0 g	2 cloves
Parsley, chopped	1 bunch	2 Tbsp
Nutmeg	1.0 g	1/2 tsp
Eggs	3 eggs	3 eggs
Saffron, flakes	5 flakes	5 flakes

Cook rice, but don't overcook.
Cook offal meats for 15 minutes. Cut into smaller pieces. Save 120 ml (1/2 cup)
of meat stock.
Soak bread crumbs in 90 ml (3 oz fl) of meat stock.
Immerse saffron in 30 ml (2 Tbsp) of meat stock.
Grind all other meat through 5 mm (1/4") plate.
Beat the eggs.
Mix meats with all ingredients and rice.
Prepare sheep stomach. The stomach is cleaned with white vinegar then rinsed
very well before filling. The stomach is cut with scissors into smaller sheets.
Each sheet is filled with sausage mix, folded over and sewn with twine. Fill
casing bags loosely as the rice will expand a little.
Cook in water at 80° C (176° F) for 30-40 minutes depending on the diameter of
the bag.
Refrigerate.

Notes
Chiretas are usually served hot as a main dish. They are also sliced, dipped in an
egg-flour batter, and fried to a golden color.

Güeña

Güeña is a Spanish dry diameter small sausage, popular in La Nueva which is the region of Castilla-La Mancha and Madrid.

Lean pork	300 g	0.66 lb
Pork belly	400 g	0.88 lb
Pork liver, lungs, heart	300 g	0.66 lb

Ingredients per 1 kg (2.2 lb) of meat

Salt	28 g	4.5 tsp
Cure #1	2.5 g	1/2 tsp
Black pepper	2.0 g	1 tsp
Pimentón, sweet	25 g	4 Tbsp
Pimentón, hot	2.0 g	1 tsp
Nutmeg	1.0 g	1/2 tsp
Cloves, ground	0.3 g	1/8 tsp
Garlic	3.5 g	1 clove

Cook lungs and heart in water for 30 minutes. Drain and cool.
Scald liver in hot water for 5 minutes. Drain and cool.
Grind all meats through 6 mm (1/4") plate.
Mix with all ingredients. Hold for 12 hours in refrigerator.
Stuff into 20-24 mm sheep casings forming 10-15 cm (4-6") links.
Dry at 12-15° C (53-59° F), 75-80% humidity for 14 days.

Notes
Fry in oil or grill and serve with eggs and potatoes on sandwiches or in stews.

Imperial de Bolaños

Imperial de Bolaños is a type of finely ground salchichón. When salchichón is stuffed into casing smaller than than 40 mm, it may be called *longaniza imperial*. It originates in Bolaños de Calatrava, a city situated in the Ciudad Real province in the autonomous community of Castile-La Mancha, Spain.

Lean pork	750 g	1.55 lb
Back fat or		
hard fat trimmings	250 g	0.55 lb

Ingredients per 1 kg (2.2 lb) of meat

Salt	20 g	3 tsp
Cure #1	2.5 g	1/2 tsp
Pepper	4.0 g	2 tsp
Nutmeg	0.5 g	¼ tsp
Oregano	1.0 g	1 tsp

Grind lean pork and fat through 3 mm (1/8") plate.

Mix ground meats with salt and spices. Hold for 24 hours in refrigerator.

Stuff the mixture into 38-40 mm natural casings forming straight links 30 cm (12") long.

Dry/ferment at 20-27° C (68-80° F), 90-85% humidity, for 30 hours.

Dry at 15-12° C (59-53° F), 85-75% humidity, for 15 days.

Store at 10-12° C (50-53° F), <70% humidity or refrigerate.

Notes

The sausage is ready to eat without cooking.

Imperial de Lorca

Imperial de Lorca is a well-known dry longaniza from Lorca. Lorca is a municipality and city in the autonomous community of Murcia in southeastern Spain and this is where the sausage originates from. When salchichón is stuffed into casing smaller than than 40 mm, it may be called *longaniza imperial.*

Lean pork	700 g	1.54 lb
Pork belly	300 g	0.66 lb

Ingredients per 1 kg (2.2 lb) of meat

Salt	25 g	4 tsp
Cure #1	2.5 g	1/2 tsp
White pepper	3.0 g	1.5 tsp
Nutmeg	0.5 g	1/4 tsp

Grind lean pork and belly through 6 mm (1/4") plate.
Mix ground meats with salt and spices. Hold for 24 hours in refrigerator.
Stuff into 38-40 mm calf casings forming links 20 cm (8") long.
Dry at 15-12° C (59-53° F), 85-75% humidity for 15-20 days.
Store at 10-12° C (50-53° F), <70% humidity or refrigerate.

Notes
Consume raw.

Llangonisa Rotja - Alicantina

Llangonisa Rotja or Llonganissa Alacantina (in Valencian language which is a dialect of Catalan) is a longaniza sausage popular in País Valenciano region of Spain. This all pork dry sausage is stuffed into small diameter natural casing and dried for about 3 weeks. Then it is ready to eat, but may be fried or grilled.

Pork, semi-fat*	700 g	1.54 lb
Pork, lean	300 g	0.66 lb

Ingredients per 1 kg (2.2 lb) of meat

Salt	28 g	4.5 tsp
Cure #1	2.5 g	1/2 tsp
Pepper	4.0 g	2 tsp
Pimentón	10 g	5 tsp
Cloves, ground	0.3 g	1/8 tsp

Grind meats through 8-10 mm (3/8") plate.

Mix ground meat with salt and spices. Hold in refrigerator for 24 hours.

Stuff into 20-22 mm sheep or hog casings. Form links about 35-40 cm (13-16") long.

Dry at 16-12° C (59-53° F), 75-85% humidity for 15-20 days.

Store at 10-12° C (50-53° F), <65% humidity or in refrigerator.

Notes

* pork shoulder (butt) is a good choice.

Consume raw, fried or grilled.

Lomo Embuchado

Spanish cured loin. The loin is marinated, stuffed into casings and dried whole. If the loin comes from pigs of Iberian breed, a distinction is made and we speak of Iberian loin. The embuchado loin is eaten raw, cut into thin slices and served as a tapa, sometimes in a sandwich.

| Whole loin | 2-3 kg | 4.4-6.6 lb |

Ingredients per 1 kg (2.2 lb) of meat

Coarse salt for salting loin, *as needed.*

Cure #2	5.0 g	1 tsp
Pimentón, sweet	25 g	4 Tbsp
Pimentón, hot	5.0 g	1 tsp
Oregano, ground	2.0 g	1 tsp
Cumin, ground	1.0 g	1/2 tsp
Bay leaf, ground	0.25 g	1/8 tsp
Garlic, smashed	7.0 g	2 cloves
White wine or vinegar	30 ml	2 Tbsp
Olive oil	60 ml	2 oz fl

Trim off the skin and connective tissue from the loin. Using force rub in a generous amount of coarse salt (as needed) all over loin. The loin should rest in a suitable container on a layer of salt and be well covered with salt all around leaving no exposed areas. Hold in refrigerator for 24 hours.
Brush off the salt, wash briefly in running water and pat dry with paper towels. Mix all ingredients with wine and oil together to form the marinade paste. Remainder: *multiply the above ingredients per weight of loin.* No more salt is needed.
Apply the paste all around the loin. Hold in refrigerator for 48 hours.
Stuff the loin into pork bungs that will tightly accommodate the piece.
Ferment/dry at 22-24° C (72-75° F), 85-90% humidity, for 2 days.
Dry at 15→12° C (59-53° F), 85→75% humidity for 2 months. The loin should lose about 35% of its original weight.
Store at 10-12° C (°F), <75% humidity.

Notes

The size of the casing is chosen to fit the loin snugly. A little oil is occasionally applied to the surface of the loin to make the operation easier. One end of the loin is tied with butcher twine and the loin is pulled through the casing. Then both ends are tied and a hanging loop is created. Pork bung is a traditionally used casing for drying loins and its structure (surface holes) is perfect for extended drying. Artificial casings can also be used as long as they are permeable (allow moisture and smoke to go through). The drying cycle is shorter so weigh the loin to verify that it lost 33% of its original weight.

Lomo Embuchado de Huelva (Caña de Lomo)

Caña de Lomo (Lomo Embuchado de Huelva) originates in Huelva, an old port city in southwestern Spain, the capital of the province of Huelva in the autonomous region of Andalusia. To the north of the city there is a number of mountain ranges and national parks with many oak forests (*dehesa*) where Iberian pigs roam free and feed between December and April on oak acorns (*bellota*). During that time an average Iberian pig (Pata Negra) consumes 10-11 kg (22 lbs) of acorns each day. This diet influences the flavor and the texture of its meat and fat.

Whole Iberian pig pork loin   2-3 kg   4.4-6.6 lb

Ingredients per 1 kg (2.2 lb) of meat

Coarse salt for salting loin, *as needed.*
Cure #2	5.0 g	1 tsp
Pimentón, sweet	30 g	5 Tbsp
Pimentón, hot	2.0 g	1 tsp
Garlic, diced	7.0 g	2 cloves
Olive oil	60 ml	2 oz fl
White wine	30 ml	2 Tbsp

Trim off the skin and connective tissue from the loin. Using force rub in a generous amount of coarse salt (as needed) all over loin. The loin should rest in a suitable container on a layer of salt and be well covered with salt all around leaving no exposed areas. Hold in refrigerator for 24 hours.
Brush off the salt, wash briefly in running water and pat dry with paper towels. Mix all ingredients with wine and oil together to form the marinade paste.
Remainder: *multiply the above ingredients per weight of loin.*
Apply the paste all around the loin. Hold in refrigerator for 48 hours.
Stuff the loin into pork bungs that will tightly accommodate the loin.
Dry at 14-15° C (58-59° F), 75% humidity for 2-3 months depending on diameter. If needed, the temperature was regulated by burning wood in the drying chamber, so the loin was also cold smoked. The loin should lose about 33% of its original weight. Store at 10-12° C (°F), <75% humidity.

Notes
Consume raw.
The size of the casing is chosen to fit the loin snugly. A little oil is occasionally applied to the surface of the loin to make the operation easier. One end of the loin is tied with butcher twine and the loin is pulled through the casing. Then both ends are tied and a hanging loop is created. Pork bung is a traditionally used casing for drying loins and its structure (surface holes) is perfect for extended drying. Artificial casings can also be used as long as they are permeable (allow moisture and smoke to go through). The drying cycle is shorter so weigh the loin to verify that it lost 33% of its original weight.

Lomo Embuchado de Segovia

Lomo embuchado is a Spanish pork loin which is cured with salt, garlic and paprika and stuffed into a natural or artificial permeable casing. The loin is left to dry for 2-3 months depending on its diameter. As its name suggests Lomo Embuchado de Segovia originates in Segovia city in Segovia province of Castilla-León region of Spain.

| Whole loin | 2-3 kg | 4.4-6.6 lb |

Ingredients per 1 kg (2.2 lb) of meat

Coarse salt for salting loin, *as needed.*

Cure #2	5.0 g	1 tsp
Pimentón, sweet	30 g	5 Tbsp
Pimentón, hot	2.0 g	1 tsp
Oregano	3.0 g	3 tsp
Garlic	10 g	3 cloves
Olive oil	60 ml	2 oz fl

Trim off the skin and connective tissue from the loin. Using force rub in a generous amount of salt (as needed) all over loin. The loin should rest in a suitable container on a layer of salt and be well covered with salt all around leaving no exposed areas. Hold in refrigerator for 24 hours.

Brush off the salt, wash briefly in running water and pat dry with paper towels.

Mix all ingredients with wine and oil together to form the marinade paste.

Remainder: *multiply the above ingredients per weight of loin.*

Apply the paste all around the loin. Hold in refrigerator for 48 hours.

Wipe off the paste and stuff the loin into 55-70 mm beef bungs (tripa cular). The length of stuffed loin around 70-90 cm (28").

Ferment/dry at 18-22° C (64-72° F), for 15 days.

Dry at 12-14° C (53-57° F), 75-80% humidity for 6-8 weeks until the sausage loses 33% of its original weight.

Notes

Consume raw.

The size of the casing is chosen to fit the loin snugly. A little oil is occasionally applied to the surface of the loin to make the operation easier. One end of the loin is tied with butcher twine and the loin is pulled through the casing. Then both ends are tied and a hanging loop is created. Pork bung is a traditionally used casing for drying loins and its structure (surface holes) is perfect for extended drying. Artificial casings can also be used as long as they are permeable (allow moisture and smoke to go through). The drying cycle is shorter so weigh the loin to verify that it lost 33% of its original weight.

Lomo Embuchado Ibérico

Lomo Embuchado Ibérico is a very popular sausage in the province of Salamanca in Castilla-León region of Spain.

Whole iberian pork loin   2-3 kg   4.4-6.6 lb

Ingredients per 1 kg (2.2 lb) of meat

Cure #1 - see brine instructions below

Pimentón, sweet	30 g	4 Tbsp
Pimentón, hot	2.0 g	1 tsp
Oregano, dry	3.0 g	3 tsp
Bay leaf, crushed	1 leaf	1 leaf
Garlic, smashed	7.0 g	2 cloves
Lime juice	15 ml	1 Tbsp

Trim off the skin and connective tissue from the loin. Hold in refrigerator for 24 hours at 0-2° C (32-35° F).

Make a strong curing solution of Baume 20° (80° Salometer) by dissolving 290 g of salt and 40 g of cure #1 in 1250 ml of water. This amount of brine is enough for 2-3 kg loin.

Immerse loin into the curing solution, keep it submerged and hold in refrigerator for 3-4 days. Wash the loin briefly with water to remove salt crystals, then soak it in cold water for 12-24 hours to equalize salt distribution. Hang it to dry until the loin stops dripping water. Pat it dry with paper towels.

Stuff loin into 50-80 mm veal or beef bungs. The length of stuffed loin around 50-70 cm (20-28").

Ferment/dry at 18-20° C (64-68° F), 80-85% humidity, for 24-48 hours.

Dry at 12-14° C (53-57° F), 75-80% humidity, for 2-3 months until the loin loses about 33% of its original weight.

Notes

The inside color of the sausage is vivid red interfaced with streaks of white fat.

Old kitchen stoves used wood for fuel and had removable top plates. Removing the plates or partially covering fire allowed control of room temperature or application of smoke. As an additional bonus the sausages acquired different flavors from foods which were being cooked on the stove. In traditional home production, after stuffing, the loin was hung above the kitchen stove for 3-4 days. Then the drying continued in any suitable chamber for about 3 months.

Lomo Ibérico de Bellota

The famous Iberian black pig, popularly known as *Pata Negra* due to its characteristic black hoof, still wanders free in "dehesas", an indigenous oak forest of the southern Spanish region of Andalusia. Pata Negra pigs feed exclusively on fallen oak acorns, known as "bellota", for three months prior to slaughter. This special diet of acorns, herbs and grass, along with lots of exercise gives Iberian meat its delicate flavor and a texture. The pig fat inherits properties of foods the animal consumes and as fat is the carrier of flavor, the Iberic meat develops wonderful flavor and texture, the meat of Lomo Ibérico de Bellota is marbled with acorn flavored fat. The very famous Spanish ham "Jamón Ibérico" is also made from black Iberian pigs. The Andalusian area in where oak forests grow is known as the Valle de Pedroches and lies in Córdoba Province, Andalusia, southern Spain. This valley was called Fahs al-Ballut by the Moorish rulers of ancient Spain, meaning "Valley of the Acorns."

Iberian pig pork loin	2-3 kg	4.4-6.6 lb

Ingredients per 1 kg (2.2 lb) of meat

Coarse salt for salting loin, *as needed.*

Cure #2	5.0 g	1 tsp
Pimentón, sweet	25 g	4 Tbsp
Pimentón, hot	6.0 g	1 Tbsp
Nutmeg	1.5 g	3/4 tsp
Oregano	4.0 g	4 tsp
Garlic, smashed	10.0 g	3 cloves
Olive oil	45 ml	3 Tbsp
Lemon juice	15 ml	1 Tbsp

Remainder: *multiply the above ingredients per weight of loin.*
Trim off the skin and connective tissue from the loin. Using force rub in a generous amount of salt (as needed) all over loin. The loin should rest in a suitable container on a layer of salt and be well covered with salt all around leaving no exposed areas. Hold in refrigerator for 24 hours.
Brush off the salt, wash briefly in running water and pat dry with paper towels.
Mix spices, cure #2, lemon juice and oil. Rub in all over the loin. Marinate in refrigerator for 48 hours.
Stuff the loin into 55-70 mm pork or beef bungs, about 50-70 cm (20-28") long.
Dry/ferment at 18-20° C (64-68° F), 80-85% humidity, for 24-48 hours.
Dry at 12-14° C (53-57° F), 75-80% humidity, for 3 months.

Notes
Consume raw.
The loin is clear red on outside and vivid red on inside.
In traditional production the temperature was controlled by slow-burning of oak logs.

Lomo Ibérico Extremeńo

Lomo Ibérico Extremeńo originates in Extremadura, a western Spanish region bordering Portugal and comprises the provinces of Cáceres and Badajoz. It's a remote area of mountains, forests, lakes/ plenty of oak trees and reserves. Black Iberian pigs roam in the area and consume acorns from oak groves. This special diet of acorns, herbs and grass, along with lots of exercise gives Iberic meat its delicate flavor and a texture.

Iberian pig pork loin   2-3 kg   4.4-6.6 lb

Ingredients per 1 kg (2.2 lb) of meat

Cure #1 - see brine instructions below
Pimentón de la Vera   25 g   4 Tbsp
Oregano, dry   3.0 g   3 tsp
Garlic, smashed   15 g   4 cloves

Trim off the skin and connective tissue from the loin. Hold in refrigerator for 24 hours at 0-2° C (32-35° F).
Make a strong curing solution of Baume 20° (80° Salometer) by dissolving 290 g of salt and 40 g of cure #1 in 1250 ml of water. This amount of brine is enough for 2-3 kg loin.
Immerse loin into the curing solution, keep it submerged and hold in refrigerator for 3-4 days. Wash the loin briefly with water to remove salt crystals, then soak it in cold water for 12-24 hours to equalize salt distribution. Hang it to dry until the loin stops dripping water. Pat it dry with paper towels.
Mix spices with a small amount of water or white wine to create paste.
Remainder: multiply the above ingredients per weight of loin.
Rub the paste into the loin all around and hold for 48 hours in refrigerator.
Stuff into 55-70 mm pork bung forming straight links about 45-60 cm (18-24") long.
Hold in a drying chamber at 10-12° C (50-53° F), 80% humidity, for 40 days.
Hold at room temperature (or in drying chamber) at 18° C (64° F) or lower until fully cured which will take about 3-4 months, depending on the diameter of the sausage and drying conditions.

Lomo Picado

Lomo picado is a formed loin made of large loin trimmings. A similar product to molded ham, the difference is that the ham pieces are held together under pressure in a mold and cooked in water, and loin pieces are stuffed tightly in a casing and fermented and dried. This of course results in a different texture and flavor.

Loin pieces must be well trimmed of any fat, silver screen (film) and connective tissue otherwise they will not stick together well. They should be cold and cut with a sharp knife to obtain a clean surface. The salt will do the rest, the cells will release proteins which will dissolve in salt and this solution known as "exudate" will glue individual meat cuts together.

Pork loin pieces	1 kg	2.2 lb

Ingredients per 1 kg (2.2 lb) of meat

Salt	25 g	4 tsp
Cure #2	3.0 g	1/2 tsp
Dextrose	2 g	1/2 tsp
Sugar	3.0 g	1/2 tsp
Pimentón, sweet	25 g	4 Tbsp
Pimentón, hot	5.0 g	1 tsp
Oregano, ground	2.0 g	1 tsp
Thyme, ground	0.5 g	1/4 tsp
Rosemary	0.3 g	1/8 tsp
Garlic, diced	7.0 g	2 cloves

Trim off the skin and connective tissue from loin pieces which should be about 1-3 cm (1/4 - 1") in size.
Mix meat with all ingredients well together. Hold in refrigerator for 48 hours.
Stuff tightly into 50-80 mm pork bungs, synthetic permeable casings or blind cap (caecum).
Ferment at 20-22° C (68-72° F), 95→90% humidity, for 48 hours.
Dry at 15→12° C (59-53° F), 85→75% humidity for 2-3 months, depending on diameter. The loin should lose around 33% of its original weight.
Store at 10-12° C (°F), <75% humidity.

Notes
Using smaller diameter casings will result in a shorter drying time.

Longanisa

Longanisa is a Filipino version of a Spanish Longaniza sausage. Longaniza is also popular in Argentina, Chile, Mexico and all other Spanish speaking countries including the Caribbean Islands like Cuba and the Dominican Republic. And of course there are different varieties of Longaniza. In 1565 Spanish Conquistador, Miguel López de Legazpi arrived in Cebu, Philippines from Mexico (New Spain) and established the permanent Spanish settlement that lasted over three hundred years. This brought catholic religion, Spanish law, administration, and new culture. Culinary arts were no exception and Spanish sausages were introduced as well. They had to be somewhat modified due to a different hot and humid climate, but their names remained the same. The most popular sausage in the Philippines is Longanisa (in Spain called Longaniza) and it has a distinctive flavor in each region of the country: Lucban is heavy on garlic and oregano, Guagua is saltier with more vinegar than finger-sized sausages from Guinobatan. Traditional Longanisa may be dried (conditions permitting) and sometimes smoked, however, it can be kept fresh or frozen and cooked. Unlike Spanish longaniza, Filipino Longanisa can be made of chicken or even tuna.

Pork 70/30 (lean/fat)	1000 g	2.20 lb

Ingredients per 1 kg (2.2 lb) of meat

Salt	18 g	3 tsp
Pepper	2.5 g	1 tsp
Sugar	2.5 g	½ tsp
Paprika	6.0 g	3 tsp
Garlic	7.0 g	2 cloves
Oregano, rubbed	2.0 g	2 tsp
Onion, diced	30 g	1/3 onion
White vinegar	50 ml	1/5 cup
Cold water	50 ml	1/5 cup

Cut pork into small cubes or grind through 10-12 mm (3/8-1/2") plate.
Mix all ingredients with water and pour over ground meat and mix well together.
Stuff into 32 mm or smaller hog casings and twist them into 4-5" (10-12 cm) links. Using cotton twine, tie the ends of each sausage link tightly, then cut between each link to separate.
Store in refrigerator.
Cook before serving - fry on a frying pan until golden brown.

Longaniza

Longaniza is a Spanish long and slim sausage which can be fresh, dry or smoked and dried. The sausage mix composition and processing steps are similar to that of chorizo, but longanizas are much longer, around 30-50 cm (12-30").

Pork, semi-fat	800 g	1.76 lb
Back fat	200 g	0.44 lb

Ingredients per 1 kg (2.2 lb) of meat

Salt	28 g	4.5 tsp
Cure #1	2.5 g	1/2 tsp
Pepper	4.0 g	2 tsp
Pimentón, sweet	20 g	3.5 Tbsp
Pimentón, hot	2.0 g	1 tsp
Oregano, ground	1.0 g	1/2 tsp
Nutmeg	0.5 g	1/4 tsp
Garlic	3.5 g	1 clove
Wine	15 ml	1 Tbsp
Water	60 ml	2 oz fl

Smash garlic and using mortar and pestle grind it with wine into the paste.
Grind meat and back fat through 10-12 mm (3/8-1/2") plate.
Mix meat, fat and all ingredients adding water as necessary to produce a firm paste. Hold the paste for 48 hours in refrigerator.
Stuff into 34-36 mm pork or beef casings forming 40-60 cm (16-24") sections.
Dry/ferment at 22-24° C (72-75° F) for 24 hours, 90-85% humidity.
Dry sausages for 16 days at 12-15° C (53-59° F), 75-80% humidity.
Store at 10° C (50° F) in a cool and ventilated area or refrigerate.

Longaniza Andaluza

Longaniza from Andalusia, the southern region of Spain.

Pork, semi-fat	1000 g	2.2 lb

Ingredients per 1 kg (2.2 lb) of meat

Salt	28 g	4.5 Tbsp
Cure #1	2.5 g	1/2 tsp
Pepper, black	2.0 g	1 tsp
Pimentón, sweet	25 g	4 Tbsp
Oregano, ground	1.0 g	1/2 tsp
Cinnamon	1.0 g	1/2 tsp
Garlic, smashed	3.5 g	1 clove
White wine	30 ml	1 oz fl
Water	60 ml	2 oz fl

Grind meat through 12 mm (1/2") plate.

Mix meat with all ingredients. Hold for 48 hours in refrigerator.

Stuff into 36 mm pork or beef casings, making sections 40-60 cm (16-24") long.

Apply a thin smoke at 22-24° C (72-75° F) (smoking step optional) or dry sausages at 22-24° C (72-75° F) for 24 hours.

Dry at 15-12° C (59-54° F), 75-80% humidity for 15 days.

Store sausages at 10-12° C (50-53° F), <70% humidity or refrigerate.

Notes

Shoulder butt is a good cut for this sausage.

Longaniza de Aragón

Longaniza de Aragón is a Spanish semi-dry sausage popular in the region of Aragón. The sausage is made with lean pork, pork belly, back fat, and aromatic spices such as cinnamon, cloves, nutmeg and anise. It includes typical chorizo spices like oregano and garlic, *but no pimentón*, just regular pepper. The color of longaniza differs from that of chorizo due to the lack of pimentón.

Pork, lean	750 g	1.65 lb
Pork belly	150 g	0.33 lb
Back fat	100 g	0.22 lb

Ingredients per 1 kg (2.2 lb) of meat

Salt	28 g	4.5 tsp
Cure #1	2.5 g	1/2 tsp
Sugar	3.0 g	1/2 tsp
Pepper	2.0 g	1 tsp
Nutmeg	0.5 g	1/4 tsp
Star anise, ground	0.3 g	1/8 tsp
Cloves	0.3 g	1/8 tsp
Cinnamon	1.0 g	1/2 tsp
Oregano, dry	2.0 g	2 tsp
Garlic	7.0 g	2 cloves
Water	30 ml	2 Tbsp

Grind meat and fat through 8 mm (3/8") plate.

Mix ground meats with all ingredients. Hold the mixture for 24-36 hours in refrigerator.

Stuff into 22-32 mm pork or sheep casings, making horseshoe loops about 40 cm (16") long. Hold for 8-10 hours in refrigerator or at low temperature.

Hang the sausages for 3-4 days at 15-20° C (59-68° F), 60-70% humidity. At this point longaniza can be classified a semi-dry sausage which is served fried or cooked.

To make a dry sausage continue drying at 12-15° C (53-59° F), 75-90% for 1-2 weeks depending on diameter. The dry sausage can be consumed raw.

Longaniza de Mezcla

Depending on a region of Spain this longaniza can be made from lean pork, semi-fat pork, including some offal meat (lungs, heart) or pork and beef.

Beef, lean	550 g	1.21 lb
Pork, semi-fat (shoulder)	350 g	0.77 lb
Pork back fat	100 g	0.22 lb

Ingredients per 1 kg (2.2 lb) of meat

Salt	28 g	4.5 tsp
Cure #1	2.5 g	1/2 tsp
Pepper	4.0 g	2 tsp
Pimentón, sweet	10 g	5 tsp
Pimentón, hot	10 g	5 tsp
Oregano, ground	1.0 g	1/2 tsp
Garlic	3.5 g	1 clove
Wine	15 ml	1 Tbsp
Water	60 ml	2 oz fl

Smash garlic and using mortar and pestle grind it with wine into the paste.
Grind meat and back fat through 12 mm (1/2") plate.
Mix meat, fat and all ingredients adding water as necessary to produce a firm paste.
Hold the paste for 48 hours in refrigerator.
Stuff into 25-35 mm veal casings forming 40-60 cm (16-24") sections. Prick air pockets with a needle.
Ferment at 24° C (75° F) for 12 hours, 90-85% humidity.
Dry sausages for 12-14 days at 12-15° C (53-59° F), 75-80% humidity.
Store at 10° C (53° F) in a cool and ventilated area or refrigerate.

Longaniza de Pascua

Longaniza de Pascua is a Valencian small diameter dry sausage made at Easter time ("Pascua" means Easter in Spanish). This snack type sausage is made with pork and veal and the drying process is relatively short due to the small diameter of the sausage.

Pork, lean	300 g	0.66 lb
Veal	300 g	0.66 lb
Semi-fat pork	400 g	0.88 lb

Ingredients per 1 kg (2.2 lb) of meat

Salt	25 g	4 tsp
Cure #1	2.5 g	1/2 tsp
Black pepper	4.0 g	2 tsp
Anise, ground	1.0 g	½ tsp

Grind all meats through 8-10 mm (3/8") plate.
Mix meat with salt and spices.
Stuff into 12 mm sheep casings forming 20-30 cm (8-12") long links.
Dry at 18→12° C (64→59° F) for 7-10 days.
Store at 10-12° C (50-53° F) in a cool and ventilated area or refrigerate.

Longaniza de Payés

The name of this longaniza is derived from the catalan word "pagès" which means "peasant." Longaniza de Payés is a narrow and long dry sausage covered with mold.

Lean pork, shoulder	800 g	1.76 lb
Pork belly	200 g	0.44 lb

Ingredients per 1 kg (2.2 lb) of meat

Salt	28 g	4.5 tsp
Cure #1	2.5 g	1/2 tsp
Black pepper	2.0 g	1 tsp
Dextrose	2.0 g	1/2 tsp
Sugar	2.0 g	1/2 tsp
Sweet sherry	15 ml	1 Tbsp

Grind meat and fat through 6 mm (1/4") plate.

Mix meat, fat and all ingredients. Hold the paste for 48 hours in refrigerator.

Stuff into 55 mm pork middles. Prick air pockets with a needle.

Dry/ferment at 24° C (75° F) for 12 hours, 90-85% humidity.

Dry sausages for 30 days at 12-15° C (53-59° F), 75-80% humidity.

Store at 10° C (53° F) in a cool and ventilated area or refrigerate.

Longaniza Dominicana

Traditional Dominican longaniza prepared with the juice of bitter oranges (*naranja de Sevilla*) or lime, garlic, oregano and salt.

Lean pork (shoulder)	700 g	1.54 lb
Back fat or		
hard fat trimmings	300 g	0.66 lb

Ingredients per 1 kg (2.2 lb) of meat

Salt	21 g	3.5 tsp
Cure #1	2.5 g	1/2 tsp
Sugar	5.0 g	1 tsp
Pepper	2.0 g	1 tsp
Paprika, sweet	6.0 g	3 tsp
Oregano, rubbed	6.0 g	6 tsp
Garlic, smashed	7.0 g	2 cloves
Juice of bitter oranges	60 ml	2 oz fl
Olive oil	15 ml	1 Tbsp

Grind pork through 8 mm (3/8") plate.

Mix ground meat with salt and cure #1 until sticky. Add all remaining ingredients and mix well together. Marinade for 12 hours in refrigerator.

Stuff firmly into 36 mm hog casings.

Dry at 20° C (68° F) for 2 days.* (To make dry sausage continue drying at 12-15° C (53-59° F), 75-80% humidity, for 14 days).

Refrigerate.

Cook before serving by pan frying or grilling.

Notes

For a hotter version add 1 g (1/2 tsp) of cayenne pepper or 1 tablespoon of Tabasco sauce.

* traditionally, the sausage was dried in the sun for 2 days.

Longaniza Fresca

Longaniza Fresca is a fresh sausage popular in Castellón de la Plana province of País Valenciano region of Spain. Castellón, is the capital city of the province of Castellón. The sausage is made with quality lean pork, lean cuts from shoulder are suitable, and pork belly. Aromatic spices such as cinnamon and nutmeg compliment the rest and the grilled sausage is a treat to enjoy.

| Lean pork | 400 g | 0.88 lb |
| Pork belly | 600 g | 1.32 lb |

Ingredients per 1 kg (2.2 lb) of meat

Salt	18 g	3 tsp
White pepper	2.0 g	1 tsp
Cinnamon	0.5 g	¼ tsp
Nutmeg	0.3 g	1/8 tsp

Grind meats through 10 mm (3/8") plate.
Mix with salt and spice.
Stuff into 22-24 mm sheep casings forming 10 cm (4") long links.
Refrigerate.

Notes
Cook fully before serving by frying or grilling.

Longaniza Murciana

Longaniza sausage is produced in many regions of Spain. This fresh longaniza originates from Murcia. It is made of pork and stuffed into small diameter casings. Longaniza can be of fresh variety which must be kept refrigerated and fully cooked before serving, or it can be dried in air becoming a dry sausage that can be eaten without cooking.

Lean pork	600 g	1.32 lb
Pork belly, skinless	400 g	0.88 lb

Ingredients per 1 kg (2.2 lb) of meat

Salt	18 g	3 tsp
Black pepper	2.0 g	1 tsp
Pimentón, sweet	20 g	3.5 Tbsp
Garlic	3.5 g	1 clove
Aniseed, whole seeds	3 seeds	3 seeds
Cinnamon	0.5 g	1/4 tsp
White wine	15 ml	1 Tbsp

Grind all meats through 3 mm (1/8") plate.
Mix meats with salt, wine and all spices.
Hold for 12 hours in refrigerator.
Stuff into 18-22 mm sheep casings forming 35-40 cm (13-16") loops or strings with 3 links, 12 cm (5") each.
Keep refrigerated.

Notes
Cook before serving.

Longaniza Navarra

Longaniza Navarra is a Spanish semi-dry or dry sausage originating in Navarra region of Spain. There are different varieties of longaniza depending whether it's made in Cataluńa, Aragon, Navarra, Andalucia or other Spanish regions. They are usually stuffed into 30-34 mm pork casings. Longaniza sausage is also made in Argentina, Chile and in Caribbean. This leads to different recipes each influenced by local conditions, for example in Dominican Republic longaniza is flavored with juice of bitter orange or lemon.

Pork belly	1000 g	2.2 lb

Ingredients per 1 kg (2.2 lb) of meat

Salt	25 g	4 tsp
Cure #1	2.5 g	½ tsp
Dextrose	2.0 g	1/2 tsp
Sugar	3.0 g	1/2 tsp
Pimentón	12 g	6 tsp
Garlic, smashed	7.0 g	2 cloves

Grind meat with 8 mm (3/8") plate.
Mix meat with all ingredients. Hold for 12 hours in refrigerator.
Stuff firmly into 30-34 mm hog casings forming long loops.
Dry/ferment at 24° C (75° F) for 12 hours, 90-85% humidity.
Dry at 15-12° C (59-54° F), 80% humidity for 8 days.
Store sausages at 10-12° C (50-53° F), <70% humidity or refrigerate.

Notes
The sausage is usually cooked or fried.

Longaniza Salamantina

Longaniza Salamantina is a dry sausage that originates in Salamanca, a city in northwestern Spain that is the capital of the Province of Salamanca in the community of Castile and León. It is made from Iberian pig whose meat is known for its superior texture and flavor.

Lean iberian* pork	750 g	1.55 lb
Pork belly or meat trimmings with attached fat	250 g	0.55 lb

Ingredients per 1 kg (2.2 lb) of meat

Salt	25 g	4 tsp
Cure #1	2.5 g	1/2 tsp
Pimentón, sweet	20 g	3.5 Tbsp
Oregano	3.0 g	3 tsp
Garlic, smashed	3.5 g	1 clove
White wine	15 ml	1 Tbsp

Cut or grind meats through 12 mm (1/2") plate.
Mix meats with salt and spices. Hold for 24 hours in refrigerator.
Stuff in 30-36 mm hog casings forming loops about 50 cm (20") long.
Dry/ferment at 17-18° C (62-64° F), 95→80% humidity for 24 hours.
Dry at 12-14° C (53-58° F), 70-75% humidity for 15-30 days.
Store sausages at 10-12° C (50-53° F), <70% humidity or refrigerate.

Notes
* from Iberian pig.
When the sausage was made in home conditions without the possibility of temperature and humidity control, the drying period varied from 1 to 2 months. The sausage maker, drawing on his experience had to decide when the sausage was done.
Consume raw or cooked.

Mondejo or Mondeju

Mondejo or Mondeju is a popular sausage in Gipuzkoa, Basque Country. This small province faces the Bay of Biscay in the north and shares its border with France in the east. Mondejo is made from sheep meat, vegetables, onions, leeks, eggs and it is stuffed into sheep casings. It looks like white blood sausage (*morcilla blanca*), but it is thinner and of yellowish color.

Sheep stomach	400 g	0.88 lb
Sheep fat	150 g	0.33 lb
Leeks	300 g	0.66 lb
Onions	150 g	0.33 lb

Ingredients per 1 kg (2.2 lb) of meat

Salt	18 g	3 tsp
Pepper	2.0 g	1 tsp
Nutmeg	1.0 g	1/2 tsp
Eggs	3 eggs	3
Parsley, chopped	1 bunch	3 Tbsp

Grind all meat and fat through 6 mm (1/4") plate.
Beat the eggs and mix with meats and all other ingredients.
Stuff the mixture into sheep casings forming a ring.
Cook in water at 80° C (176° F) for 2 hours. Serve or cool in air and refrigerate.

Notes
Serve with potatoes and cabbage or with spinach, fresh red peppers and olive oil. When made with sheep blood the sausage is called Mondejo Negro, leeks, parsley and eggs are not added.

Morcilla

Morcilla is a blood sausage, very popular in Spain and Latin America. A typical recipe follows below.

Pork blood	250 g	0.55 lb
Fat (beef suet, pork back fat, belly, pork fat trimmings	250 g	0.55 lb
Rice	250 g	0.55 lb
Onions, diced	250 g	0.55 lb

Ingredients per 1 kg (2.2 lb) of meat

Salt	18 g	3 tsp.
Black pepper	2.0 g	1 tsp
Pimentón, sweet	10.0 g	5 tsp
Pimentón, hot	4.0 g	2 tsp
Cinnamon	1.0 g	½ tsp
Cloves, ground	0.5 g	1/4 tsp
Oregano, ground	2.0 g	1 tsp

Peel onions and chop them finely. Mix them with rice and leave overnight in a suitable container. The rice will absorb onion juice and will increase in volume. Dice fat into 1/2" cubes.

Stuff loosely into 32-36 mm hog casings as the rice will still increase in volume during cooking. Make 12" rings.

Cook in a hot water at 80° C (176° F) for about 60 minutes. Use a needle to prick any sausage that comes to the top to remove air. Don't increase temperature as the casings may burst.

The color should be dark brown-red with white pieces of fat.

Notes

The remaining morcilla stock known as *calducho* is used for cooking.

Morcilla Achorizada

Morcilla achorizada is a popular blood sausage around Cordoba, Andalusia. The name is derived from chorizo as both sausages contain pimentón. Both are dried and look somewhat similar on outside.

Back fat, fat trimmings	300 g	0.66 lb
Blood	100 ml	0.22 lb
Pork trimmings		
with attached fat	200 g	0.44 lb
Pork skins	100 g	0.22 lb
Offal meat: pork heart,		
lungs, stomach, diaphragm	300 g	0.66 lb

Ingredients per 1 kg (2.2 lb) of meat

Salt	28 g	4.5 tsp
Pimentón, sweet	20 g	4 Tbsp
Pimentón, hot	2.0 g	1 tsp
Oregano, ground	1.0 g	1/2 tsp
Smashed garlic	3.5 g	1 clove

Cook heart, lungs, stomach, skins in hot water (below boiling point) until soft.
Grind through 5 mm (1/4") plate.
Grind meat and fat trimmings through 5 mm (1/4") plate.
Dice hard fat (back fat) into 6 mm (1/4") cubes.
Mix meat, fat and all ingredients together.
Stuff into 30-32 mm pork or sheep casings.
Dry in a low humidity, cool and well ventilated room, 12-15° C (53-59° F).

Morcilla Andaluza

Spanish blood sausage from Andalusia - the province in the south of Spain.

Onion	650 g	1.43 lb
Back fat, pork fat trimmings		
or lard	250 g	0.55 lb
Blood	100 ml	3.3 oz fl

Ingredients per 1 kg (2.2 lb) of materials

Salt	12 g	2 tsp
Pepper	2.0 g	1 tsp
Cumin	2.0 g	1 tsp
Pimentón, sweet	5.0 g	2.5 tsp
Garlic, diced	3.5 g	1 clove
Oregano, rubbed	1.0 g	1 tsp
Cilantro, finely cut	1.0 g	1 tsp
Cayenne	0.3 g	1/8 tsp
Cloves, ground	0.3 g	1/8 tsp

Grind fat through 1/8" (3 mm) plate.

Boil the onions until soft, drain and cut into little cubes. Cool. Mix onions with blood.

Place a frying pan on low heat, add ground fat and melt it down, stirring often. Mix onions, liquid fat and spices together.

Stuff into 36 mm hog casings making rings.

Cook in water at 80° C (176° F) for 30 minutes.

Cool and refrigerate.

Notes

To serve, fry in butter or barbecue.

Morcilla Asturiana

Morcilla Asturiana is a popular blood sausage in the Asturias region of Spain. The sausage is heavily smoked so it is almost black when finished. Onions are added raw or precooked.

Back fat, kidney fat	500 g	1.10 lb
Pork or beef blood	100 g	100 ml
Onions	400 g	0.88 lb

Ingredients per 1 kg (2.2 lb) of meat

Salt	18 g	3 tsp
Cure #1	1.0 g	1/4 tsp
Pimentón, sweet	15 g	2.5 Tbsp
Pimentón, hot	4.0 g	2 tsp
Oregano, dry	2.0 g	2 tsp

Dice fat into 6 mm (1/4") cubes.

Chop the onions. Mix fat, blood, onions and spices together.

Stuff into beef middles or 45 mm pork casing making 10-15 cm (4-6 inch) long links.

Start smoking with oak wood at 28-30° C (82-86° F), high humidity. As the smoking progresses start lowering temperature and humidity. This process continues for 6-7 days.

Notes

Occasionally the onions are diced and cooked in water. Then they are drained, placed on the table and cooled.

Morcilla Asturiana is dried longer when it is added to Fabada Asturiana (bean stew).

Morcilla Asturiana has a strong sharp smoky flavor that is not enjoyed on its own. It is better suited to be served with stews.

Morcilla Blanca

White sausage (*Morcilla blanca, "blanco"* means white in Spanish) is a variety of morcilla which is made without blood, so technically speaking it is not a blood sausage, but a cooked sausage (*salchicha cocida*). This nomenclature is not reserved to Spanish sausages, but is also used by other countries: England – *White Pudding* (English call blood sausage a "pudding", France – *Boudin Blanc* (blanc means white in French), Poland – *Biała Kaszanka* (biały means white in Polish, blood sausage is usually called Kaszanka or Kiszka Krwista). The processing steps remain the same as the ones for black morcilla, however, without blood the sausage develops a lighter color.

Lean pork	500 g	1.10 lb
Fat (pork back fat, belly, fat trimmings, dewlap, jowls)	300 g	0.66 lb
Cream	200 ml	7 oz fl

Ingredients per 1 kg (2.2 lb) of material

Salt	18 g	3 tsp
White pepper	3.0 g	1 ½ tsp
Cinnamon	1.0 g	½ tsp
Cloves, ground	0.5 g	1/4 tsp
Nutmeg	1.0 g	½ tsp
Whole egg, beaten	1 egg	1
Onion, chopped	60 g	1 onion
Parsley, chopped	1 Tbsp	1 Tbsp

Chop onion finely and fry in a little fat (oil) until glassy and gold.
Grind pork and back fat through 3 mm (1/8") plate.
Mix the beaten egg, cream and all ingredients in a blender. If no blender is available, mix manually.
Pour over ground meat and mix everything well together.
Stuff into 32-36 mm hog casings, forming 15 cm (6") links.
Cook in water at 80° C (176° F) 40 min. Do not boil, the sausages may burst open.
Store in a refrigerator.

Notes:
Eat cold, heat in water, fry or grill.
Lean pork - meat can come from shoulder, rear leg (ham), pork head, lean meat trimmings, tongue, as well as a small amount of liver or kidneys.
Optional - adding saffron flakes will create a sausage with a yellowish color.

Morcilla Blanca de Cazorla

White sausage from Cazorla originates in Sierras de Cazorla natural park in Andalusia, southern Spain.

Lean pork	500 g	1.10 lb
Fat (pork back fat, belly, fat trimmings, dewlap, jowls)	300 g	0.66 lb
Dry wheat bread	200 g	0.44 lb

Ingredients per 1 kg (2.2 lb) of material

Salt	18 g	3 tsp
White pepper	3.0 g	1 ½ tsp
Cinnamon	1.0 g	½ tsp
Cloves, ground	0.5 g	1/4 tsp
Nutmeg	1.0 g	½ tsp
Whole egg, beaten	2 eggs	2
Cream	60 ml	2 oz fl
Garlic, smashed	3.5 g	1 clove
Parsley, chopped	2 Tbsp	2 Tbsp
Saffron, flakes	5	5
Water	30 ml	2 Tbsp

Place saffron flakes in 30 ml of water.
Slice dry bread into small pieces and soak in water until soft. Drain and squeeze out the excess water.
Grind pork and back fat through 3 mm (1/8") plate.
Mix the beaten eggs, water, cream and all ingredients in a blender. If no blender is available, mix manually.
Pour over ground meat and mix everything well together.
Stuff into 32-36 mm hog casings, forming 15 cm (6") links.
Cook in water at 80° C (176° F) for 40 min. Do not boil, the sausages may burst open.
Store in a refrigerator.

Notes:
Eat cold, heat in water, fry or grill.
Lean pork - meat can come from shoulder, rear leg (ham), pork head, lean meat trimmings, tongue, as well as a small amount of liver or kidneys.
Adding saffron flakes will create sausage with a yellowish color.

Morcilla Blanca de Jaén

White Sausage of Jaén (Morcilla Blanca de Jaén) is a popular product of Jaén province of southern Spain, in the eastern part of the autonomous community of Andalusia. The Jaén province is surrounded by mountain ranges and national parks. Olive oil, which is delicious and in abundant supply throughout the province, gives flavor and personality to the cuisine of this area. The oak forests known as "dehesas" provide an abundant supply of acorns which are the main food of free roaming Iberian pigs. The capital of Jaén province is Jaén city, also known as the "Holy Kingdom". This is because the area we know today as Jaén province was long ago a kingdom ruled first by Moors and then by Christians.

Pork head meat	250 g	0.55 lb
Meat from other animals *	500 g	1.10 lb
Pork dewlap, fat trimmings	250 g	0.55 lb

Ingredients per 1 kg (2.2 lb) of meat

Salt	28 g	5 tsp
Pimentón, sweet	6.0 g	3 tsp
Sugar	5.0 g	1 tsp
Eggs	4 eggs	4 eggs
White pepper	2.0 g	1 tsp
Parsley, chopped	1 Tbsp	1 Tbsp
Nutmeg	0.3 g	1/8 tsp
Cinnamon	0.5 g	¼ tsp
Almonds	28 g	1 oz
Garlic, smashed	3.5 g	1 clove
Sherry wine	30 ml	2 Tbsp

Grind meats through 6 mm (1/4") plate. Beat the eggs.
Mix meats with eggs and all ingredients. Hold for 24 hours in refrigerator.
Stuff into 30 mm pork or beef casings forming rings about 25-40 cm (10-16") long. Tie the ends together.
Hold at 20-25° C (60-77° F), 75-85% humidity, for 10 days.
Store at 20-22° C (60-71° F) 70-75% humidity or refrigerate.

Notes
This is the traditional sausage recipe for making Morcilla Blanca de Jaén.
* The recipe includes half of its meats from other animals, light poultry meat, for example a chicken breast. Beef or wild game will make the sausage darker. The sausage was not cooked, but cured.
Today the sausage is cooked and most recipes list head meat (the tongue included), dewlap and pork belly.
Occasionally saffron is added to paint the texture of the sausage yellow.
Consume raw, fried or cooked in water.

Morcilla Blanca Provenzal

Morcilla Blanca is a Spanish sausage which is related to blood sausages by name only as it is made without blood. You may translate it as White Blood Sausage and this is how it is known in countries such as England, France, Germany, Poland and Spain. La Provence is a southern region of France

Lean pork	600 g	1.54 lb
Fat (beef or pork)	250 g	0.66 lb
Cream	150 g	5 oz fl

Ingredients per 1 kg (2.2 lb) of material

Salt	12 g	2 tsp
White pepper	3.0 g	1 ½ tsp
Cinnamon	1.0 g	½ tsp
Cloves, ground	1.0 g	½ tsp
Nutmeg	1.0 g	½ tsp
Egg white	2	2
Parsley, finely chopped	1 Tbsp	1 Tbsp
Onion	60 g	1 small

Chop onion finely. Fry in lard until glassy.

Grind pork with onions through 1/8" (3 mm) plate.

Grind fat through 1/8" (3 mm) plate.

Mix the egg white, cream and all spices in a blender. If no blender available, whisk the egg and mix manually with other ingredients.

Pour over meat and mix everything well together.

Stuff into 32-36 mm hog casings, make 6" (15 cm) links.

Cook in water at 80° C (176° F) for 40 min.

Cool for 10 minutes in cold water, drain, hang or spread on the table to let the moisture evaporate.

Refrigerate.

Morcilla de Álava

This rice and onions blood sausage originates in Álava, a province of Spain and a historical territory of the Basque Country.

Onions	450 g	0.99 lb
Rice, cooked	200 g	0.44 lb
Pork fat	200 g	0.44 lb
Blood	150 ml	5 oz fl

Ingredients per 1 kg (2.2 lb) of material

Salt	12 g	2 tsp
Pepper	2.0 g	1 tsp
Pimentón, sweet	10 g	5 tsp
Pimentón, hot	4.0 g	2 tsp
Oregano, dry	2.0 g	2 tsp
Garlic, diced	7.0 g	2 cloves
Cinnamon	1.0 g	1/2 tsp
Cloves, ground	1.0 g	1/2 tsp
Nutmeg	1.0 g	1/2 tsp

Cook the rice, but don't overcook.

Grind fat through 5 mm (1/4") plate.

Chop the onions finely and fry in a little lard until glassy. Remove from heat and stir in salt and spices.

Add blood and rice and mix all together.

Stuff into 36 mm pork casings.

Cook in water at 80° C (176° F) for 40 minutes.

Cool and refrigerate.

Notes

Serve raw, cooked, fried or grilled.

Morcilla de Arroz

Every country with a rich tradition in sausage making has its own version of blood sausage with rice and so does Spain.

Pork fat: kidney fat, back fat, belly fat, fat trimmings	250 g	0.55 lb
Rice, cooked	100 g	0.22 lb
Blood	400 ml	0.88 lb
Onions	250 g	0.55 lb

Ingredients per 1 kg (2.2 lb) of material

Salt	28 g	4.5 tsp
Pimentón, sweet	20 g	3/5 Tbsp
Anise, ground	1.0 g	1/2 tsp
Cinnamon	1.0 g	1/2 tsp

Cook rice until semi-done, don't overcook.

Chop the onions and fry in a little fat on low heat until glassy and gold, then add rice and mix together. Take off the heat and let cool.

Add spices and blood and mix all well together.

Stuff loosely (the rice may expand) into 45-50 mm pork middles.

Cook in water at 80° C (176° F) for 50-60 minutes.

Immerse in cold water for 10 minutes, then spread on the table or hang to let the moisture evaporate.

Refrigerate.

Morcilla de Arroz (Castellón de la Plana)

Adding rice or onions to blood sausages is a common practice. This thick and short blood sausage contains both, rice and onions and is very popular in Castellón de la Plana, the capital city of the province of Castellón in the Valencian region of Spain by the Mediterranean Sea.

Rice, cooked	400 g	0.88 lb
Blood	200 g	0.44 lb
Fat, lard	300 g	0.66 lb
Onions	100 g	0.22 lb

Ingredients per 1 kg (2.2 lb) of material

Salt	12 g	2 tsp
Black pepper	4.0 g	2 tsp
Cinnamon	1.0 g	1/2 tsp
Cloves, ground	0.3 g	1/8 tsp
Coriander	1.0 g	1/2 tsp
Nutmeg	0.5 g	1/4 tsp
Oregano, dry	2.0 g	2 tsp

Cook rice. Chop onions finely.
Mix rice with blood, spices and diced lard or ground fat.
Stuff into 35-40 mm beef casings, linking every 10 cm (4").
Cook in water at 80° C (176° F) for 30 minutes.
Refrigerate.

Notes
The sausage is usually fried when served.

Morcilla de Burgos

Morcilla de Burgos received the prestigious Protected
Designation of Origin (PDO) certificate on September
5, 2018. Burgos is a city in northern Spain and the
historic capital of Castile in Castilla-León region.

IGP MORCILLA
DE BURGOS

The traditional Morcilla Burgalesa is made without meat. The main ingredients
are onions, rice, lard, sometimes suet, blood and spices. The general consensus is
that the sausage should be bland, greasy and spicy. The color of the sausage varies
from brown to almost black. The texture of the sausage is crumbly and somewhat
greasy with easily recognizable soft grains of rice and a noticeable presence of
onion. Its aroma is a subtle combination of onions and spices.

Composition of the sausage:

Horcal onion-mild, slightly sweet local onion, added at 35% or more.
Rice, 15-30%.
Lard or suet, 10-22%.
Blood, 12% or more.
Salt and spices.

Horcal (*Allium cepa L. var. horcal*) is a large, slightly sweet onion that grows in
Burgos and Palencia provinces. This onion is also used in Morcilla de León. The
properties and the amount of horcal onion play a major role in the development
of taste and flavor of Morcilla de Burgos.

Onions	420 g	0.92 lb
Rice, cooked	210 g	0.46 lb
Lard	210 g	0.46 lb
Pork blood	160 ml	5.33 oz fl

Ingredients per 1 kg (2.2 lb) of material

Salt	12 g	2 tsp
Pepper	2.0 g	1 tsp
Pimentón, sweet	10 g	5 tsp
Pimentón, hot	2.0 g	1 tsp
Oregano, rubbed	3.0 g	3 tsp
Thyme, rubbed	1.0 g	1 tsp
Coriander	1.0 g	1/2 tsp
Cumin	1.0 g	1/2 tsp
Cinnamon	0.5 g	1/4 tsp
Cloves, ground	0.3 g	1/8 tsp
Anise, ground	0.2 g	1/8 tsp

Cook rice, but do not overcook. Chop the onions finely.

Mix onions with rice, spices and blood. Place lard in a pot and apply low heat, stirring often. When the lard starts to melt mix it with other ingredients.

Stuff into 35-45 mm natural casings linking every 20 cm (8"). Depending on the size of the casings the diameter of the sausage varies from 30-100 mm and its length from 15-35 cm (6-14"). Both ends are clipped or tied with twine which becomes a hanging loop.

Cook in water at 80° C (176° F) for 40 minutes.

Air cool to 8-10° C (47-50° F) and refrigerate.

Notes

The sausage can be made with raw or semi-cooked rice.

Serve by frying, cooking in water or eating raw.

Morcilla de Burgos has a wonderful onion flavored mild flavor and can be enjoyed on its own.

Morcilla de Calabaza (*Pumpkin Blood Sausage*)

Pumpkin blood sausage is not cooked, just scalded shortly and then dried. Sausages made with pumpkin flesh whether morcillas or chorizos, dry well and are characterized by a long shelf life.

Fat: fat trimmings,
back fat, belly .... 600 g   1.32 lb
Pork blood   100 ml 0.22 lb
Pumpkin, cooked and drained   300 g   0.66 lb

Ingredients per 1 kg (2.2 lb) of material

Salt	25 g	4 tsp
Pepper, black	4.0 g	2 tsp
Pimentón, sweet	35 g	6 Tbsp
Pimentón, hot	5.0 g	1 Tbsp
Oregano	1.0 g	1 tsp
Nutmeg	0.5 g	1/4 tsp
Garlic, smashed	3.0 g	1 clove

Cut fat trimmings into small cubes.
Make pumpkin puree, place in a drain bag and drain for 6 hours or overnight.
Mix fat, blood, pumpkin and spices.
Stuff into 36-40 mm pork or beef casings.
Cook in water at 80° C (176° F) for 15 minutes.
Dry in air to evaporate moisture. Dry at 12-15° C (53-59° F) for 2 weeks.
Store at <12° C (53° F) or refrigerate.

Note
To make 1 kg of cooked pumpkin about 4 kg of raw pumpkin is needed.

Pumpkin puree: cut pumpkin into smaller sections, remove seeds and fiber. Cook pumpkin for 25 minutes in water, 15 minutes in steam or bake for 30 minutes at 176° C (350° F). Remove the skin (it peels off easily) and cut the pieces into smaller parts. Place the pumpkin flesh in a food processor and emulsify it into the puree. Don't add any water as pumpkin has plenty of it. Place pumpkin puree in a draining bag, place some weight on top and let it drain overnight.

Morcilla de Calabaza de Mezcla (*Blood Sausage with Pumpkin, Rice and Onions*)

Blood sausage made with pumpkin, pork blood, back fat, onions and spices. All stuffed into natural or artificial casings and cooked.

Pork back fat	200 g	0.44 lb
Blood	200 ml	0.44 lb
Pumpkin	300 g	0.66 lb
Cooked rice	100 g	0.22 lb
Onions	100 g	0.22 lb
Potatoes	100 g	0.22 lb

Ingredients per 1 kg (2.2 lb) of material

Salt	18 g	3 tsp
Pepper	2.0 g	1 tsp
Pimentón, sweet	10 g	5 tsp
Pimentón, hot	6.0 g	3 tsp
Nutmeg	1.0 g	1/2 tsp
Cloves, ground	0.5 g	1/4 tsp
Cumin	1.0 g	1/2 tsp
Oregano, rubbed	2.0 g	2 tsp
Garlic, diced	3.5 g	1 clove
Parsley, chopped	1 bunch	3 Tbsp
Mint, chopped	1 tsp	1 tsp

Dice onions and cook in water for 45 minutes. Drain. Spread on the table and let the steam and moisture evaporate.

Cut pumpkin into smaller sections, remove seeds and fiber. Cook pumpkin for 25 minutes in water, 15 minutes in steam or bake for 30 minutes at 176° C (350° F). Remove the skin (it peels off easily) and cut the pieces into smaller parts. Place the pumpkin flesh in a food processor and emulsify it into puree. Don't add any water as pumpkin has plenty of it. Place pumpkin puree in a draining bag, place some weight on top and let it drain overnight.

Cook the rice.

Boil potatoes and drain them.

Grind fat through 3 mm (1/8") plate.

Grind the pumpkin, onions and potatoes through 3 mm (1/8") plate.

Except blood, mix everything together: fat, spices, pumpkin, potatoes and rice. Add the blood and mix all together.

Stuff into 36 mm pork casings forming U-shaped loops about 50 cm (20") long. Tie the ends together with twine.

Dry at 12-15° C (53-59° F), 75-85% humidity for 30 days.

Store at <12° C (53° F), <70% humidity or refrigerate.

Morcilla de Cebolla (*Blood Sausage with Onions*)

A large number of Spanish blood sausages are made with filler material such as onions, rice, bread or pumpkin. Following blood, onions are the next most popular ingredient in blood sausages anywhere. Unlike other sausage types where a small amount of raw or powdered onion is added for flavor, in Spanish blood sausages onion becomes an important ingredient and is added in substantial amounts. This is a basic recipe for making a typical blood sausage with onions.

Pork fat, lard	175 g	0.38 lb
Pork blood	125 ml	4.16 fl oz
Onions, cooked*	700 g	1.54 lb

Ingredients per 1 kg (2.2 lb) of material

Salt	21 g	3.5 tsp
Black pepper	2.0 g	1 tsp
Pimentón, sweet	8.0 g	4 tsp
Pimentón, hot	8.0 g	4 tsp
Cilantro, ground	1.0 g	1/2 tsp
Oregano, ground	1.0 g	1/2 tsp
Caraway	1.0 g	1/2 tsp
Garlic, smashed	3.0 g	1 clove

Dice the onion and cook in water for 30-45 minutes adding a little salt. Drain and cool.
Dice fat (lard) into cubes.
Mix fat, onions, blood and spices.
Stuff into 36-40 mm pork or beef casings.
Immerse sausages into boiling water and cook at 80° C (176° F) for 45 minutes.
Immerse in cold water for 10 minutes, then cool in air and refrigerate.

Notes
* it takes about 5 parts of raw onions to produce one part of cooked onion. In this case 700 x 5 = 3,500 g = 3.5 kg
Morcilla de Cebolla has a mild taste and can be enjoyed on its own.

Morcilla de Cebolla de León

Blood sausages are very popular in Castlla-León region of Spain: Morcilla de Burgos, Morcilla de Valladolid or Morcilla De Cebolla de León. Morcilla de Cebolla de León is made with blood, lard or kidney fat, and rice. Although many Spanish sources insist that the real Morcilla de Cebolla from León should be made with only two basic materials: onions and pork blood. There are 96 varieties of Spanish onions, Morcilla de Cebolla de León is usually made with an early onion maturing in May-June known as "babosa" onion. It is a mild white onion with a large amount of moisture.

Onions	700 g	1.54 lb
Kidney fat, back fat or lard	160 g	0.35 lb
Blood	100 ml	3.33 oz
Rice	40 g	1.41 oz

Ingredients per 1 kg (2.2 lb) of material

Salt	12 g	2 tsp
Black pepper	4.0 g	2 tsp
Pimentón, sweet	12 g	6 tsp
Cinnamon	1.0 g	½ tsp
Aniseed, ground	0.5 g	1/4 tsp

Cut fat into 18 mm (3/4") pieces.
Dice onions into 18 mm (3/4") cubes. Place in a boiling water and cook for 80 minutes. Add rice, lower the heat and cook for 20 minutes more. Drain.
Mix fat, onions, spices and blood together.
Stuff into 30-40 mm beef or pork casings. Form links 15-18 cm (6-7") long.
Cook in water at 85° C (185° F) for 30 minutes.
Drain and cool in air.

Notes
Cook by boiling, frying or grilling before serving.
Local "babosa" onion also known as "cebolla horcal", is preferred for this sausage.

Morcilla de Cebolla Valenciana

Morcilla de Cebolla Valenciana is Valencian blood sausage made with onions. This blood sausage keeps extremely well if the onions are cooked which removes much of the moisture.

Onions	600 g	1.32 lb
Back fat	300 g	0.66 lb
Blood	100 ml	3.33 oz fl

Ingredients per 1 kg (2.2 lb) of material

Salt	12 g	2 tsp
Pepper	4.0 g	2 tsp
Oregano, ground	2.0 g	1 tsp
Aniseed, ground	0.5 g	¼ tsp
Cloves	0.3 g	1/8 tsp

Peel onions and cut in half. Cook in water for 60 minutes, then drain and cool.
Grind back fat and onions through 3 mm (1/8") plate.*
Mix onions, blood, salt, spices and fat together.
Stuff into 25 mm natural casings making 12 cm (5") long links.
Cook in water at 80° C (176° F) for 30 minutes.
Hang at room temperature (15° C/59° F) for 2-3 days. This is the optional drying/conditioning step which improves the flavor of the sausage and strengthens the casings so the sausage does not fall apart when fried.
Keep refrigerated.

Notes
* you could grind ½ of fat and manually dice remaining ½ of fat into 6 mm (1/4") cubes.
The sausage is usually fried or grilled.

Morcilla de Despojos (*Blood Sausage with Offal Meat*)

Spanish blood sausage made with offal meat. Despojos means offal meat (liver, heart, lungs, kidneys), stomach, entrails - the less noble cuts of meat which spoil relatively fast.

Dewlap	250 g	0.55 lb
Liver, heart, lungs	375 g	0.82 lb
Blood	125 ml	4.16 oz fl
Onions, raw	250 g	0.55 lb

Ingredients per 1 kg (2.2 lb) of material

Salt	25 g	4 tsp
Pimentón, sweet	15 g	7 tsp
Pimentón, hot	12 g	6 tsp
Parsley, chopped	3.0 g	1 Tbsp
Cloves, ground	1.0 g	1/2 tsp
Oregano	0.5 g	1/2 tsp
Mint	0.5 g	1/2 tsp
Garlic, smashed	3.5 g	1 clove

Cook liver, heart, and lungs in water until soft. Drain and cool. Grind through 5 mm (1/4") plate.

Chop the onion finely, place in a drain bag, place weight on top and let it drain for 6 hours.

Cut dewlap and any fat into small cubes.

Mix all meats, fat, onions, spices and blood together.

Stuff into 50-65 mm beef middles.

Smoke first day with hot smoke, then smoke/dry with cold smoke until sausages develop black color.

Morcilla de la Sierra de Huelva

This Spanish blood sausage is popular in Sierra de Huelva, a municipality and the mountain range in the province of Huelva in Andalusia, Spain. Morcilla de la Sierra de Huelva is made with lean pork, blood, fat and a large proportion of offal meat. The proportion of meats can vary, but the blood should be applied at 7-20%.

Lean pork	400 g	0.88 lb
Offal meat: heart, lungs, pancreas, stomach *......	200 g	0.44 lb
Fat and fat trimmings	200 g	0.44 lb
Blood	200 ml	6.66 oz fl

Ingredients per 1 kg (2.2 lb) of material

Salt	30 g	5 tsp
Pepper	4.0	2 tsp
Pimentón	15.0 g	7 tsp
Cumin	1.0 g	½ tsp
Garlic, diced	7.0 g	2 cloves

Cook offal meat in water (below the boiling point) until soft. Drain and cool.
Grind meats and fat through 6 mm (1/4") plate.
Mix meat and fat with salt and all spices. Hold for 12-24 hours in refrigerator.
Stuff into 24-26 mm sheep casings or 34-36 mm pork casings. Make rings about 25 cm (10") long.
Dry 24-26 mm sausages for 15-20 days at 12-18° C (53-72° F), 80-85% humidity. Dry 34-36 mm sausages for 30-60 days at 12-18° C (53-72° F), 80-85% humidity.

Notes
* Any other leftovers like tongue, mask meat (face) or skins.
Consume 34-36 mm sausages raw and 24-26 mm sausages fried or cooked.

Morcilla de Lengua

Spanish version of a blood sausage made with tongue. Blood sausages made with tongue are characterized by large chunks of tongue and visible cubes of white fat in different sizes.

Back fat	300 g	0.66 lb
Pork skins	200 g	0.44 lb
Pork tongue	300 g	0.66 lb
Blood	200 ml	0.44 lb

Ingredients per 1 kg (2.2 lb) of material

Salt	20 g	3.5 tsp
Cure #1	2.0 g	1/3 tsp
Black pepper	2.0 g	1 tsp
Marjoram	0.5 g	1/4 tsp
Nutmeg	0.5 g	1/4 tsp
Cloves, ground	0.5 g	1/4 tsp

Dice tongue into 15-20 mm (1/2-3/4") cubes. Mix with 1/3 salt and 1/3 cure #1 and place for 24 hours in refrigerator. The tongues will develop a nice red color.
Cut/grind skins, cover with a little water and slow cook (below boiling point) until a gelatin paste is obtained.
Dice partially frozen back fat into 6-8 mm (1/4-3/8") cubes. Place cubes in a strainer and scald them briefly with hot water 90° C (194° F) which will remove any melted fat.
Keep blood warm in a double pot (arrangement baño de Maria) or in a bowl immersed in warm water.
In a warm bowl start mixing: tongue cubes, fat cubes, gelatin paste (skins), spices, and blood. The mixture must be warm otherwise the gelatin will prematurely harden.
Stuff warm mixture into 80-120 mm beef cap end or pork blind caps (caecum). Cook in water first at 90° C (194° F) for 15 minutes, then at 80° C (176° F) for 60-90 minutes.
Immerse the sausages in cold water for 30 minutes. Insert the sausage between two wooden boards, and place a heavy weight on top. Hold for 24 hours at low temperature or in refrigerator. Then cold smoke (*optional step*) for 6 hours. Store at 10° C (53° F) or refrigerate.

Morcilla de Pan (*Blood Sausage with Bread*)

Every country with a rich tradition in sausage making has its own version of blood sausage with bread and so does Spain.

Pork fat: kidney fat, back fat, belly fat, fat trimmings	300 g	0.66 lb
Dry wheat bread or rolls	300 g	0.66 lb
Blood	200 ml	0.44 lb
Onions, raw, chopped	200 g	0.44 lb

Ingredients per 1 kg (2.2 lb) of material

Salt	25 g	4 tsp
Pimentón, sweet	12 g	6 tsp
Cumin	2.0 g	1 tsp
Cloves	0.3 g	1/8 tsp

Slice dry bread very thinly. Melt the fat in skillet. Add onions, spices and bread and mix together. Remove from heat.

Add blood and mix all together. Hold in refrigerator for 24 hours.

Stuff into 36-40 mm pork casings.

Cook in water at 80° C (176° F) for 40 min.

Hang in a cool place to dry.

Refrigerate.

Morcilla de Pícaro

Morcilla de Pícaro originates in region of Murcia in Spain. The sausage contains typical ingredients such as fat, blood and onions, however, it is aromatized with oregano, cloves and cinnamon. Presentation of Morcilla de Picaro is very attractive as it is in a shape of a string of round balls.

Lard	350 g	0.77 lb
Pork blood	200 ml	6.66 oz fl
Onions	450 g	0.99 lb

Ingredients per 1 kg (2.2 lb) of material

Salt	12 g	2 tsp
Pimentón	6.0 g	3 tsp
Cinnamon	1.0 g	1/2 tsp
Cloves, ground	0.3 g	1/8 tsp
Oregano, dry	3.0 g	3 tsp
Pine nuts	28 g	1 oz

Peel the onions. Cook in water for 60 minutes, then drain and cool.
Grind lard and onions through 3 mm (1/8") plate.
Mix onions, lard, blood, salt, spices and nuts together.
Stuff into 40-45 mm pork middles making 4-6 cm (2") balls. Keep 4 balls in one string.
Cook in water at 80° C (176° F) for 20 minutes.
Cool and store in refrigerator.

Notes
Serve fried, grilled or in stews.

Morcilla de Sangre de Oveja (Buskantza or Mondejos)

Morcilla de Sangre de Oveja-Buskantza, Mondejos. Morcilla de Sangre de Oveja (blood sausage made with sheep blood) is a popular blood sausage in the País Vasco region of Spain. The sausage is made with sheep meat and sheep blood, onions and rice. It is very similar to Morcilla Odolki or Odoste, another blood sausage made in the same region, however, Morcilla Odolki or Odoste is made with pork blood and pork fat.

Sheep blood	120 ml	4 oz fl
Sheep fat	240 g	0.5 lb
Onions	600 g	1.32 lb
Rice	40 g	0.70 oz

Ingredients per 1 kg (2.2 lb) of material

Salt	15 g	2.5 tsp
Pepper	12 g	6 tsp
Oregano, ground	4.0 g	2 tsp

Cook rice, but do not overcook.

Chop onions into smaller sections and cook in water for 45 minutes. Drain, spread on the table and cool.

Grind onions and sheep fat through 6 mm (1/4") plate.

Mix all materials with spices and blood.

Stuff into 32-36 mm sheep casings forming straight links or rings.

Cook in water at 80° C (176° F) for 30 minutes.

Dry in air. The sausage is ready to eat.

Store in refrigerator.

Notes

Serve cooked or fried with red chilies (pimientos rojos) or in stews.

Morcilla de Tocino

Spanish blood sausage made with with a large amount of fat.

Back fat	500 g	1.10 lb
Pork skins	250 g	0.55 lb
Blood	250 ml	0.55 lb

Ingredients per 1 kg (2.2 lb) of material

Salt	25 g	4 tsp
Cure #1	1.5 g	1/4 tsp
Black pepper	2.0 g	1 tsp
Marjoram	0.5 g	1/4 tsp
Oregano	0.5 g	1/4 tsp
Nutmeg	0.5 g	1/4 tsp
Cloves, ground	0.3 g	1/8 tsp

Keep blood warm in a double pot (arrangement baño de Maria) or in a bowl immersed in warm water.

Cut/grind skins, cover with a little water and slow cook (below boiling point) until a gelatin paste is obtained.

Dice partially frozen back fat into 5 mm (1/4") cubes. Place cubes in a strainer and scald with hot water, 90° C (194° F). Drain in a strainer.

In a warm bowl start mixing: fat cubes, gelatin paste (skins), spices, and blood. The mixture must be warm otherwise the gelatin will prematurely harden.

Stuff warm mixture into 45-65 mm beef middles.

Cook in water first at 90° C (194° F) for 15 minutes, then at 80° C (176° F) for 30-45 minutes.

Immerse the sausages in cold water for 10 minutes, then hang in a cool room to cool and evaporate the moisture. Next day cold smoke the sausages.

Store at 10° C (53° F) or refrigerate.

Morcilla de Valladolid

Morcilla de Valladolid originates in Valladolid, a city in Spain and the de facto capital of the autonomous community of Castile and León region in Spain. Like other morcillas produced in Castilla-León region (*Morcilla de Burgos, Morcilla de Cebolla de León*) this blood sausage is made with rice, onions, fat and blood.

Rice	410 g	0.90 lb
Kidney fat or lard	290 g	0.64 lb
Onions	200 g	0.44 lb
Blood	100 ml	3.33 oz fl

Ingredients per 1 kg (2.2 lb) of meat

Salt	12 g	2 tsp
Pepper, black	1.0 g	1/2 tsp
Cloves, ground	0.25 g	1/8 tsp
Pimentón, sweet	6.0 g	3 tsp
Oregano, ground	1.0 g	1/2 tsp

Cook the rice, but do not overcook.
Dice fat into 10-12 mm (3/8-1/2") cubes.
Chop the onions.
Mix rice, onions, fat, blood and spices.
Stuff into 40-70 mm pork or beef casings. Make links 20 cm (8") long or form rings.
Cook in water at 80° C (176° F) for 40-60 minutes.
Immerse for 10 minutes in cold water. Air dry and refrigerate.

Notes
Serve fried or cooked.

Morcilla Dulce Canaria

Morcilla Dulce Canaria is a sweet blood sausage immensely popular in Canary Islands, an autonomous region of Spain. There are seven main islands: Tenerife, Fuerteventura, Gran Canaria, Lanzarote, La Palma, La Gomera and El Hierro. Sweet blood sausages are available on all islands although some differences in sausage recipes can be expected due to local preference. This blood sausage is very popular in the city of Santa Cruz de Tenerife, the capital of Santa Cruz de Tenerife province. Morcilla Dulce and Chorizo Rojo de Teror (Sweet Chorizo from Teror) are the two most popular sausages in Canary Islands.

Lean pork (shoulder butt)	190 g	0.41 lb
Kidney fat, lard	120 g	0.26 lb
Sweet potato	130 g	0.28 lb
Blood	560 ml	18.66 oz fl

Ingredients per 1 kg (2.2 lb) of material

Sugar	30 g	2 Tbsp
Raisins	15 g	½ oz
Almonds, sliced	30 g	1 oz
Oregano, dry	2.0 g	2 tsp
Thyme, dry	1.0 g	1 tsp
Cinnamon	1.0 g	½ tsp
Nutmeg	0.3 g	1/8 tsp
Cloves, ground	0.3 g	1/8 tsp
Aniseed	0.3 g	1/8 tsp
Bread, crushed	2 slices	2 slices

Grind lean pork through 6 mm (1/4") plate.
Grind uncooked sweet potatoes through 6 mm (1/4") plate.
Dice cold fat into 6 mm cubes.
Slice almonds into 3 mm (1/8") wafers or crush into large pieces.
Mix ground meats with all ingredients slowly adding blood. Hold the mixture at room temperature, approximately at 16° C (59° F), 75% humidity, for 6 hours.
Stuff into 40 mm pork casings, forming links 10 cm (4") long.
Cook at 80° C (176° F) for 25 minutes.
Cool in air for 2-3 hours.
Store in refrigerator.

Notes
Mint is sometimes added.
The sausage is usually served fried.

Morcilla Dulce de Soria

Sweet blood sausage from Soria is a popular product of Soria province in
Spain's central Castile and León region. The sausage consists of pork blood,
lard, rice, sugar, dry fruits, bread, salt and spices.

Pork blood	300 ml	0.55 lb
Lard	300 g	0.66 lb
Rice, cooked	250 g	0.55 lb
Wheat bread, dry	150 g	0.33 lb

Ingredients per 1 kg (2.2 lb) of meat

Salt	12 g	2 tsp
Sugar	20 g	4 tsp
Raisins	30 g	1 oz
Pine nuts, fried	30 g	1 oz
Cinnamon	1.0 g	1/2 tsp
Star anise, ground	0.5 g	1/4 tsp

Cook the rice.

Fry pine nuts in butter or lard until light brown.

Break or slice dry bread thinly.

Mix lard with all spices, then add rice, bread, raisins, nuts and blood and mix all
together.

Stuff into 36 mm pork casings forming 40 cm (16") long loops. Tie the ends
together.

Cook in water at 80° C (176° F) for 30 minutes.

Immerse for 10 minutes in cold water. Air dry and refrigerate.

Notes

Serve with vegetables, bean stews, lentils or pastry.

Morcilla Dulce Riojana

Blood sausages are very popular in Spain especially in the province of La Rioja where they are served in many different forms. Generally there are two types: one made with rice and onions (*morcilla riojana*) and another made with blood, rice, bread and sugar called *morcilla dulce riojana* (*dulce* means "sweet" in Spanish). They are served with cooked dishes, in bean stews or simply fried and eaten together with fried tomato.

Pork blood	170 ml	5.66 oz fl
Kidney fat, lard	220 g	7.76 oz
Rice, cooked	220 g	7.76 oz
Sugar	220 g	7.76 oz
White bread	170 g	5.60 oz

Ingredients per 1 kg (2.2 lb) of material

Salt	6.0 g	1 tsp
Cinnamon	1.0 g	½ tsp
Star anise, ground	0.5 g	¼ tsp

Cook the rice, but don't overcook.
Grind fat through 3 mm (1/8") plate.
Break white of bread in smaller pieces and mix with blood, rice, sugar, spices and fat.
Stuff into 32-36 mm pork casings.
Cook in water at 80° C (176° F) for 30 minutes.
Refrigerate.

Notes
The sausage is ready to eat raw but is usually fried or grilled. The appearance of the sausage is black on inside and outside with visible white specks of rice.

Morcilla Extremeña de Badajoz

Morcilla Extremeña from Badajoz originates in Extremadura, a western Spanish region bordering Portugal which comprises the provinces of Cáceres and Badajoz. Morcillas of all types are popular in Extremadura and often include filler material such as potatoes (*Morcilla Extremeña Patatera*) or pumpkin (*Morcilla Extremeña de Calabaza*).

Pork belly	850 g	1.87 lb
Pork blood	150 ml	5 oz fl

Ingredients per 1 kg (2.2 lb) of meat

Salt	18 g	3 tsp
Black pepper	2.0 g	1 tsp
Pimentón, sweet	20 g	3 Tbsp
Oregano, dry	2.0 g	2 tsp
Coriander	2.0 g	1 tsp
Garlic, diced	7.0 g	2 cloves

Grind pork belly through 6 mm (1/4") plate.
Mix ground meat with blood and spices.
Stuff into 28-32 mm pork casings forming 30 cm (12") rings. Tie the ends together.
Dry at around 15° C (59° F) for 3 weeks.

Notes
Consume cooked, fried or in stews.

Morcilla Francesa

Morcilla Francesa is a Spanish version of a French blood sausage.

Back fat, belly fat	100 g	0.22 lb
Blood	500 ml	1.10 lb
Skins	250 g	0.55 lb
Milk, full	25 ml	2 Tbsp
Onions, raw	125 g	0.27 lb

Ingredients per 1 kg (2.2 lb) of material

Salt	30 g	5 tsp
Black pepper	1.0 g	1/2 tsp
Marjoram	0.5 g	1/4 tsp
Nutmeg	0.5 g	1/4 tsp

Chop onions finely and fry in lard on low heat until glassy and golden.

Dice fat into small cubes, place in a strainer and scald with hot water.

Cut/grind skins, cover with a little water and slow cook (below boiling point) until a gelatin paste is obtained.

Place a mixing bowl in warm water (arrangement type baño Maria) and start mixing: onions, fat cubes, gelatin, spices, milk and blood. The mixture must be warm otherwise the gelatin will prematurely harden.

Stuff warm mixture into 36-40 mm pork or beef casings.

Cook in water at 80° C (176° F) for 45 minutes, moving sausages around during the first 15 minutes.

Spread sausages on the table, cool and let the moisture evaporate.

Refrigerate.

Morcilla Gallega from La Coruña

Morcilla Gallega from La Coruña is a Galician sweet blood sausage made with blood, sugar, onions and pine nuts (piñones). La Coruña is a city and municipality of Galicia, Spain. Sweet blood sausage (morcilla dulce) is popular in many regions of Spain: Canaria, La Rioja, Castilla y Léon (Soria), Aragón, however, galician sausage is probably the sweetest as it contains not only sugar but also sweet fruits such as apples, figs or raisins.

Blood	300 g	0.66 lb
Lard or back fat	150 g	0.33 lb
White bread (no crust)	150 g	0.33 lb
Sugar	150 g	0.33 lb
Onions	30 g	1.05 oz
Dry fruit		
(figs, raisins, nuts)	200 g	0.44 lb
Pine nuts	20 g	0.70 oz

Ingredients per 1 kg (2.2 lb) of material

Salt	12 g	2 tsp

If back fat is used freeze it partially then grind through 3 mm (1/8") plate.
Grind onions through 3 mm (1/8") plate.
Break nuts and figs into smaller pieces.
Break bread into small chunks and mix with all ingredients and lard (except blood).
Stir blood to prevent coagulation.
Mix blood with sausage paste.
Stuff into 30-50 mm natural casings.
Cook in water at 80° C (176° F) for 30 minutes.
Dry at 12-16° C (53-59 F), 75-85% humidity for 2 weeks.
Store at 10-12° C (50-53° F), <70% humidity or refrigerate.

Notes
In traditional production after cooking the sausage was hung in the kitchen for up to 5 months.
Morcilla Gallega is usually fried and often served with lightly grilled or fried apples.
There are versions of the sausage that include apples or potatoes.

Morcilla Lebaniega

Morcilla Lebaniega is a blood sausage made in municipality of Liébana in Cantabria region of Spain. This short, large diameter sausage is made with blood, fat, red onions, spices and bread. It is aged between 2-3 months.

Back fat, kidney fat, dewlap, fat trimmings	350 g	0.77 lb
Pork blood	300 ml	10 oz fl
Wheat bread, dry	350 g	0.77 lb

Ingredients per 1 kg (2.2 lb) of material

Salt	15 g	2.5 tsp
Black pepper	2.0 g	1 tsp
Red onions	80 g	1 small
Garlic, diced	7.0 g	2 cloves
Oregano, dry, rubbed	3.0 g	3 tsp

Soak dry wheat bread or rolls in water or bouillon.* Drain and squeeze the excess water out.

Dice 1/3 of hard fat into 6 mm (1/4") cubes. Grind remaining 2/3 of fat through 6 mm (1/4") plate.

Chop onions and fry in ground fat until glassy. Add drained bread and all spices during this step.

Mix all together with blood and cubed fat.

Stuff into pork caps (caecum), stomachs or bladders.

Cook at 80° C (176° F) for 2-3 hours.

Dry at 12-15°C (53-59° F) for 2-3 months. The sausage is ready to eat - serve raw, fried or boiled.

Notes

* bread soup (*sopa de pan*) is made in countless variations all over Europe and South America. Unused dried bread is broken into smaller pieces and cooked in a small amount of water or chicken stock. Salt, olive oil, pepper, garlic, sometimes cooked potato, egg or bacon are often added. The simplest version is to dissolve a bouillon cube in water and soak bread in it (no cooking necessary).

Soaked dry bread combines well with other ingredients. In Cantabria a high quality and delicious local wheat bread called *Pan Lebaniego* will be used. Using bread for blood sausage is a common occurrence in many countries, for example Polish blood sausage made with buckwheat groats is known as "Kaszanka", but if made with bread or rolls it is called "Bułczanka" (the Polish word for roll is "bułka"). There were food shortages countries damaged by war and unused bread or rolls were always saved and later added to sausages or meat hamburgers. A quality wheat roll like Portuguese roll will not spoil at room temperature as long as kept at low humidity.

Morcilla Lustre

Blood sausage that shines (*lustre* means "shine") is an English translation for this Spanish sausage which is made with cooked lungs, chopped heart, pork belly, cumin, parsley, and mint. All stuffed into natural or artificial casings and cooked.

Pork trimmings,		
lungs, heart, skins	300 g	0.66 lb
Pork belly	300 g	0.66 lb
Blood	400 ml	0.88 lb

Ingredients per 1 kg (2.2 lb) of material

Salt	12 g	2 tsp
Pimentón, sweet	10 g	5 tsp
Cumin	2.0 g	1 tsp
Mint, chopped	5.0 g	1 Tbsp
Parsley, chopped	1 bunch	3 Tbsp
Garlic	3.5 g	1 clove

Trim hearts of veins and connective tissue.
Cook meats in water (below the boiling point) until soft.
Grind meats through 3 mm (1/8") plate.
Grind pork belly through 3 mm (1/8") plate.
Mix meats, all ingredients and blood together.
Stuff into 36 mm pork casings. Form loops 45 cm (16") long, tie the ends with twine.
Cook in water at 80° C (176° F) for 40 minutes.
Store at 10-12° C (50-53° F), <70% humidity or refrigerate.

Notes
Serve with potatoes, cabbage or fry in oil.

Morcilla Lustre Malagueña

Blood sausage that shines (*lustre* means "shine"). This basic and simple to make sausage is very popular in Malaga, Andalusia region in Spain where it is often eaten with tomatoes and wheat rolls.

Blood	1000 ml	1.05 qt

Ingredients per 1 kg (2.2 lb) of material

Salt	20 g	3.5 tsp
Cumin, ground	6.0 g	3 tsp
Oregano, ground	6.0 g	3 tsp

Mix blood with salt and spices.
Stuff into 36 mm pork casings. Slip the end of the casings over the narrow part of the funnel and pour the sausage mass into the casing forming one long sausage. Take twine and tie off the sausage into 20 cm (8") links leaving them together.
Cook in water at 80° C (176° F) for 45 minutes.
Cool and refrigerate.

Notes
Cook before serving. Remove the skin, slice the sausage into 12 mm (1/2") sections and dry them lightly in oil. In a skillet fry some tomatoes, add tomato sauce, add sausage and bring to a boil. Serve with bread.

Morcilla Odolki or Odoloste

Morcilla Odolki also known as Odoloste is a popular blood sausage in País Vasco region of Spain. The sausage is made with onions and rice though leeks are also sometimes added. In Vasco-Castellan dialect the words Odolki or Odoloste denote "morcilla" which is blood sausage and the word "odol" signifies "blood." Morcilla Odolki is a light-colored blood sausage due to its white colored ingredients: lard, rice, onions and a small proportion of blood (12%). Morcilla Odolki or Odoloste is very similar to Morcilla de Sangre de Oveja, Buscantza, Mondejos, another blood sausage made in the same region, but Morcilla de Sangre de Oveja is made with sheep blood and sheep meat.

Pork blood	120 ml	4 oz fl
Onions	600 g	1.32 lb
Lard	240 g	8.4 oz
Rice, cooked	40 g	1.41 oz

Ingredients per 1 kg (2.2 lb) of material

Salt	12 g	2 tsp
Pepper	2.0 g	1 tsp
Oregano, dry	2.0 g	2 tsp

Cook the rice, but don't overcook. Cook onions and leeks (if used).
Grind onions and lard through 6 mm (1/4") plate.
Mix all materials with spices and blood.
Stuff into 32-36 mm hog casings forming 10 cm (4") links.
Cook in water at 80° C (176° F) for 30 minutes.
Cool and dry in the air.
Store in refrigerator.

Notes
In some areas leeks are added.

Morcilla Porteña

Argentinian blood sausage. Buenos Aires locals are referred to as porteños.

Pork shoulder	150 g	0.33 lb
Pork back fat or		
pork fat trimmings	100 g	0.22 lb
Pork skins	300 g	0.66 lb
Pork blood	200 ml	0.44 lb
Onions	150 g	0.33 lb
Flour, general purpose	50 g	0.11 lb
Vital wheat gluten or		
whole wheat flour	50 g	0.11 lb

Ingredients per 1 kg (2.2 lb) of material

Salt	15 g	2.5 tsp
Pepper	2.0 g	1 tsp
Oregano, rubbed	2.0 g	2 tsp
Thyme, rubbed	1.0 g	1/2 tsp
Cumin	1.0 g	1/2 tsp
Nutmeg	1.0 g	1/2 tsp

Cook skins in hot water (below the boiling point) until soft. Drain and cool.
Finely dice the onion. Scald in hot water for 5 minutes. Drain.
Grind pork shoulder through 3/8" (10 mm) plate.
Grind back fat, skins and onions through 1/4" (5 mm) plate.
Mix ground meat, fat, skins with blood and all other ingredients.
Stuff into 36 mm hog casings making rings.
Cook in water at 80° C (176° F) for 35 minutes.
Cool and refrigerate.

Notes
To serve, fry in butter or barbecue.

Morcilla Riojana de Arroz

Morcilla Riojana is a very popular blood sausage in La Rioja region of Spain. The sausage is black with visible specks of white rice.

Pork blood	300 ml	10 oz fl
Kidney fat, lard	130 g	4.58 oz
Onions	140 g	4.94 oz
Rice, cooked	430 g	15.16 oz

Ingredients per 1 kg (2.2 lb) of material

Salt	9.0 g	1.5 tsp
Black pepper	2.0 g	1 tsp
Cinnamon	2.0 g	1 tsp
Nutmeg	0.5 g	¼ tsp

Chop onions and boil them for 45 minutes. Drain and spread on the table to cool.
Cook rice until semi-cooked.
Grind fat with 6 mm (1/4") plate.
Mix fat, onions, rice, blood and spices.
Stuff into 45-60 mm beef or pork casings. Form rings.
Cook in water at 80° C (176° F) for 45-60 minutes.

Notes
The sausage can be eaten raw, fried or cooked.

Morcilla Rondeña

Morcilla Rondeña is a blood sausage made with lard and seasoned with cloves, coriander, cumin, oregano, paprika and pepper. Ronda is a mountaintop city in Spain's Malaga province of Andalusia region in Spain.

Back fat, fat trimmings	600 g	1.32 lb
Blood	400 g	0.88 lb

Ingredients per 1 kg (2.2 lb) of meat

Salt	12 g	2 tsp
Pepper	2.0 g	1 tsp
Pimentón, sweet	6.0 g	3 tsp
Oregano, dry	1.0 g	1 tsp
Coriander	0.5 g	1/4 tsp
Cumin	0.5 g	1/4 tsp
Cloves, ground	0.3 g	1/8 tsp
Garlic, smashed	3.5 g	1 clove

Cut fat into small pieces.
Mix with all spices. Slowly add blood mixing everything together.
Stuff into 38-42 mm beef middles or pork casings. Form rings 35-40 cm (14-16") long.
Cook in water at 80° C (176° F) for 45 minutes.
Dry at 15° C (59° F) for 2 days.
Refrigerate.

Notes
Consume raw, cooked or in stews.
In traditional production the sausages were stored in oil or lard.

Morcilla Serrana

Morcilla Serrana, also called fat blood sausage (*morcilla gorda*) is a blood sausage popular in Andalusia and Extremadura regions of Spain. Iberian pigs grow in oak forests in this part of the country so the sausage is made from iberian pork, belly, pepper, garlic, and pimentón. Stuffed into natural casings in the shape of a loop and dried for about one month.

Lean iberian pork	600 g	1.32 lb
Pork belly, jowls, fat meat trimmings	200 g	0.44 lb
Pork blood	200 ml	0.44 lb

Ingredients per 1 kg (2.2 lb) of meat

Salt	25 g	4 tsp
Cure #1	2.5 g	1/2 tsp
Black pepper	2.0 g	1 tsp
Pimentón, sweet	20 g	5 tsp
Pimentón, hot	5.0 g	2 tsp
Sugar	2.0 g	1/2 tsp
Oregano, ground	2.0 g	1 tsp
Garlic	3.5 g	1 clove

Grind meat and fat through 10 mm (3/8") plate.
Mix ground meat and fat with all ingredients and hold for 24 hours in refrigerator.
Mix the mass with blood.
Stuff into 40-50 mm natural casings, forming loops.
Dry at 12-15° C (53-59° F) for 30-35 days, 75-85 % humidity.
Store at <12° C (53° F), <70% humidity or refrigerate.

Morcilla Toledana

In addition to typical ingredients like blood, fat and onions, Morcilla Toledana contains pumpkin which gives it a different personality. Adding pumpkin to a sausage is fairly common, it is included for example in Spanish Chorizo de Calabaza or in Portuguese Chouriço de Abóbora de Barroso-Montalegre which carries the prestigious PGI award. As its name implies Morcilla Toledana originates in Toledo, a city and municipality located in central Spain; it is the capital of the province of Toledo and the autonomous community of Castile–La Mancha region.

Back fat or		
hard fat trimmings	200 g	0.44 lb
Pumpkin	300 g	0.66 lb
Onions	350 g	0.77 lb
Pork blood	150 ml	5 oz fl

Ingredients per 1 kg (2.2 lb) of material

Salt	12 g	2 tsp
Pimentón	10 g	5 tsp
Coriander, ground	2.0 g	1 tsp
Thyme	1.0 g	1 tsp
Caraway, ground	0.5 g	¼ tsp

Chop onions and cook in water for 30 minutes. Drain.
Cut the pumpkin into halves, discard the seeds and boil for 20 minutes. Separate the pumpkin flesh from the skin.
Grind fat through 8-10 mm (3/8") plate.
Mix all materials, spices and blood together. Hold for 24 hours in refrigerator.
Stuff the mixture into 28-30 mm pork casings. Form 30 cm (12") links or rings.
Cook in water at 80° C (176° F) for 40 minutes.
Cool in air.

Notes
The sausage is usually cooked and served hot.

Morcilla Vasca

Morcilla Vasca originates in País Vasco region of Spain where every municipality and village has its own way of making a blood sausage. The basic formula remains the same, what varies is the choice of filler material and selection of spices. In Álava rice is popular, in Gipuzkoa and Bizkaia onions and leeks are preferred. Usually pork blood and fat are applied, but there are areas where morcillas are made with sheep blood and sheep fat (known as buskantzas or mondejus) what gives them a much stronger flavor.

Blood	250 g	0.55 lb
Onions	250 g	0.55 lb
Pork head meat, pork belly	150 g	0.33 lb
Filler material: leeks, cooked rice, pumpkin*....	350 g	0.77 lb

Ingredients per 1 kg (2.2 lb) of material

Salt	18 g	3 tsp
Pepper, black	3.0 g	1.5 tsp
Cayenne pepper	2.0 g	1 tsp
Nutmeg	1.0 g	½ tsp
Pine nuts	28 g	1 oz
Almonds, crushed	28 g	1 oz

Traditionally pork head meat was added with pork belly. Split pork heads (without eyes and brains) were slowly boiled (often with meat scraps, bones, skins and offal meat) until meat would separate from bones. Then while still warm the meat was removed from head and chopped or ground together with pork belly.
Chop onions finely.
Mix meats, onions, nuts, salt, spices, filler material and blood together.
Stuff into large 45-50 mm diameter pork casings.
Cook at 80° C (176° F) for 45 minutes.
Store in refrigerator.

Notes
* the choice of material depends on its popularity in particular areas.
Pork heads might be hard to obtain so use jowls, shoulder or leg meat.

Morcilla Vasca - Argentinian

This Morcilla Vasca is an Argentinian sweet blood sausage, not to be confused with Morcilla Vasca from Spain.

Dry wheat rolls or bread	300 g	0.66 lb
Wheat flour	100 g	0.22 lb
Blood	450 ml	0.99 lb
Sugar	100 g	0.22 lb
Onions	50 g	1 small

Ingredients per 1 kg (2.2 lb) of material

Salt	6.0 g	1 tsp
White pepper	1.0 g	1/2 tsp
Pine nuts	15 g	1/2 oz
Raisins	15 g	1/2 oz
Figs, chopped	15 g	1/2 oz
Crushed walnuts	15 g	1/2 oz
Cinnamon	2.0 g	1 tsp
Nutmeg	1.0 g	1/2 tsp
Star anise, ground	0.5 g	1/4 tsp
Thyme, ground	1.0 g	1/2 tsp
Oil, for frying onion	30 ml	2 Tbsp

Break or slice dry bread into smaller pieces.
Chop onions finely and fry in oil, lard or butter until golden, but not brown.
Mix salt, sugar and spices with blood. Add bread, onions and nuts and mix together. Add flour and mix all together. If the mixture is too thick add a little water.
Mix nuts, spices, sugar, flour, onions, bread and blood together.
Stuff into 36 mm pork casings making rings about 30 cm (12") long. Tie the ends together.
Cook in water at 80° C (176° F) for 45 minutes.
Cool in cold water for 15 minutes. Remove from water and let the moisture evaporate.

Notes
To serve fry in oil and butter on both sides. Cut in slices and sprinkle with powdered sugar.

Morcón Andaluz

A typical Andalusian morcón that can be found in the province of Huelva and other areas. Morcón is a type of short (8", 20 cm) chorizo like sausage which is stuffed into pig blind cap (caecum also known as cecum), an intestine called in Spanish "morcón", thus its name. The large diameter dry sausage is very popular in the regions of Andalusia and Extremadura and in the province of Salamanca in Castilla-León. Morcón sausage has a dark red color, deep flavor and aroma. Best morcón is produced from Iberian pigs that feed on oak acorns.

Pork butt (shoulder), neck meat or both,
preferably from iberian pig .... 1000 g   2.20 lb

Ingredients per 1 kg (2.2 lb) of meat

Salt	28 g	4.5 tsp
Cure #2	2.5 g	1/2 tsp
Pimentón, sweet	25 g	4 Tbsp
Pimentón, hot	5.0 g	1 Tbsp
Garlic, smashed	12 g	4 cloves
White wine	60 ml	2 oz fl

Manually cut pork meat with fat into 20-30 mm (3/4 - 1-1/2") cubes.
Mix all ingredients with meat together. Hold for 24 hours in refrigerator.
Stuff firmly into pork cap (caecum) large intestine, around 18-25 cm (8-10") long. Reinforce lengthwise and across with twine.
Dry at 12-15° C (53-59° F), 75-80% humidity for 2-3 months. The total time depends on the diameter of the sausage and temperature/humidity. In natural chambers without control of temperature and humidity the drying time could be from 3-4 months or even longer.*
Store at 12° C (53° F), 65% humidity.

Notes
* It is hard to maintain steady temperature and humidity in natural chambers. In traditional production the temperature was maintained by burning oak wood when necessary. Cure #2 was not added either.
Finished product exhibits a strong red color and is about 12-15 cm (5-6") thick, and 25-30 cm (12-14") long. Net weight around 1 kg (2.2 lb).
Store in a cool, dry and lightly ventilated dark place.
Consume raw.

Morcón Extremeño

Morcón is a very lean sausage that looks like an oval small rugby ball. The sausage is very popular in Extremadura region of Spain. Morcón Extremeño is made from local iberian pig which is renown for its superior meat. Sliced morcón displays a vivid red color due to the large amount of pimentón used in its manufacture.

Lean pork *	1000 g	2.2 lb

Ingredients per 1 kg (2.2 lb) of meat

Salt	28 g	4.5 tsp
Cure #2	2.5 g	1/2 tsp
Pimentón, sweet	30 g	5 Tbsp
Garlic, smashed	15 g	5 cloves
Olive oil	30 ml	2 Tbsp

Cut meat with attached fat into 25 mm (1") pieces.
Mix with salt and spices. Hold for 24 hours in refrigerator.
Stuff into pork blind cap (caecum) casing. The casing is about 18-25 cm long. Reinforce lengthwise and across with butcher twine. The stuffed morcón looks like an oval small rugby ball.
Ferment/dry at 20° C (68° F), 85-90% humidity, for 48 hours.
Dry at 10-15° C (50-59° F), 80% humidity, for 2-3 months. The total time depends on the diameter of the sausage and temperature/humidity. In natural chambers without control of temperature and humidity the drying time could be from 3-4 months or even longer.
Store at 12° C (53° F), 65% humidity.

Notes
* at least 30% lean meat from pork shoulder (butt) or neck area.
In traditional production the temperature in natural chambers was maintained by burning oak wood when necessary. Cure #2 was not added.
Consume raw.

Morcón de Lorca

This is a traditional recipe for making Morcón de Lorca. Pork head and dewlap is used and the sausage is stuffed in pork bladder or stomach. As the name implies the sausage originates in the municipality of Lorca in Murcia region of Spain. Morcón de Lorca breaks established rules for making morcón as practiced in Extremadura, Castilla-León and Andalusia and is made with different cuts of meat, without pimentón, and is cooked.

Pork head meat and dewlap   1000 g   2.2 lb

Ingredients per 1 kg (2.2 lb) of meat

Salt	20 g	2.5 tsp
Cure #1	2.5 g	1/2 tsp
White pepper	4.0 g	2 tsp
Aniseed, ground	0.3 g	1.8 tsp
Cinnamon	1.0 g	1.2 tsp
Nutmeg	0.5 g	1/4 tsp
Cloves	0.3 g	1/8 tsp
Egg, beaten	1 egg	1 egg

Cook split heads and dewlaps in water at 95° C (203° F) until meat can be separated from bones. Drain and spread on the table. Cool until comfortable to handle; separate meat from bones.
Cut or grind meats into 12 mm (1/2") pieces.
Mix meats with salt, spices and beaten egg.
Stuff into pork bladders or stomachs.
Cook in water at 80° C (176° F) for about 150 minutes or until the sausage reaches 72° C (160° F) internal temperature.
Refrigerate.

Notes
This is a large sausage, about 15 cm (6") in diameter if stuffed in bladders.
The sausage can be kept at cool temperature and low humidity for 30-45 days.
It was customary to store the sausage covered with oil and pimentón.
The texture of the sausage looks much better if meat is cut manually.

Morcón Gaditano

Morcón Gaditano comes from Cádiz, a city and port in southwestern Spain. It is the capital of the province of Cádiz in Andalusia. The word "gaditano" describes a native of Cádiz city.

Pork butt (shoulder), neck meat or both,
preferably from iberian pig .... 1000 g   2.20 lb

Ingredients per 1 kg (2.2 lb) of meat

Salt	28 g	4.5 tsp
Cure #2	2.5 g	1/2 tsp
Pepper	2.0 g	1 tsp
Pimentón, sweet	30 g	5 Tbsp
Garlic, diced	12 g	4 cloves

Cut meat into 25 mm (1") pieces.
Mix meat with salt and spices.
Stuff into pork large intestine blind cap (caecum) casing. The casing is about 18-25 cm long. Reinforce lengthwise and across with twine. The stuffed morcón looks like an oval small rugby ball.
Hold at 10° C (50° F), 90% humidity, for 8-10 days.
Dry at 12-14° C (53-57° F), 80% humidity, for 2-3 months. The total time depends on the diameter of the sausage and temperature/humidity. In natural chambers without control of temperature and humidity, drying time could be 3-4 months or even longer.
Store at 12° C (53° F), 65% humidity.

Notes
In traditional production the temperature was maintained by burning oak wood when necessary. Cure #2 was not added.
Consume raw.

Moronga

Moronga is a blood sausage popular in Spanish speaking countries of Central America, Mexico, Cuba and Puerto Rico.

Pork skins	100 g	0.22 lb
Back fat or		
pork fat trimmings	100 g	0.22 lb
Pork blood	400 ml	0.88 lb
Tomatoes, diced	200 g	0.44 lb
Onions, diced	100 g	0.22 lb
Jalapeños, diced	50 g	0.11 lb
Flour	50 g	0.11 lb

Ingredients per 1 kg (2.2 lb) of material

Salt	15 g	2-1/2 tsp
Pepper	1.0 g	1/2 tsp
Mint, peppermint,		
or spearmint, chopped	15 g	2 Tbsp
Oregano, rubbed	2.0 g	2 tsp
Garlic	3.5 g	1 clove

Cook skins in water (below the boiling point) until soft. Drain and cool.
Grind skins through 1/8" (3 mm) plate.
Cut fat into 1/4" (6 mm) cubes.
Mix fat, skins, blood and all ingredients together.
Stuff loosely into 36 mm hog casings.
Cook in water at 80° C (176° F) for 35 minutes.
Place in cold water for 10 minutes.
Dry briefly and refrigerate.

Mortadela Bolonia

The name mortadella originates from the Latin words myrtle (mirtatum) and mortar (mortario) and the sausage was made the same way in Italy for hundreds of years. This sausage is the pride of the Italian city of Bologna. The sausage may have originated in Italy but it has world wide appeal and every European country has its own version. It is also popular in Argentina, Bolivia, Brasil, Chile, Colombia, Costa Rica, Ecuador, Paraguay, Peru, Uruguay and Venezuela. Mortadela Bolonia is an emulsified large diameter sausage of pink color with visible cubes of white fat, whole peppercorns and pistachio nuts.

Pork, lean	650 g	1.43 lb
Jowls, belly or fat trimmings	200 g	0.44 lb
Back fat	150 g	0.33 lb

Ingredients per 1 kg (2.2 lb) of meat

Salt	18 g	3 tsp
Cure #1	2.5 g	½ tsp
Soy protein concentrate	15 g	1/2 oz
White pepper	2.0 g	1 tsp
Whole peppercorns	4.0 g	2 tsp
Coriander	0.5 g	¼ tsp
Anise, ground	1.0 g	½ tsp
Mace	1.0 g	½ tsp
Caraway, ground	0.5 g	¼ tsp
Pistachios, whole	30 g	1 oz
Red wine	30 ml	1 oz fl
Cold water	90 ml	3 oz fl

Dice partially frozen back fat into ¼" cubes for use as show meat.
Grind all meats through ¼" (6 mm) plate, refreeze and grind again through ⅛" (3 mm) plate.
Mix ground meats with all ingredients (except whole peppercorns, pistachios, fat cubes and water).
Emulsify sausage mass in a food processor adding cold water.
Mix emulsified meat paste with cubed fat, pistachios and whole peppercorns.
Stuff into 100 mm (4") fibrous casings.
Cook sausages in water at 80° C (176° F), until meat reaches 70° C (158° F) internal temperature which will take about 2 hours.
Cool and refrigerate.

Notes
If a food processor is not available, grind meats once more adding cold water.

Mortadela Cordobesa

Spanish mortadela popular in Cordoba made with cubes of white fat about the size of a grain of rice and whole pitted green olives.

Pork, lean	650 g	1.43 lb
Jowls, belly		
or fat trimmings	150 g	0.33 lb
Pork skins	50 g	0.10 lb
Back fat	150 g	0.33 lb

Ingredients per 1 kg (2.2 lb) of meat

Salt	18 g	3 tsp
Cure #1	2.5 g	½ tsp
Soy protein concentrate	15 g	1/2 oz
White pepper	2.0 g	1 tsp
Whole peppercorns	4.0 g	2 tsp
Coriander	0.5 g	¼ tsp
Garlic powder	3.0 g	1 tsp
Anise, ground	1.0 g	½ tsp
Mace	1.0 g	½ tsp
Caraway, ground	0.5 g	¼ tsp
Whole olives, pitted	50 g	1.76 oz
Red wine	30 ml	1 oz fl
Cold water	90 ml	2 oz fl

Cook skins in hot water (below a boiling point) for 60 minutes. Cool, then grind through 3 mm (1/8") plate.
Dice partially frozen back fat into 6 mm (1/4") cubes for use as show meat.
Grind all meats through 6 mm (1/4") plate, refreeze and grind again through 3 mm (1/8") plate.
Mix ground meats, skins with all ingredients (except whole peppercorns, olives, fat cubes and water).
Emulsify sausage mass in a food processor adding cold water.
Mix emulsified meat paste with cubed fat, olives and whole peppercorns.
Stuff into 100 mm (4") synthetic casings.
Cook sausages in water at 80° C (176 ° F), until meat reaches 70° C (158° F) internal temperature which will take about 2 hours.
Cool and refrigerate.

Notes
If a food processor is not available, grind meats once more adding cold water.

Moscancia

Moscancia, a sausage made with blood, suet, onions, pimentón and other spices, stuffed into beef casings and cooked. Occasionally made with sheep fat and garlic.

Pork fat	300 g	0.33 lb
Onions	300 g	0.66 lb
Pork blood	400 ml	0.88 lb

Ingredients per 1 kg (2.2 lb) of meat

Salt	12 g	2 tsp
Pimentón, sweet	10 g	5 tsp
Pimentón, hot	5.0 g	2 tsp
Olive oil	60 ml	2 oz fl

Grind pork fat through 3 mm (1/8") plate.
Chop onions finely. Cook the onions in a frying pan in oil until glassy and golden. Cool.
Mix ground fat, blood, onions, and spices.
Stuff into 32-34 mm pork casings.
Cook at 80° C (176° F) for 30 minutes.
Refrigerate.

Notes
Cut the sausage into slices and serve over cooked rice.

Obispo de Tenancingo

It is claimed that this Mexican sausage was made in the past with brains as it was originally called "brain sausage" (*rellena de sesos*), but there is no proof of it today. The story goes that in 1950 a group of clerics were preparing a Tenancingo visit for the local bishop (*obispo*) and treated him to a new and original sausage. Someone exclaimed "this delicacy deserves Obispo" (the bishop) and the rest is history - the locals started to ask: "give me the sausage that the bishop likes".

Pork shoulder (picnic), leg meat	400 g	0.88 lb
Pork back fat, belly, jowls, fat trimmings	300 g	0.66 lb
Skins	100 g	0.22 lb
Tomatoes, red	100 g	0.22 lb
Onions	100 g	1 onion

Ingredients per 1 kg (2.2 lb) of material

Salt	18 g	3 tsp
Black pepper	4.0 g	2 tsp
Paprika, sweet	6.0 g	3 tsp
Paprika, hot	2.0 g	1 tsp
Manzana chile peppers*	30 g	1 oz
Epazote**	12 leaves	
Garlic, diced	7.0 g	2 cloves

Cook skins and any meat with bones in water, until soft. Cool and separate meat from bones when still warm.
Grind meat and fat through 10 mm (3/8") plate.
Grind skins through 3 mm (1/8") plate.
Cut a cross on top of the tomato and insert for 40 seconds into hot water.
Remove from water and peel off the skin.
Dice tomatoes and onions.
Mix meat, fat and all ingredients. Stuff into a large diameter casing such as pork caecum (blind cap) or stomach. Refrigerate.
Serve hot, usually by baking.

Notes
* manzana chili peppers are hot peppers, rated 10,000-30,000 on Scoville scale, about twice as hot as jalapeños. The pepper is called *manzana chile* due to its shape that resembles apple (apple is "manzana" in Spanish).
** epazote is a is a strong tasting and smelling herb-plant popular in Mexico. Its pungent flavor has notes of oregano, anise, citrus, and mint. If hard to find, you can substitute 12 leaves with with 1/3 cup chopped cilantro.
The following ingredients are often added: raisins, nuts, pine nuts and peanuts.

Paltruch-Bisbot

Paltruch also known as *Bisbot* or *Bisbe* is a Spanish blood sausage (blood head cheese) very popular in Gerona (in Catalan language Girona) which is the city and municipality in the region of Catalonia. It is a type of a very thick butifarra and it goes by many names: paltruc, bull, bisbe negre, bisbot negre, obispo negro, butifarra de barilla. When made without blood it changes its name to paltruch blanco, bisbe blanc, bull blanc or bisbot.

Dewlap, jowls	140 g	4.93 oz
Tongue	160 g	5.64 oz
Heart, lungs, liver, stomach	200 g	7.05 oz
Head meat	120 g	4.23 oz
Back fat, hard fat trimmings	130 g	4.58 oz
Pork blood	250 ml	8.33 oz fl

Ingredients per 1 kg (2.2 lb) of meat

Salt	20 g	3.5 tsp
Black pepper	5.0 g	2.5 tsp
Cinnamon	1.0 g	½ tsp
Nutmeg	0.5 g	¼ tsp
Cloves, ground	0.3 g	1/8 tsp

Cut back fat into 3 mm (1/8") strips, about 8 cm (3") long.
Grind all meats through 2-3 mm (1/8") plate.
Mix blood with salt and spices.
Mix ground meats, fat and blood well together.
Stuff into pork blind caps (caecum), about 20 cm (8") long.
Cook in water at 80° C (176° F) for 120 minutes.
Keep in refrigerator.

Notes
Consume cold.
The sausage is also stuffed in pork bungs.

Patatera

Potato sausage (*patatera*) is not a unique product that is limited to Spain only, but can be found in other countries as well, for example Swedish Potato Sausage (*Potatis Korv*). Taking under consideration the fact that plenty of meat products are served with potatoes it should not come as a surprise that combining meat with potatoes inside of the casing will also create a great product.

Lean pork	100 g	0.22 lb
Back fat, belly, fat trimmings	400 g	0.88 lb
Cooked potatoes	500 g	1.10 lb

Ingredients per 1 kg (2.2 lb) of material

Salt	15 g	2.5 tsp
White pepper	2.0 g	1 tsp
Allspice	1.0 g	1/2 tsp
Pimentón, sweet	4.0 g	2 tsp
Garlic, smashed	3.5 g	1 clove
Water	60 ml	2 oz fl

Boil the potatoes. Drain.
Grind meats, potatoes and onions through 3/8" (10 mm) plate.
Mix meat with salt, pepper and spices until sticky. Add potatoes and mix again.
Stuff into 36 mm hog casings. Refrigerate.
Cook before serving.

Perro

Perro is a popular semi-dry sausage from Valencia. It is made with pork head meat, back fat, skins, blood, pepper, cinnamon and cloves.

Lean pork from pork head or other meat trimmings	300 g	0.66 lb
Back fat or pork belly	400 g	0.88 lb
Pork skins	100 g	0.22 lb
Blood	200 ml	0.44 lb

Ingredients per 1 kg (2.2 lb) of meat

Salt	18 g	3 tsp
Black pepper	2.0 g	1 tsp
Pimentón, sweet	15 g	2 Tbsp
Cinnamon	2.0 g	1 tsp
Cloves, ground	0.3 g	1/8 tsp
Garlic, diced	7.0 g	2 cloves

Cook skins and meat in water until meat separates from bones. Separate meat from bones.

Grind meats through 10-12 mm (3/8-1/2") plate.

Grind skins through 3 mm (1/8") plate.

Dice back fat into 6-10 mm (1/4-3/8") cubes.

Mix meat, fat, skins with spices and blood.

Stuff into natural 36-42 mm (or larger) pork or beef casings forming straight (*vela*) or U-shaped (*sarta*) sections 25-35 cm (12-14") long. Both ends of a loop tied with twine.

Cook in water at 80° C (176° F) for 60 minutes.

Dry at 12-15° C (53-59° F) for 3-4 days (depending on the diameter of the sausage).

Notes:

Perro is often produced in 100 mm diameter or larger casings, 25-35 cm (12-14") long. Cook in water for 2 hours and dry for 14 days or more.

The sausage is consumed raw.

Queso de Cabeza

Argentinian head cheese.

Pork meat rich in connective tissue*	1000 g	2.2 lb

Ingredients per 1 kg (2.2 lb) of meat

Salt	15 g	2-1/2 tsp
Peppercorns	4.0 g	2 tsp
Cayenne	1.0 g	1/2 tsp
Onion	60 g	2 oz
Garlic	10 g	3 cloves
Bay leaf	1 leaf	
Celery	1 stalk	
Leek	1 stalk	
Parsnip	1 root	
Carrot	1 root	
Oregano, rubbed	10 g	1 Tbsp
White wine	60 ml	2 oz fl

Place all meats in a suitable pot, add leek, celery, parsnip, carrot, onion, peppercorns and cover with 1 inch of water and wine. Bring to a boil and simmer below boiling point until meats are soft and the bones are easily removable.

Drain the meats, spread on the table and allow to cool. Save meat stock, discard vegetables.

When the meats are still warm, separate the meat from the bones. Cut larger chunks into smaller pieces, cut the skins into strips.

Mix meats with salt, garlic, oregano, cayenne adding about 1/2 cup (125 ml) of the meat stock. This meat stock is a naturally produced gelatin.

Using a ladle stuff the mixture loosely into pork stomachs or large diameter synthetic casings.

Cook in water at 80° C (176° F) for 90-120 min (depending on the size) until meat reaches 68-70° C (154-158° F) internal temperature.

Spread head cheeses on a flat surface and let the steam out. Flatten with weight and cool to 6° C (43° F) or lower.

Clean head cheeses of any fat and aspic that accumulated on the surface and cut off excess twine.

Keep refrigerated.

Notes

* head, leg meat, pork skins, snouts, meats with connective tissue.
Eat cold with a roll and lemon juice or vinegar.

Queso de Puerco (*Chilean head cheese*)

Chilean version of head cheese. The same technology is used all over the world, what is different is the selection of spices. In Spanish speaking countries oregano, cumin, vinegar and hot source are usually included, in norther European countries, marjoram and caraway may be added. Garlic is added everywhere.

Split pork head, or head meat.
Pork shoulder (picnic), front leg, feet.
White vinegar, aji source*.
Soup greens: carrots, onions, leek, parsley, bay leaf, oregano.
Spices: salt, whole black pepper, oregano, diced garlic, cumin.

Creating meat stock (gelatin). Immerse meats in a pot, add soup greens, bay leaves and whole black peppers and cover with 5 cm (2") of water. Bring to a boil and simmer for 2-3 hours until the meat can be separated from bones. If the water level drops too much add a little water.

Drain the meats and spread on the table to cool. *Save the meat stock* as this will become the natural gelatin that will hold meats together. Place meat stock in refrigerator.

When the meat is still warm but comfortable to work with, separate all meats including snouts, ears, and skins from the bones. If the split heads come with tongue, use it as well. Cut all meats into smaller parts.

Recover meat stock from refrigerator and discard any fat from the surface. Add salt, diced garlic, cumin, oregano and aji source to meat stock until you are satisfied with the result.

Mixing. Start mixing meats gradually adding meat stock. Add some vinegar to taste, this is optional as most people eat head cheese with lemon or vinegar. You cannot spoil the product by adding too much or not enough of the meat stock. Adding more of the stock will produce head cheese with more gelatin, a kind of meat jelly. Some people like more jelly, some like less.

Stuffing. Fill pork stomach or a large diameter synthetic casing with the mixture. It is usually done with a ladle.

Cooking. Cook in water at 80° C (176° F) for 90-120 min (depending on the size) until meat reaches 68-70° C (154-158° F) internal temperature.

Conditioning. Spread head cheeses on a flat surface and let the steam out. Flatten pork stomachs with weight and cool to 6° C (43° F) or lower. Round synthetic casings are not flattened.

Storing. Clean head cheeses of any fat and aspic that accumulated on the surface. Keep refrigerated.

Notes

Eat cold with a roll and lemon juice or vinegar. How you serve head cheese depends much on local customs and preference.

* Ají is a spicy sauce that often contains tomatoes, cilantro (coriander), ají pepper, onions, lemon juice and water. If you cannot get it use Tabasco sauce.

Relleno de Huéscar

Relleno de Huéscar originates in Huéscar in the province of Granada, Andalusia region of Spain. The sausage is made from pork, chicken, cured ham, eggs, bread, garlic and parsley. Other meats like rabbit, chicken, turkey or goose may be used. The sausage is of light yellowish color due to saffron spice.

Pork meat	150 g	0.33 lb
Dry ham	150 g	0.33 lb
Chicken breast	150 g	0.33 lb
Dry wheat bread	300 g	0.66 lb
Eggs	250 g	4 eggs

Ingredients per 1 kg (2.2 lb) of material

Salt	12 g	2 tsp
White pepper	2.0 g	1 tsp
Nutmeg	1.0 g	1/2 tsp
Garlic	3.0 g	1 clove
Saffron, a few flakes	5 flakes	5
Parsley, chopped	1 bunch	1
Lime juice	15 ml	1 Tbsp
Water	120 ml	4 oz fl

Immerse saffron flakes in 120 ml of water.
Grind pork and chicken through 6 mm (1/4") plate.
Dice ham into 6 mm (1/4") cubes.
Slice dry bread thinly.
Beat the eggs.
Mix all meats with bread, water, spices and eggs until a uniform soft mass is obtained.
Stuff into 36-40 mm pork casings.
Cook in water at 80° C (176° F) for 45 minutes. Immerse for 5 minutes in cold water. Spread on a table to cool and let the moisture evaporate.
Refrigerate.

Sabadiego or Sabadeña

Sabadiego also known as *Sabadeña* or *Chorizo Sabadiego* is a popular sausage in Noreña, a municipality in the Asturias region of Spain. The name means "Saturday Sausage" (*Sabado* means Saturday). In Spain and in other European Christian countries the consumption of any meat was strictly forbidden on Friday, with noble meats on Saturday as well. This was rigidly observed during Lent, a 40 day period of fasting preceding Easter.

It has been accepted that in the eighteenth century Alonso Marcos de Llanes Argüelles, bishop of Segovia and archbishop of Seville, Christianized this sausage with the approval of King Carlos III and also authorizing the consumption of a certain type of meat exclusively on Saturdays. This meat was called "Saturday meat" and generally used to be wild game or an injured animal. Offal meats (heart, liver, lungs, kidneys, blood, skin, stomach, tripe) were considered inferior meats and were also permitted. Thus Sabadiego (*Saturday*) sausage was invented and as long as it was made with strict adherence to church requirements (made from less noble meats) there was no conflict.

The pigs were slaughtered during Christmas or soon after so the supply of meat was short lived and Sabadiego sausage was available for only a few months. Today Sabadiego can be made at any time.

Offal meat: heart, lungs, liver, stomach	600 g	1.32 lb
Back fat, belly fat, fat trimmings	250 g	0.55 lb
Beef	150 g	0.33 lb

Ingredients per 1 kg (2.2 lb) of meat

Salt	30 g	5 tsp
Cure #1	2.5 g	1/2 tsp
Pimentón, sweet	25 g	4 Tbsp
Pimentón, hot	5.0 g	1 tsp
Oregano, ground	1.0 g	1/2 tsp
Nutmeg	1.0 g	1/2 tsp
Garlic	7.0 g	2 cloves
Wine	60 ml	2 oz fl

Cook heart, lungs, stomach in water (below boiling point) until soft. Scald liver in hot water for 5 minutes.

Grind beef and fat through 10 mm (3/8") plate. Grind offal meats through 3 mm (1/8") plate.

Mix meats, fat and all ingredients together. Hold for 12 hours in refrigerator.

Stuff into 40-50 mm pork or beef middles.

Ferment/dry at 25° C (77° F), 90% humidity for 48 hours.

Dry at 14-15° C (57-59° F), 70% humidity for 30 days.

Store at 10-12° C (50-52° F), 60-65% humidity or refrigerate.

Salami Spanish *(Salami Español)*

Traditionally made dry salami using modern starter culture technology. The salami will develop a strong color and a typical cheesy flavor that is present in traditionally produced products.

| Lean pork | 700 g | 1.54 lb |
| Back fat | 300 g | 0.66 lb |

Ingredients per 1 kg (2.2 lb) of meat

Salt	28 g	4.5 tsp
Cure #2	2.5 g	1/2 tsp
Dextrose	2.0 g	1/2 tsp
Sugar	3.0 g	1/2 tsp
Pepper	2.0 g	1 tsp
Oregano, ground	2.0 g	1 tsp
Garlic powder	1.0 g	1/2 tsp
T-SPX, starter culture	0.12 g	use scale

Trim meat from all gristle, sinews, tendons, and silver film.
Grind meat through 6 mm (1/4") plate.
Dice partially frozen fat into 6 mm (1/4") cubes.
Dilute starter culture in 15 ml (1 tablespoon) of distilled or spring water. Do not use chlorinated water.
Mix lean meat with salt, Cure #1, spices and starter culture. Add fat and mix again.
Stuff firmly into 50-60 mm hog middles forming sections 40 cm (16") long.
Ferment at 20° C (68° F) for 72 hours, 90-85% humidity.
Dry at 16 → 12° C (60-54° F), 85 → 80% humidity for 45 days (or longer depending on a diameter of the casing). The sausage is dried until around 30% in weight is lost.
Store sausages at 10-12° C (50-53° F), <75% humidity.

Notes
**Sausage can be made *without the culture,* *the traditional way:*

Mix lean meat with salt, Cure #1, spices and fat. Hold for 48 hours in refrigerator.
Stuff firmly into 50-60 mm hog middles forming sections 40 cm (16") long.
Ferment/dry at 20-25° C (68-77° F) for 48 hours, 90-85% humidity.
Dry at 16 → 12° C (60-54° F), 85 → 80% humidity for 45 days (or longer depending on the diameter of the casing). The sausage is dried until around 30% in weight is lost.
Store sausages at 10-12° C (50-53° F), <75% humidity or refrigerate.

Salchicha de Higado (*Liver Sausage*)

A basic Spanish liver sausage. Liver sausages can be spreadable, have a firm texture and be of grey, pink, yellow or almost white color. They can include rice, bread, eggs, tripe, cream and flours. Different livers can also be used: veal, pork, rabbit, goose, beef, poultry or wild game.

Lean pork	300 g	0.66 lb
Pork liver	300 g	0.66 lb
Back fat, pork belly, jowls	250 g	0.55 lb
Meat trimmings rich in		
connective tissue	50 g	0.11 lb
Pork skins	50 g	0.11 lb
Chopped onion	50 g	0.11 lb

Ingredients per 1 kg (2.2 lb) of material

Salt	12 g	2 tsp
White pepper	2.0 g	1 tsp
Allspice	1.0 g	1/2 tsp
Nutmeg	0.5 g	1/4 tsp
Meat stock from		
cooking meats	60 ml	2 oz fl

Cook pork meat (except liver), meat trimmings and skins in water at 95° C (203° F) until soft. Cook belly, back fat, jowls for 10 minutes only. Drain and cool. Save meat stock.

Fry finely chopped onion in lard until light yellow, but not brown.

Grind meat and fat through 1/4" (6 mm) plate.

Grind liver through 1/8" (3 mm) plate.

Using a food processor emulsify liver, skins and meat trimmings rich in connective tissue adding spices and 60 ml of meat stock.

Mix ground meat, fat and emulsified paste together.

Stuff into 36-40 mm hog casings.

Cook in water at 80° C (176° F) for 40-50 minutes. Immerse for 10 minutes in cold water. Drain, dry briefly and refrigerate.

Notes

Don't cook the liver, just scald it with hot water. Cooked liver loses its emulsifying properties. You can also briefly insert liver in hot water and remove it, repeating the process 3 times. The liver will change its outside color from dark red to pale.

Salchicha de Higado con Trufas (*Liver Sausage with Truffles*)

Spanish liver sausage with truffles. Truffles are the most expensive mushrooms of them all and they are often added to liver pâtés. Fortunately for Spain black truffles grow in the Pyrenees mountain range that separates the Iberian Peninsula from the rest of Europe and are often included in Spanish sausages.

Pork liver	325 g	0.71 lb
Beef	350 g	0.77 lb
Pork fat	325 g	0.71 lb

Ingredients per 1 kg (2.2 lb) of meat

Salt	24 g	4 tsp
Pepper, white	4.0 g	2 tsp
Truffles, chopped	30 g	1 oz

Immerse liver for 3-5 minutes in hot water at around 95° C (203° F) which is below boiling point. Drain and cool.
Grind liver through 3 mm (1/8") plate.
Separately grind meat and fat through 3 mm (1/8") plate.
Emulsify liver paste in a food processor. Add meat, fat, all ingredients and emulsify again.
Stuff into 45-50 mm pork or beef middles.
Cook in water at 80° C (176° F) for 60 minutes.
Cool in cold water for 10 minutes, then cool in air and refrigerate.

Notes

Don't cook the liver, just scald it with hot water. Cooked liver loses its emulsifying properties. You can also insert liver briefly in hot water and remove it, repeating the process three times. The liver will change its outside color from dark red to pale.

If there is no food processor available, grind liver paste, meat and fat second time through 3 mm (1/8") plate and then mix with all ingredients.

Salchicha de Higado con Trufas y Tomate (*Liver Sausage with Truffles and Tomato Paste*)

A delicious Spanish liver sausage with mushrooms and tomato paste.

Pork liver	300 g	0.66 lb
Pork meat, semi-fat	400 g	0.88 lb
Back fat	300 g	0.66 lb

Ingredients per 1 kg (2.2 lb) of meat

Salt	20 g	3.5 tsp
Pepper	2.0 g	1 tsp
Cardamom	0.5 g	1/4 tsp
Nutmeg	0.5 g	1/4 tsp
Onion, chopped and fried	30 g	1 oz
Tomato paste	50 g	1.76 oz
Truffles, chopped	50 g	1.76 oz

Immerse liver for 3-5 minutes in hot water at around 95° C (203° F) which is below boiling point. Drain and cool.

Chop the onion and fry in fat until glassy and gold. Do not brown the onion as it will acquire a bitter taste.

Grind liver with onion through 3 mm (1/8") plate.

Separately grind meat and fat through 3 mm (1/8") plate.

Emulsify liver paste in a food processor. Add meat, fat, all ingredients and emulsify again.

Stuff into 45-50 mm pork or beef middles.

Cook in water at 80° C (176° F) for 60 minutes.

Cool in cold water for 10 minutes, then cool in air and refrigerate.

Notes

Don't cook the liver, just scald it with hot water. Cooked liver loses its emulsifying properties. You can also insert liver briefly in hot water and remove it, repeating the process three times. The liver will change its outside color from dark red to pale.

If there is no food processor available, grind liver paste, meat and fat second time through 3 mm (1/8") plate and then mix with all ingredients.

Salchicha de Higado de Mezcla (*Liver Sausage with Pork and Beef*)

Spanish liver sausage with pork liver and beef.

Pork liver	250 g	0.55 lb
Beef	250 g	0.55 lb
Pork belly, back fat	500 g	1.1 lb

Ingredients per 1 kg (2.2 lb) of meat

Salt	21 g	3.5 tsp
Pepper	1.0 g	1/2 tsp
Allspice	0.5 g	1/4 tsp
Thyme	1.0 g	1/2 tsp

Immerse liver for 3-5 minutes in hot water at around 95° C (203° F) which is below boiling point. Drain and cool.
Grind liver through 3 mm (1/8") plate.
Separately grind meat and fat through 3 mm (1/8") plate.
Emulsify liver paste in a food processor. Add meat, fat, all ingredients and emulsify again.
Stuff into 45-50 mm pork or beef middles.
Cook in water at 80° C (176° F) for 60 minutes.
Cool in cold water for 10 minutes, then cool in air and refrigerate.

Notes
Don't cook the liver, just scald it with hot water. Cooked liver loses its emulsifying properties. You can also insert liver briefly in hot water and remove it, repeating the process three times. The liver will change its outside color from dark red to pale.

Salchicha de Ternera (*Veal Sausage*)

Small Spanish fresh sausages made from veal.

Veal	700 g	1.54 lb
Pork belly, fat trimmings	300 g	0.66 lb

Ingredients per 1 kg (2.2 lb) of meat

Salt	24 g	4 tsp
Pepper, white	4.0 g	2 tsp
Nutmeg	0.5 g	1/4 tsp
Water, cold	60 ml	2 oz fl

Grind beef and fat through 10 mm (3/8") plate.

Grind fat through 10 mm (3/8") plate.

Grind beef, adding salt and spices through 3 mm (1/8") plate or emulsify in a food processor adding 60 ml of cold water.

Mix emulsified paste with fat.

Stuff into 18 mm sheep casings, forming links 10-12 cm (4-5") long.

Refrigerate. Cook fully before serving.

Salchicha de Trufas

Spanish fresh sausage with mushrooms.

Lean pork	500 g	1.1 lb
Pork belly	500 g	1.1 lb

Ingredients per 1 kg (2.2 lb) of meat

Salt	24 g	4 tsp
Pepper, whole	4.0 g	2 tsp
Nutmeg	0.5 g	1/4 tsp
Cloves	0.3 g	1/ 8tsp
Cardamom	0.5 g	1/4 tsp
Cumin	0.5 g	1/4 tsp
Truffles, chopped	30 g	1 oz
White wine	60 ml	2 oz fl

Grind pork and fat through 10 mm (3/8") plate.

Mix ground meat with salt adding water. Add all ingredients and mix again.

Stuff into 18 mm sheep casings, forming links 10-12 cm (4-5") long.

Refrigerate. Cook fully before serving.

Salchicha de Turista

A small Spanish fresh sausage. In many countries, for example Russia, such small sausages are called "tourist" sausages as they are easy to carry and keep reasonably well. They were often called hunter's sausage as hunters would carry them in a bag as convenience food.

Lean pork	600 g	1.32 lb
Beef	300 g	0.66 lb
Pork fat	100 g	022 lb

Ingredients per 1 kg (2.2 lb) of meat

Salt	24 g	4 tsp
Cure #1	2.5 g	1/2 tsp
Pepper	2.0 g	1 tsp
Coriander	1.0 g	1/2 tsp
Caraway	0.5 g	1/4 tsp
Garlic, smashed	3.0 g	1 clove
Water	30 ml	1 oz fl

Grind pork and fat through 5 mm (1/4") plate.
Grind beef through 3 mm (1/8") plate.
Mix ground meat with salt and cure #1 until sticky. Add spices and water and mix again.
Stuff into 18-24 mm sheep casings, forming links 10-12 cm (4-5") long.
Apply smoke at 60° C (140° F) for 30 minutes,
Cook in water at 80° C (176° F) for 30 minutes.
Cool in air and refrigerate.

Salchicha de Zaratán

Salchicha de Zaratán is a small semi-cured sausage made of lean pork, pork belly and a hefty dose of pimentón which is responsible for the sausage's brilliantly red color. As its name implies the Salchicha de Zaratán originates in the city of Zaratán in Valladolid province of Castilla-León region of Spain.

Lean pork	700 g	1.32 lb
Pork belly	300 g	0.66 lb

Ingredients per 1 kg (2.2 lb) of meat

Salt	21 g	3.5 tsp
Cure #1	2.5 g	1/2 tsp
Pimentón, sweet	20 g	3 Tbsp
Pimentón, hot	5 g	1 Tbsp
Oregano, dry	1.0 g	1 tsp
Garlic, smashed	3.5 g	1 clove

Grind meats through 10 mm (3/8") plate.
Mix meats with salt and spices and hold for 30 hours in refrigerator.
Stuff into 18-20 mm sheep casings forming 15-20 cm (6-8") links.
Dry at 15-12° C (59-53° F) for 30-40 hours.
Refrigerate.

Notes
Cook before serving by: frying in fat, boiling in white or rose wine or grilling. The sausage is often cooked in apple cider. It is also added to stews, paella dishes or fried with eggs and peppers.

Salchicha Exquisita de Higado (*Excellent Liver Sausage*)

A high quality Spanish liver sausage.

Pork liver	350 g	0.77 lb
Pork meat, semi-fat	400 g	0.88 lb
Pork fat	250 g	0.55 lb

Ingredients per 1 kg (2.2 lb) of meat

Salt	21 g	3.5 tsp
Pepper	2.0 g	1 tsp
Nutmeg	1.0 g	1/2 tsp
Marjoram	0.5 g	1/4 tsp
Cloves, ground	0.3 g	1/8 tsp
Onion, chopped and fried	50 g	1.76 oz

Immerse liver for 3-5 minutes in hot water at around 95° C (203° F) which is below boiling point. Drain and cool.

Chop the onion and fry in fat until glassy and gold. Do not brown the onion as it will acquire a bitter taste.

Grind liver with onion through 3 mm (1/8") plate.

Separately grind meat and fat through 3 mm (1/8") plate.

Emulsify liver paste in a food processor. Add meat, fat, all ingredients and emulsify again.

Stuff into 45-50 mm pork or beef middles.

Cook in water at 80° C (176° F) for 60 minutes.

Cool in cold water for 10 minutes, then cool in air and refrigerate.

Notes

Don't cook the liver, just scald it with hot water. Cooked liver loses its emulsifying properties. You can also insert liver briefly in hot water and remove it, repeating the process three times. The liver will change its outside color from dark red to pale.

Salchicha Frankfurt Style *(Salchicha tipo Frankfurt)*

Spanish version of frankfurter, quite popular in Spain. The frankfurter is a cured, smoked and cooked sausage. It is a ready to eat sausage or it may be boiled, fried or grilled for serving. The frankfurter originated some 350 years ago in Frankfurt, Germany and German immigrants brought the technology to other countries. The terms frankfurter, wiener or hot dog are practically interchangeable today. When the term "beef frankfurter" is used, the sausage is made of pure beef only.

Beef	600 g	1.32 lb
Lean pork trimmings	200 g	0.44 lb
Fat pork trimmings	200 g	0.44 lb

Ingredients per 1 kg (2.2 lb) of meat

Salt	18 g	3 tsp
Cure #1	2.5 g	½ tsp
Sweet pimentón	4.0 g	2 tsp
White pepper	2.0 g	1 tsp
Coriander	2.0 g	1 tsp
Nutmeg	1.0 g	½ tsp
Cold water	150 ml	⅝ cup

Grind beef with 3 mm (1/8") plate adding 75 ml of cold water. Grind pork with 3 mm (1/8") plate adding 75 ml of cold water. Grind fat trimmings through 3 mm (1/8") plate. Mix all meats together. Place ground meats in a freezer for 30 minutes then grind them again through 3 mm (1/8") plate.
(You could grind meats and fat through 6 mm (1/4") plate, then emulsify in a food processor adding 150 ml of cold water. Add spices during emulsifying.)
Mix the sausage mass with spices together.
Stuff firmly into 24-26 mm sheep casings. Form 4-5" (10-12 cm) long links.
Hang for one hour at room temperature.
When sausages feel dry apply hot smoke 60-70° C (140-158° F) for about 60 minutes until the sausages acquire brown color.
Cook in water at 75° C (167° F) until internal meat temperature reaches 154-158° F (68-70° C). This should take about 20 minutes.
Shower with cold water for 5 minutes then cool in air.
Keep in a refrigerator.

Salchicha Madrileña *(Madrid Sausage)*

Spanish fresh sausage from Madrid.

Pork meat, semi-fat	750 g	1.65 lb
Pork belly, back fat		
or fat trimmings	250 g	0.55 lb

Ingredients per 1 kg (2.2 lb) of meat

Salt	20 g	3 tsp
Pepper, white	2.0 g	1 tsp
Nutmeg	1.0 g	1/2 tsp
Cinnamon	0.5 g	1/4 tsp
Garlic	3.5 g	1 clove
Wine	60 ml	2 oz fl

Grind pork and fat through 8 mm (3/8") plate.

Mix ground meat with salt adding wine. Add spices and mix again.

Stuff into 18 mm sheep casings, forming links 10-12 cm (4-5") long.

Refrigerate. Cook fully before serving.

Salchicha Roja *(Red Sausage)*

Spanish fresh sausage of red color due to pimentón paprika.

Lean pork	500 g	1.10 lb
Pork fat	500 g	1.10 lb

Ingredients per 1 kg (2.2 lb) of meat

Salt	20 g	3 tsp
Pepper, black	2.0 g	1 tsp
Pimentón	25 g	4 Tbsp
Cinnamon	1.0 g	1/2 tsp
Red wine	60 ml	2 oz fl

Grind pork and fat through 10 mm (3/8") plate.
Mix ground meat with salt adding water. Add spices and mix again.
Stuff into 18 mm sheep casings, leave in one coil.
Refrigerate. Cook fully before serving.

Salchicha Viena Style *(Salchicha tipo Viena)*

Spanish version of wiener, quite popular in Spain. The wiener is a cured, smoked and cooked sausage. It is a ready to eat sausage or it may be boiled, fried or grilled for serving. The wiener originated about 300 years ago in Vienna, where Austrian and German immigrants brought this sausage to other countries. The terms frankfurter, wiener or hot dog are practically interchangeable today.

Lean beef	400 g	0.88 lb
Veal	300 g	0.66 lb
Back fat, pork jowl or pork fat trimmings	300 g	0.66 lb

Ingredients per 1 kg (2.2 lb) of meat

Salt	18 g	3 tsp
Cure #1	2.5 g	½ tsp
White pepper	2.0 g	1 tsp
Pimentón, sweet	4.0 g	1 tsp
Coriander	2.0 g	1 tsp
Mace	0.5 g	⅓ tsp
Onion powder	1.0 g	½ tsp
Cold water	150 ml	⅝ cup

Grind veal with 3 mm (1/8") plate adding 75 ml cold water. Grind beef with 3 mm (1/8") plate adding 75 ml cold water. Grind fat trimmings through 3 mm (1/8") plate. Mix all meats together. Place ground meats in a freezer for 30 minutes then grind them again through 3 mm (1/8") plate.

(You could grind meats and fat through 6 mm (1/4") plate, then emulsify in a food processor adding 150 ml of cold water. Add spices during emulsifying.)

Mix the sausage mass with spices together.

Stuff firmly into 24-26 mm sheep casings. Form 4-5" (10-12 cm) long links.

Hang for one hour at room temperature.

When sausages feel dry apply hot smoke 60-70° C (140-158° F) for about 60 minutes until a brown color develops.

Cook in hot water at 75° C (167° F) until internal meat temperature reaches 154-158° F(68-70° C). This should take about 20 minutes.

Shower with cold water for 5 minutes then cool in air.

Keep in a refrigerator.

Salchichón

After chorizo, salchichón is the second most popular dry sausage in Spain. Black pepper is the principal spice used, pimentón is not added to salchichones. Technically speaking, salchichón may be considered to be the Spanish equivalent of Italian salami.

Lean pork	800 g	1.76 lb
Back fat	100 g	0.22 lb
Back fat as show meat	100 g	0.22 lb

Ingredients per 1 kg (2.2 lb) of meat

Salt	25 g	4 tsp
Cure #2	2.5 g	1/2 tsp
Dextrose	2.0 g	1/2 tsp
Sugar	3.0 g	1/2 tsp
Black pepper	3.0 g	1.5 tsp
Black pepper, whole	1.0 g	1 tsp
Nutmeg	1.0 g	1/2 tsp
Dry wine	30 ml	2 Tbsp

Grind meat through 6 mm (1/4") plate.
Grind 100 g of fat through 6 mm (1/4") plate.
Dice partially frozen 100 g of fat into 5-8 mm (1/4-3/8") cubes.
Mix all ingredients with wine, pour over the meat and fat and mix all together.
Hold for 48 hours in refrigerator.
Stuff into 60-90 mm pork bungs forming sections 30-40 cm (12-16") long.
Ferment/dry at 20° C (68° F) for 48 hours, 90-85% humidity.
Dry at 15-12° C (59-54° F), 85-75% humidity for 2-3 months.
Store sausages at 10-12° C (50-53° F), <70% humidity or refrigerate.

Salchichón de Mezcla

Spanish dry sausage (*salchichón*) made with pork and beef.

Lean pork	400 g	0.88 lb
Lean beef	400 g	0.88 lb
Pork back fat	200 g	0.44 lb

Ingredients per 1 kg (2.2 lb) of meat

Salt	25 g	4 tsp
Cure #2	2.5 g	1/2 tsp
Dextrose	2.0 g	1/2 tsp
Sugar	2.0 g	1/2 tsp
Black pepper	2.0 g	1 tsp
Black pepper, whole	1.0 g	1 tsp
Nutmeg	1.0 g	1/2 tsp
Sweet sherry wine	60 ml	2 oz fl

Grind beef through 6 mm (1/4") plate.

Grind pork meat and fat through 3 mm (1/4") plate.

Mix spices with wine, then pour over the meat and fat and mix all together. Hold for 48 hours in refrigerator.

Stuff into 60-90 mm pork bungs forming sections 30-40 cm (12-16") long.

Ferment/dry at 20° C (68° F) for 48 hours, 90-85% humidity.

Dry at 15-12° C (59-54° F), 85-75% humidity for 2-3 months.

Store sausages at 10-12° C (50-53° F), <70% humidity or refrigerate.

Salchichón de Vic

The first references written about sausage from
Vic date back to 1456. In the past this product was
produced in the farms located in the Plana de Vic as
a method of preserving meats taking advantage of the
suitable climate conditions of the area. Salchichón de
Vic also known as Llonganissa de Vic is made in the
province of Barcelona. Salchichón de Vic carries PGI,
2001 classification.

LLONGANISSA•DE VIC

INDICACIÓ GEOGRÀFICA PROTEGIDA

Lean pork (shoulder, leg)	800 g	1.76 lb
Pork belly	150 g	0.22 lb
Back fat	50 g	0.11 lb

Ingredients per 1 kg (2.2 lb) of meat

Salt	25 g	4 tsp
Sugar	3.0 g	1/2 tsp
White pepper	3.0 g	1.5 tsp
Black pepper, whole	1.0 g	1 tsp

Dice back fat into 6 mm (1/4") cubes.
Grind meats through 8 mm (3/8") plate.
Mix ground meats with all ingredients.
Hold for 24-48 hours at 4-6° C (40-43° F) or in refrigerator.
Stuff firmly into pork bungs, 50-60 cm (20-24") long.
Ferment/dry at 20° C (68° F) for 48 hours, 90-95% humidity.
Dry at 15→ 12° C (59-54° F), 80 → 75% humidity for 45 days (or longer
depending on the diameter of the casing). The sausage is dried until around 30%
in weight is lost. The sausage should develop a white mold which is expected
and desired.
Store sausages at 10-12° C (50-53° F), <70% humidity.

Notes
Consume raw.
In traditional production the fermentation step was often skipped and the stuffed
sausage was only dried for 5-11 months at room temperatures, depending on the
diameter of the casing.
Salchichón de Vic, fuet and secallona are Catalan dry sausages that employ
similar materials and ingredients, they also follow the same manufacturing steps.
Fermenting and drying times will be shorter for fuet and secallona as they
are stuffed into smaller diameter casings. Another difference is that secallona
is formed into a U-shaped loop and salchichón and fuet are straight sections
sausages.

Salchichón Gallego

Salchichón is Spanish dry sausage made usually from pork. Salchichón de Lugo is Galician version that is made from pork and beef. Because Lugo is a province in Galicia the sausage might as well be called Salchichón Gallego. Salchichón de Lugo is made with white and black pepper, the sausage is dried, but not smoked.

Pork, lean (shoulder)	650 g	1.43 lb
Beef	100 g	0.22 lb
Back fat or		
hard fat trimmings	250 g	0.55 lb

Ingredients per 1 kg (2.2 lb) of meat

Salt	25 g	4 tsp
Cure #2	2.5 g	½ tsp
Sugar	3.0 g	1/2 tsp
White pepper, ground	1.0 g	1/2 tsp
Black pepper, ground	1.0 g	1/2 tsp
Black pepper, crushed	2.0 g	1 tsp

Grind meats and fat through 3-5 mm (1/8-1/4") plate.

Mix with salt, cure #2 and pepper and hold in refrigerator for 24 hours.

Stuff into large diameter (55-60 mm) pork casings.

Dry at 15 -12° C, (59-53° F), 75-85% humidity for 2 months.

Store at 12° C (53° F), <70% humidity.

Notes

Oregano, garlic and nutmeg are often added.

Secallona-Somalla-Petador-Espetec

Secallona, Somalla, Petador, Espetec - although those names sound mysterious and exotic, the truth is that they all are dry sausages and they all can be called fuet or longaniza. The manufacturing process is basically the same, what separates them is the size. Longaniza is packed into a large diameter, fuet into medium and secallona into a small diameter casing. Secallona is very dry and wrinkled, somalla is more moist. Secallona or somalla are U-shaped and usually not covered with mold, unlike fuet which always carries white mold. Petador is the name that is common for those sausages in Catalonian city of Sabadell, 20 km north from Barcelona. Espetec or fuet is basically the same Catalonian sausage.

Lean pork	800 g	1.76 lb
Back fat	200 g	0.44 lb

Ingredients per 1 kg (2.2 lb) of meat

Salt	22 g	3.5 tsp
Cure #1	2.5 g	1/2 tsp
Dextrose	2.0 g	1/2 tsp
Sugar	3.0 g	1/2 tsp
White pepper	3.0 g	1½ tsp.

Grind lean pork and pork belly through 6-8 mm (1/4") plate.
Mix all ingredients with meat. Hold in refrigerator for 24 hours.
Stuff into 32-34 mm pork casings making straight links.
Dry at 14-15° C (54-59° F), 75-80% humidity for 12 days.
Store sausages at 10-12° C (50-53° F), <75% humidity or refrigerate.

Sobrasada de Mallorca

Sobrasada de Mallorca carries Protective Geographical Indication certificate (PGI 1996). The sausage must meet the following requirements: lean pork (30-60%), back fat (40-70%), pimentón (4-7%), salt (1.8-2.8%), spices: pepper, rosemary, thyme, oregano. Sobrasada is a very popular sausage in Balearic Islands. As the name implies this sausage originates in the island of Majorca.

Sobrasada includes a lot of pimentón, when made with sweet pimentón only it is known as sweet sobrasada ("dulce") and when hot pimentón is added it becomes hot sobrasada ("picante").

Pork, lean	380 g	0.83 lb
Pork belly	270 g	0.59 lb
Back fat, fat trimmings	350 g	0.77 lb

Ingredients per 1 kg (2.2 lb) of meat

Salt	24 g	4 tsp
White pepper	2.0 g	1 tsp
Pimentón, sweet	48 g	7 Tbsp
Thyme, ground	2.0 g	2 tsp
Oregano, ground	2.0 g	2 tsp

Grind meat and fat through 5 mm (1/4 ") plate.

Mix ground meat and fat with salt and spices. Hold in refrigerator for 24 hours.

Stuff into 40-100 mm pork casings.

Dry at 15-18° C (59-64° F), 75-80% humidity for 30-45 days depending on the diameter of the sausage.

Store at 10-12° C (50-53° F), 60-65% humidity or refrigerate.

Notes

Although Pimentón de La Vera is the highest quality pimentón, it is made from smoked peppers and *must not be added* to Sobrasada de Mallorca in order not to introduce the smoky flavor.

Neither *garlic* nor *sugar* is added to Sobrasada de Mallorca.

Majorcan Sobrasada is traditionally served on bread and topped with a variety of spreads such as honey, sugar or apricot jam.

For hot version add 6 g (1 Tbsp) of hot pimentón.

Sobrasada de Mallorca de Cerdo Negro

Sobrasada de Mallorca de Cerdo Negro must be
made from meat that comes exclusively from
black pig (*cerdo negro*) that grows in the island
of Majorca. The sausage carries Protective
Geographical Indication certificate (PGI 1996).

Pork, lean	380 g	0.83 lb
Pork belly	270 g	0.59 lb
Back fat, fat trimmings	350 g	0.77 lb

Ingredients per 1 kg (2.2 lb) of meat

Salt	24 g	4 tsp
White pepper	2.0 g	1 tsp
Pimentón, sweet	48 g	7 Tbsp
Thyme, ground	2.0 g	2 tsp
Oregano, ground	2.0 g	2 tsp

Grind meat and fat through 5 mm (1/4 ") plate.
Mix ground meat and fat with salt and spices. Hold in refrigerator for 24 hours.
Stuff into 40-100 mm pork casings.
Dry at 15-18° C (59-64° F) for 30-45 days depending on the diameter of the
sausage.
Store at 10-12° C (50-53° F), 60-65% humidity or refrigerate.

Notes

Although Pimentón de La Vera is the highest quality pimentón, it is made from
smoked peppers and *must not be added* to Sobrasada de Mallorca in order not to
introduce the smoky flavor.
Neither *garlic* nor *sugar* is added to Sobrasada de Mallorca de Cerdo Negro.
Majorcan sobrasada is traditionally served on bread and topped with a variety of
spreads such as honey, sugar or apricot jam.

Sobrasada Picante Casera

Sobrasada sausage has a characteristic reddish-orange color, that is the result of mixing ground lean pork and pork fat with paprika, salt and spices. In Balearic islands sobrasada is made from locally grown pigs.

Lean pork (<20% fat)	600 g	1.32 lb
Back fat or fat pork trimmings	400 g	0.88 lb

Ingredients per 1 kg (2.2 lb) of meat

Salt	25 g	4 tsp
Cure #1	2.0 g	1/2 tsp
Pimentón, sweet	30 g	5 Tbsp
Pimentón, hot	10 g	5 tsp
Garlic, diced	7.0 g	2 cloves

Grind pork and fat through 5 mm (1/4") plate.

Mix meat, fat, salt, cure and spices together. Hold for 12 hours in refrigerator.

Stuff into large hog casings. Different casings are used including bladder and stomach. You can used fibrous synthetic casings.

Dry for 2 months at 16-12° C (60-54° F), 85-80% humidity.

Store sausages at 10-12° C (50-53° F), <70% humidity.

Notes

Exact drying time will be determined by the type and the size of the casings used.

Sobrasada Valenciana

Sobrasada sausage from the municipality of Alicante, País Valenciano region of Spain.

Lean pork	300 g	0.66 lb
Back fat	300 g	0.66 lb
Pork belly	400 g	0.88 lb

Ingredients per 1 kg (2.2 lb) of meat

Salt	25 g	4 tsp
Cure #2	2.5 g	1/2 tsp
Pepper	4.0 g	2 tsp
Pimentón, sweet	36 g	6 Tbsp
Pimentón, hot	4.0 g	2 tsp
Cloves, ground	0.5 g	1/4 tsp

Grind meat and fat through 3 mm (1/8") plate.
Mix ground materials with all ingredients. Hold for 12 hours in refrigerator.
Stuff into 60-80 mm pork bungs forming 30 cm (1 foot) straight sections or 30-40 mm pork casings forming 30 cm (1 foot) rings.
Dry at 15-12° C (59-53° F), 65-70% humidity for 2-3 months depending on the diameter of the sausage.
Store at 10-12° C (50-53° F), <70% humidity.

Notes
Consume raw.
In Valencia the sausage is often sliced and served on bread with honey.

Chapter 5

Topics of Vital Importance

Due to a favorable climate people in Spain have been making sausages without giving much thought to ambient conditions. This empirical knowledge had worked for their ancestors and it has worked for them, however, hobbyists in humid and hot Louisiana, Florida or Philippines need to pay more attention to processing parameters. The rudimentary knowledge of stuffing spiced hamburger meat into the casing and calling it a sausage is not enough for making dry sausages.

There is enough information in the first four chapters to produce any sausage listed in the book, however, if the sausage maker wants to create his own recipes he must work with bacteria together because they and not him are developing the flavors. He needs to know more about bacteria, humidity control, fermentation, starter cultures and drying to be in firm control of the process.

Although more technical in nature this chapter provides information which will positively contribute to a better understanding of the process and will make the reader a better sausage maker. After carefully reading the sections on acidity, water activity, fermentation and drying food the reader should grasp the basic understanding of the manufacturing process.

The following information is reprinted from our book *The Art of Making Fermented Sausages.*

Mystery of Cold Smoking

The majority of hobbyists think of cold smoking as some mysterious preservation technique that will produce a unique and superb quality product. What makes matters worse is that they start to experiment with different temperatures and establish their own rules which then spread around and are accepted by newcomers entering the field of smoking meats. In most German, Polish, Russian or Spanish technology books the upper limit for cold smoking is 25° C (77° F) although 18-20° C (64-71° F) may be the average.

Cold smoking is not a preservation method, it will not preserve meat unless the meat is dried; cold smoking is an *additional* safety hurdle that helps to achieve microbiological safety of meat; the higher amount of salt is added to meat that would be cold smoked to inhibit the growth of spoilage bacteria.

Cold smoking was nothing else but a drying method whose purpose was *to eliminate moisture so that bacteria would not grow*. This technique developed in North Eastern European countries where the climate was harsh and winters severe. When meats were cold smoked for 2-3 weeks, the meat became preserved, but *it was drying that made the meat safe*. If the same meat was dried at 54° F (12° C) without any smoke present, it would be preserved all the same.

As the temperature had to be higher than freezing temperatures outside, the slowly burning fire provided suitable temperatures for drying. The meats were flavored with cold smoke which not only helped to preserve the product but gave it a wonderful aroma. The meat, however, was preserved by drying and the benefit of smoke flavor was just an added bonus.

A large smokehouse was also a storage facility where smoked meats hung in a different area where they continued to receive some smoke, although on a much smaller scale. This prevented any mold from growing on the surfaces of hams or sausages, as molds need oxygen to grow. It was established that meats dried best when the temperatures were somewhere between 10-16° C (50–60° F) and although the temperature of the smoke leaving the firebox was higher, it would be just right by the time it made contact with meat. Whole logs of wood were burnt. The fire was allowed to die out when people went to sleep. In the morning the fire would be re-started again. So when you see an old recipe saying that ham or sausage was smoked for 2 weeks, well it really was not, as it probably received smoke for about 1/3 of the time. *Cold smoking is not a continuous process*, it is stopped a few times to allow fresh air into the smoker.

Smoking Slow Fermented/Dry Sausages

Fermented and dry sausages which are not subjected to heat treatment can be smoked with cold smoke only. When making traditional slow-fermented sausages we apply fermentation temperatures around 18-25° C (66-77° F) and about 12-16° C (53-60° F) when drying. *Cold smoking is basically drying with smoke.* Think of cold smoke as a part of the drying/fermentation cycle and not as the flavoring step. *If the temperature of the smoke is close to the fermentation temperature, there is very little difference between the two*. The sausage will ferment and the drying will continue. If we applied heavy smoke for a long time, that would definitely inhibit the growth of color and flavor forming bacteria which are so important for the development of flavor in slow-fermented sausages.

As drying continues for a long time and cold smoking may be a part of it, it makes little difference whether cold smoke is interrupted and then re-applied again.

Smoking sausages made with offal meat (liver and blood sausages, head cheese) is less popular, but it is sometimes performed. In such cases the sausage is *cooked first,* cooled down to around 15-18° C (59-64° F) and then briefly smoked with *cold smoke* at 18° C (64° F) to develop some flavor and color.

Photo 5.1 & 5.2 Using the weather to his advantage, Waldemar Kozik has no problems with cold smoking sausages in Catskill Mountains of New York.

Fermenting Sausages

In simple terms *meat fermentation is spoilage of meat by bacteria.* Leaving meat at room temperature to itself will result in a spoilage, but if the process is properly controlled, the result is a quality fermented product.

Learn how to work with and how to control bacteria. After all, they and not you, make the sausage, you are just the driver. Making fermented sausages is a combination of the art of the sausage maker and unseen magic performed by bacteria. The friendly bacteria are working together with a sausage maker, but the dangerous ones are trying to wreak havoc. Using his knowledge the sausage maker monitors temperature and humidity which allows him to control reactions that take place inside the sausage. This game is played for quite a while and at the end a high quality product is created.

Meat fermentation is accomplished by lactic bacteria, either naturally present in meat or added as starter cultures. These bacteria *feed on sugars* and produce lactic acid and small amounts of other components. Increased amount of lactic acid results in higher acidity (lower pH) what not only creates for some a highly desirable product, but also prevents the growth of spoilage and pathogenic bacteria. *The main product of fermentation is lactic acid and the main cause is an increased acidity of meat.* The more sugar that is metabolized by the lactic acid bacteria, more lactic acid is produced, a higher acidity of meat is obtained and the sausage becomes more sourly. Sugar must be present for fermentation to occur. Fruits, bell peppers, paprika, rice, pumpkin, potatoes, cabbage, groats, bread, honey, raisins, dry milk, grains - all contain sugar and will support fermentation.

Meat contains naturally present lactic bacteria and a very small mount of its own sugar (glycogen, less than 1%) so obviously no significant fermentation can take place, *unless we add more sugar.* Adding sugar to sausages is not practiced in Spain so the fermentation is rather weak and the sausages do not become sourly. The color and flavor producing bacteria have enough time to develop the great flavor. *The speed of fermentation is directly proportional to the temperature* so the fermentation proceeds faster at higher temperatures. If the fermentation temperature drops to <53° F (12° C), the lactic acid bacteria may stop metabolizing sugar. *How acidic the sausage becomes depends on the amount and type of sugar introduced.* In traditionally made slow-fermented dry sausages, the proper fermentation can take place only if there is a sufficient number of lactic bacteria in the meat to begin with. To increase their number a long curing step was performed which allowed lactic acid bacteria to grow. This marinating step (*reposo*) - applying *adobo* paste to meat has been always included in the traditional production of Spanish dry sausages. Unfortunately, spoilage and pathogenic bacteria were growing as well, although at a much slower rate due to the effects of salt and nitrate. In the latest production methods huge numbers of lactic acid bacteria in the form of *starter cultures* are introduced into the meat right at the beginning of the process what guarantees healthy and strong fermentation.

These armies of beneficial bacteria start competing for food with other bacteria types, decreasing their chances for growth and survival. Fermentation stops when no more lactic acid is produced by bacteria. Keep in mind that during fermentation bacteria break down sugar into lactic acid and oxygen dioxide. Lactic acid, like all acids has a sourly taste, take for example vinegar, and people are not particularly fond of sourly flavored sausages. This is what we obtain when a fast-fermented semi-dry salami is produced. Those type of sausages are popular in the USA because they are produced fast and they are cheap. They have little in common with traditionally produced Italian salami or Spanish dry sausages.

The main purpose of the fermentation is to increase the microbiological safety of the sausage by increasing the acidity of the meat. It is a biological process that preserves the meat and provides a distinctive flavor. Fermentation does not improve the taste of the sausage, on the contrary fast fermented sausages develop a sour and tangy taste. Fermentation is performed by increasing the temperature of the sausage after stuffing. This triggers an increased activity of all types of bacteria and allows new reactions to take place..

There is no golden rule which will cover fermentation parameters such as temperature, time and relative humidity. This can vary from one manufacturer to another. Many manufacturers don't own climate controlled fermentation chambers and use chambers which depend on weather conditions that prevail during a particular season. As weather changes from year to year, sausages which are made in the same season may be subjected to different temperatures, humidities, and winds the next year and this makes constant quality of the product difficult to control.

The End of Fermentation

Without performing pH acidity tests it is impossible to predict exactly when the fermentation ends and the drying begins, as both processes are closely related.

The sausage pH, not the time, is the factor that determines when the fermentation is completed.

When the lowest pH reading is obtained we may assume that the fermentation stage has ended. The question is even harder to answer in the case of slow-fermented products which are made with little sugar as this results in a slow and small pH drop. Once the fermentation starts, it will continue until the sugar supply is exhausted providing that there is sufficient moisture inside the sausage (Aw > 0.95). Then the sausage enters the drying stage at a lower temperature although in reality *it starts drying already in the fermentation stage*. Because acidity accumulation (pH drop) is directly proportionate to the amount of introduced sugar, the amount of added sugar should not be higher than 0.5% (5 g/1kg of meat). If less than 0.3% sugar is added the acidity will not reach pH 5.0 and curing and flavor bacteria will work at their fullest.

As the pH of the sausage drops below pH 5.3 moisture removal becomes easier. At around pH 4.8 a point is reached, called the *isoelectric point*, when water holding forces become weaker and the sausage starts drying fast. Slow-fermented sausages usually do not develop so much acidity. When making a traditional fermented sausage, the pH values should not fall below 4.8-5.0 as this will inhibit the action of color and flavor forming bacteria which are sensitive to acidity.

Starter Cultures

Starter cultures have been used by the industry for a number of years, first in dairy products like yogurt and cheeses, then in fermented meat like salami. They are easily available and sausage makers use them more and more. Any traditionally dried sausage like Italian salami or Spanish chorizo will pass through a fermentation stage as long as sugar is available to bacteria. Naturally present in meat lactic acid producing bacteria will start producing lactic acid. Because no sugar is usually added to Spanish sausages there is no fermentation and the sausage begins to dry. Fermenting starter cultures contain millions of bacteria so it would be useless to add them to meat if they have no food (sugar). There are also cultures that help to develop the color and flavor. Mold developing cultures might be of special interest to a hobbyist as they guarantee development of healthy mold on any air dried sausage. Follow the listed rules when applying starter cultures:

- Do not add starter culture during mixing meat with spices.
- Do not add starter cultures when meats are submitted to curing for 6-24 hours (*adobo* process).
- Add starter culture to meat just before stuffing.
- About 30 minutes before adding culture, mix the culture with a little distilled or spring water.

Mold developing cultures are applied to the surface of the sausage so follow the instructions. The following culture can be used for making Spanish dry sausages.

T-SPX (*Pediococcus pentosaceus, Staphylococcus xylosus*), produced by Chr. Hansen is an aromatic culture with mild acidification. The high concentration of *Pediococus pentosaceus* gives a controlled and moderate pH drop. The acidification gives a mild lactic acid taste. *Staphylococcus xylosus* gives good color formation and stability. Furthermore *Staphylococcus xylosus* gives a very round and mild flavor which is very typical for South European salami types such as Milano. The culture has been specifically selected for traditional fermentation profiles applying fermentation temperatures not higher than 75° F (24° C). When making a traditional fermented sausage, the pH values should not fall below 4.8-5.0 as this will inhibit the action of color and flavor forming bacteria which are sensitive to acidity. To meet this requirement when applying T-SPX culture *fermentation temperatures must be kept in the 68-75° F (20-24° C) range and only a small amount of glucose (dextrose) should be added (0.2-0.3%, 2-3 g per 1 kg /2.2 lb of meat).*

Drying Sausages

When water is eliminated, bacteria cannot eat, they will not grow and will eventually die. This is the basic concept of drying foods.

A very large number of Spanish meat products is air dried and not cooked at all. This is possible due to the favorable mild climate, relatively low humidity in most of the country and prevailing winds. Say chorizo in Spain and it is assumed that the sausage has been dried, mention the name in South America and you may get a fresh sausage suitable for grilling.

There are processors of dry products that limit the entire process to one long drying step. The stuffed sausage is introduced into the drying chamber at 6-15° C (42-58° F), where it remains for the rest of the process. Color and flavor forming bacteria (*Staphylococcus, Kocuria*) are aerobic (need oxygen to survive) and are concentrated close to the surface of the sausage where they easily find oxygen. They are sensitive to changing water activity levels and very fast drying at low humidity levels will prematurely dry out the surface of the sausage. A gray surface ring is a typical example. Like other bacteria, they need moisture to grow and the dry surface area will affect their growth. This will affect the development of proper color and flavor.

Drying basically starts already in the fermentation stage with the humidity kept at a high level of about 90-95%. Air flow is quite fast (0.8 m/sec) to permit fast moisture removal but the high humidity level moisturizes the surface of the casing preventing it from hardening. Drying continues after the fermentation stage and more moisture is removed from the sausage. This becomes easier in time as the increasing *acidity weakens the forces that bind water*. As the Aw (water activity) keeps dropping lower, the humidity level is decreased to about 0.85-90%. As the sausage now contains less moisture, less moisture appears on the surface and maintaining previous fast air flow may harden the surface of the casing so the air speed is decreased to about 0.5 m/sec (1.8 miles/per hour) which corresponds to a slow walk. The process continues until the desired amount of dryness (weight loss) is obtained. At home conditions *this can be calculated by weighing test sausages*.

Drying is usually performed at 18→12° C (66-53° F) and decreasing humidity, from about 85% to 65-70%. Higher temperatures and humidity over 75% will promote the development of mold on the surface of the sausage. When making slow fermented sausages without starter cultures, drying temperatures should fall in 12-15° C (54-59° F) range. *Staph. aureus* starts growing faster at 15.6° C (60° F) and obviously it is best to avoid this and higher temperatures.

After 3 months of drying the sausage will last almost indefinitely as long as it is kept in a cool (12° C, 44° F) and dark place at about 60% humidity. If the humidity is very low, the sausage will lose too much moisture which will make sausage production less profitable.

It should be noted that in slow-fermented sausages yeasts and molds often appear during the drying process. This induces a "reversed" fermentation as these microorganisms consume some of the lactic acid that was produced during fermentation and leave behind a small amount of ammonia which is alkaline. This alkalinity will lower the overall acidity of the sausage and is the main factor contributing to a milder flavor in slow drying sausages. One may say why not to dry a sausage very quickly and be done with all this pH and bacteria. Well there are basically two reasons:

1. The outside layer of the sausage must not be hardened as it may prevent the removal of the remaining moisture. It may affect the curing of the outside layer which will develop a gray ring that will be visible when slicing the sausage.

2. Bacteria naturally found in meat and/or introduced starter cultures need moisture to grow. They have to go through the so called "lag phase" first. They have been deep frozen, they are drowsy and need time to wake up. Only then can they metabolize sugar and produce lactic acid. Once when a sufficient pH drop is obtained, lactic acid bacteria slow down growing and more moisture can be removed.

Removing water content by drying a sausage is a slow process. We could dry sausages at higher temperatures by applying fast air speed, but that would only harden their surfaces, trapping the moisture inside causing the sausages to spoil. Slow controlled drying is the method applied to traditionally made slow-fermented sausages which require three months or more to produce. As the process proceeds, water starts to evaporate making meat stronger against spoilage and pathogenic bacteria. There eventually comes a point when there are no bacteria present and the meat is microbiologically stable. It will not spoil as long as it is kept at low temperatures and at low humidity levels. If the temperature and humidity go up, new bacteria will establish a colony on the surface and will start moving towards the inside of the sausage. The mold immediately appears on the surface.

Sausages dry from inside out. For a correct drying process, there must be a balance between moisture diffusion towards the surface and moisture evaporation from the surface. If diffusion is faster than evaporation, moisture will accumulate on the surface of the sausage causing it to be slimy. Yeasts and molds will soon follow. If evaporation is faster than diffusion, the outside surface area of the sausage will dry out and harden, and will act as a barrier to subsequent moisture removal. As a result moisture will be trapped inside of the sausage creating favorable conditions for the growth of spoilage and pathogenic bacteria.

Drying is affected by:

- humidity - higher humidity, slower drying.
- temperature - higher temperature, faster drying.
- air flow - faster air flow, faster drying.

For the perfect drying the humidity of the drying room should be 5% lower than the water activity (Aw) within the sausage. This requires water activity measurements and computer operated drying chambers where parameters such as temperature, humidity and air speed are continuously monitored and readjusted. This relationship remains constant and every time the water level drops the humidity is lowered accordingly. Water activity (Aw) can be lowered faster in a sausage which contains more fat than a leaner sausage. Meat contains about 75% of water but the water content of fat is only about 10-15%. A fatter sausage containing less meat also contains less water and will dry out faster.

Increasing the acidity of the meat facilitates drying and the movement of moisture towards the surface is much smoother. As the pH drops, it approaches the isoelectric point of the myofibrillar proteins (actin and myosin) where their ability to bind water reaches a minimum. This happens around pH of 4.8-5.3. In simple words, *lowering pH aids in the removal of moisture.* Depending on the method of manufacture, diameter of a casing and the content of fat in a sausage mass, fermented sausages lose from 5-40% of their original weight.

Air Speed

Air speed is a factor that helps remove moisture and stale air, and of course it influences drying. Sausages will dry faster at higher temperatures, but in order to prevent the hardening of the sausage surface long term drying must be between 12-15° C (53-59° F). The speed of drying does not remain constant, but changes throughout the process: it is the fastest during the beginning of fermentation, then it slows down to a trickle. At the beginning of fermentation humidity is very high due to the high moisture content of the sausage.

When starter cultures are used, the temperature is at the highest during fermentation, as some cultures are designed to ferment at 35-45° C (95-113° F. *Such temperatures enormously* speed up moisture removal from the sausage. The surface of the sausage contains a lot of moisture which must be continuously removed otherwise slime and mold might appear. If the sausages are soaking wet during fermentation, the humidity should be lowered. At the beginning of fermentation the fastest air speed is applied, about 0.8-1.0 m/sec. *The speed of 3.6 km/h (2.2 mile/hour) corresponds to the speed of 1 meter/second.* Ideally the amount of removed moisture should equal the amount of moisture moving to the surface.

Fermentation is performed at high humidity (92-95%) to prevent case hardening. If the humidity were low and the air speed fast, the moisture would evaporate from the surface so fast that the moisture from the inside of the sausage would not make it to the surface in time. The surface of the casing will harden creating a barrier to the subsequent drying process. *In slow fermented sausages* this will create a big problem as the inside of the sausage may never dry out and the product will spoil. As the sausage enters the drying stage, less moisture remains inside and the humidity and air speed are lowered.

After about one week the air speed is only about 0.5 m/sec and after another week it drops to *0.1 m/sec (4 inches/sec)*. It will stay below this value for the duration of the drying. Fast moisture removal is not beneficial in *fast-fermented sausages* either. Lactic acid bacteria need water to grow and if we suddenly remove this moisture, they would produce lactic acid at a slower rate. The technology of making fast-fermented sausages relies on a rapid pH drop and not on drying so the air speed control is less critical.

Humidity Control

Humidity or better said the "relative humidity" defines how much water is present in the air at a particular temperature. The air always contains some water vapor and although we don't see it, it is there and it has a certain mass. *The higher the temperature the more water can be held by air and vice versa.* Humidity changes throughout the day and is dependent upon temperature. *When the temperature goes up, the humidity goes down and vice versa.* This means that there is higher humidity in the air at night when temperatures are lower. When the clouds come in and it starts to drizzle, the humidity goes up immediately. There is more humidity in areas containing many lakes, rivers or being close to the sea shore. Arid areas such as deserts or mountains have less water and subsequently less humidity.

This humidity behavior can be used to our advantage when a large drying chamber or smokehouse is located outside. The amount of moisture in the air is fixed for at least some time but raising the temperature lowers the relative humidity. As you cannot change the physical location of the drying chamber, you have to learn how to work around it.

- There are portable devices (humidifiers and dehumidifiers) which can be placed inside of the drying chamber. They are inexpensive and have a thermostat which allows automatic humidity control.

- In smaller chambers such as an old refrigerator box, the simplest humidifier is a bowl filled with water that is placed inside. The larger the surface area of the dish, the more evaporation will take place.

- To increase humidity, sausages can be periodically sprayed or immersed briefly in water.

- Humidity testers are inexpensive and there is no excuse for not having one.

- In a home freezer or refrigerator humidity varies between 40-50%.

Understanding Acidity (pH)

Bacteria hate acidity and this fact plays an important role in the production and stabilization of fermented sausages.

The term "pH" is a measure of acidity; the lower its value, the more acidic the food. Acidity may be natural as in most fruits for example lemon, or added as in pickled food. The acidity level in foods can be increased by adding lemon juice, citric acid, vinegar, or lowered by adding alkaline foods like baking soda, milk or water. Bacteria will not grow when the pH is below the minimum or above the maximum limit for a particular bacteria strain. Pure water is said to be neutral, with a pH close to 7.0. Solutions with a pH less than 7 are said to be *acidic* and solutions with a pH greater than 7 are basic or *alkaline*. All bacteria have their own preferred acidity level for growth, generally around neutral pH (7.0). As the pH of foods can be adjusted, this procedure becomes a potent weapon for the control of bacteria.

The thermal resistance of microorganisms decreases as the pH of their medium is lowered. Most bacteria, particularly *Clostridium botulinum*, will not grow below pH 4.6. Therefore acidic foods having pH below 4.6 do not require as severe heat treatment as those with pH above 4.6 (low acid) to achieve microbiological safety. *The pH value of 4.6 is the division between high acid foods and low acid foods.* Low acid foods have pH values higher than 4.6. They include red meats, seafood, poultry, milk, and all fresh vegetables except for most tomatoes. There are varieties that have a lower pH level and there are varieties which also have a higher pH level. Tomatoes are usually considered an acidic food.

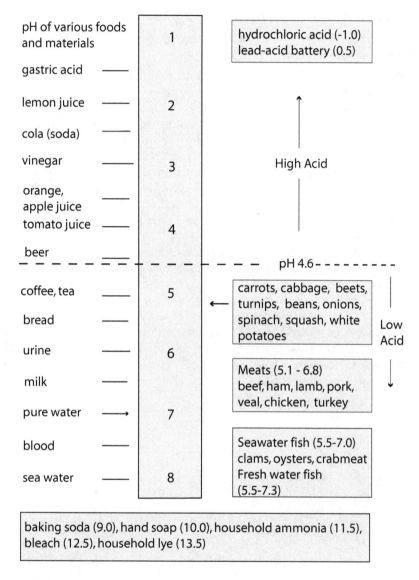

Fig. 3.5 pH of different foods.

A pH drop is accomplished by lactic acid bacteria, which consume sugar and produce lactic acid. This increases the acidity of the meat. The acidity can also be increased by adding additives such as Gdl (glucono-delta-lactone) and/or citric acid. Such ingredients have to be carefully selected as they will alter the flavor of the sausage. Combining different meats and fats will produce a sausage mass of a certain pH, and the pH meat meter will provide the initial value of the pH of the mix. Foods with a low pH value (high acidity) develop resistance against microbiological spoilage. Pickles, sauerkraut, eggs, pig feet, anything submerged in vinegar will have a long shelf life. Even ordinary meat jelly (head cheese) will last longer if some vinegar is added and this type of head cheese is known as "souse." Look at the list of ingredients when buying meat marinade. The list invariably includes items like vinegar, dry wine, soy sauce, lemon juice, and ingredients which are acidic or salty by nature. Although those ingredients are added mainly to tenderize meat by unwinding the protein structure, they also contribute to inhibiting the growth of bacteria. A sausage can be made safe by acidity alone if its pH is 5.3 or lower, but its flavor will be sour. To avoid this most sausages are additionally submitted to drying or cooking as these steps add safety and less acidity is needed.

The table on the right shows a pH value below which the listed bacteria will not grow. *Almost all fermented sausages produced in the USA today are manufactured by lowering the pH of the meat.* It is a profitable and risk free method for commercial producers, although the taste and flavor of the product leaves much to be desired. Generally a pH of less than 5.0 will severely restrict or completely stop the growth of harmful bacteria.

Name	Min pH
Salmonella	3.8
Cl.botulinum	5.0
Staph.aureus	4.2
Campylobacter	4.9
Listeria	4.4
E.coli	4.4
Shigella	4.0
Bacillus	4.3

Understanding Water Activity (Aw)

All microorganisms need water to live, when enough of the water is removed they will stop growing and die. This statement explains the science of drying foods.

The amount of water available to microorganisms is defined as water activity. Water activity (Aw) is an indication of how tightly water is "bound" inside of a product. It does not say how much water is there, but how much water is *available* to support the growth of bacteria, yeasts or molds. Adding salt or sugar "binds" some of this free water and lowers the amount of available water to bacteria which inhibits their growth. A scale is used to classify foods by their water activity, it starts at 0 (bone dry) and ends on 1 (pure water). Below certain Aw levels microbes cannot grow. United Stated Department of Agriculture guidelines state that: *"A potentially hazardous food does not include... a food with a water activity value of 0.85 or less."*

Freshly minced meat possesses a very high water activity level around 0.99, which is a breeding ground for bacteria. *Adding salt to meat* drops this value immediately to 0.96-0.98 (depending on the amount of salt), and this already creates a safety hurdle against the growth of bacteria. It was also discovered that the addition of sugar would preserve foods such as candies and jellies. Both factors contribute to lowering the water activity of the meat. This may be hard to comprehend as we don't see water evaporating suddenly when salt is added to meat.

Water activity (Aw) of foods	
Pure water	1.00
Fresh meat & fish	0.99
Bread	0.99
Salami	0.87
Aged cheese	0.85
Jams & jellies	0.80
Plum pudding	0.80
Dried fruits	0.60
Biscuits	0.30
Milk powder	0.20
Instant coffee	0.20
Bone dry	0.00

Although the addition of salt to meat does not force water to evaporate, it does something similar: it immobilizes free water and prevents it from reacting with anything else, including bacteria. It is like stealing water from bacteria, the salt locks up the water creating less favorable conditions for bacteria to grow and prosper. As we add more salt, more free water is immobilized, however, a compromise must be reached as adding too much salt will make the product unpalatable. Too much salt may impede the growth of friendly bacteria, the ones which work with us to ferment the sausage. The manipulation of water content in processed meat is very important to the successful production of the traditionally made slow-fermented sausages. Water exists in meat as:

Bound (restricted or immobilized water) - structurally associated with meat proteins, membranes and connective tissues. This water (3-5% of total water) can only be removed by high heat and is not available for microbial activities.

Free or bulk water - held only by weak forces such as capillary action. This free water is available for microorganisms for growth.

It can be seen in the table that except *Staphylococcus aureus*, the growth of other bacteria (spoilage and pathogenic) is severely restricted below Aw 0.92. This is why drying is such an effective method of preventing bacteria growth and preserving foods in general.

Minimum Aw for microorganism growth	
Molds	0.75
Staphylococcus aureus	0.85
Yeasts	0.88
Listeria	0.92
Salmonella	0.93
Cl.botulinum	0.93
E.coli	0.95
Campylobacter	0.98

References

Antonio Madrid Vicente, *Carnes, embutidos y jamones de España*, 2014
Augusto Jurado, *El cerdo y sus chacinas*, 2008
Aug. Valessert, *Cría y aprovechamiento del cerdo. Salchichería*, 1893
Bhavbhuti M. Kehta, *Fermentation Effects on Food Properties*, 2016
Carmen Márquez Sereno, *Elaboración de curados y salazones cárnicos*, 2014
Cesáreo Sanz Egaña, *Chacinería moderna*, 1940
Cesáreo Sanz Egaña, *Enciclopedia de la carne*, 1967
Cesáreo Sanz Egaña, *La matanza familiar*, 1949
Daniel Marcos Aguiar, *Embutidos Crudos Curados Españoles*, 1990
Fidel Toldra, *Handbook of Fermented Meat and Poultry*, 2007
Fidel Toldra, *Dry Cured Meat Products*, 2002
Francisco Léon Crespo, *Embutidos andaluces*, 1988
Francisco Cervantes, *D.O. España jamones y embutidos*, 2012
José Bello Gutériez, *Jamón Curado*, 2008
Ministerio de Agricultura, *Tripas para embutidos*, 1960
Ministerio de agricultura, pesca y alimentación, *Catalogo de embutidos y jamones curados de España*, 1983
Ministerio de agricultura, pesca y alimentación, *Principios basicos de elaboración de embutidos*, 1989
Stanley and Adam Marianski, *The Art of Making Fermented Sausages*, 2009
Thomas Malmertoft, *Manual de charcutería artenasal*, 2016

Historical Books

Spanish-Arabic Cuisine During Almohad Empire (La cocina hispano-magrebí durante la época almohade) translated from XIII century anonymous arabic manuscript into Spanish by Ambrosio Huici Miranda ISBN: 978-84-9704-958-0

The Book of Sent Sovi: Medieval recipes from Catalonia,
ISBN: 978-1855661646 in English
Libro de Sent Soví, ISBN: 978-84-96238-70-1 in Spanish

Useful Links

The Sausage Maker www.sausagemaker.com distributor of sausage making equipment and supplies.

Allied Kenco www.alliedkenco.com distributor of sausage making equipment and supplies.

La Tienda www.latienda.com Spanish hams, hams, sausages and other quality food products from Spain.

INDEX

314

T

Temperature 78, 304
Traditional Speciality Guaranteed
        (TSG) 20
Truffles 68
T-SPX starter culture 83, 300

V

Vela 72

W

Water 308
  bound 308
  Bound 308
  free 308
  Free 308
Water Activity (Aw) 307
Wieners 43
Wine 68
Wood 76

Y

Yeasts 302

More books by Stanley and Adam Marianski